*Praise for* CL

## *Growth Co*

"I started using the *Growth Company Guide* in the late 90s and I have both the 1993 and 2000 editions. Our company has grown from $3.8 million annual revenues in 1995 to a projected $100 million in revenues in 2007. You can bet that I have picked up this valuable book many times as we have navigated the challenges of financing this kind of growth. It is a solid piece of work and the latest update adds even more information useful in today's financial markets."

> *Terri Jondahl, CEO, CAB Incorporated*
> *Atlanta's Fastest Growing Private Companies List 2007*

"The *Growth Company Guide* is an incredibly comprehensive resource for anyone involved in the capital-raising process. It's a soup-to-nuts perspective on the essential as well as subtle deal characteristics that can make or break a successful transaction."

> *Kathy Harris, Partner, Noro-Moseley Partners*

"The best, most thorough, objective, "plain English", corporate finance guide for business owners, executives, financiers, and advisors on the market today. It will be required reading for all of our new and incoming analysts."

> *Mark Loeffler, Managing Director, VRA Partners, LLC*

"An excellent compilation of the terms we use everyday in helping to finance companies, explained in easy-to-understand language and updated for the changing environment of private equity."

> *Thomas A. Avery, Managing Director*
> *Raymond James & Associates*

"This book should be basic reading for any entrepreneur who is considering raising outside capital."

> *Michael D. Long, Managing Partner, MSouth Equity Partners*

"Terribly helpful to the first time entrepreneur who is basically unfamiliar with the rough and tumble world of venture firms and venture partners. Bravo!"

> *Steven G. Anderson, President/Founder, CryoLife, Inc. (NYSE)*

"Since reading the first draft of the *Growth Company Guide* back in the mid 1980s until today, it has been and is my reference of choice for my many business plan students, clients, and non-clients for the understanding it brings to the various aspects of the new venture funding process. Clint has written and maintained as current an important encyclopedic work in the venture field that everyone, i.e., entrepreneurs, students, and professional practitioners have to have."

*Robert G. Schwartz, EWU Foundation Chairholder*
*Distinguished Professor of Entrepreneurship*
*Eastern Washington University*

"We worked with the author on one of our portfolio companies from fundraising through a very successful exit. His book provides valuable insight into the give-and-take of the venture funding and company growth processes."

*Will Griffith, General Partner, Technology Crossover Ventures*

"This book is a great reference guide for those involved in organizing and funding a growing company. It provides an easy to understand description of the common terms, deal structures, and many other related matters you will be faced with in financing a company, regardless of what stage you are at. I like how the book is laced with down-to-earth practical advice. I also like how he provides insight on the perspective of others during the process of raising growth capital. Clint's book is clearly a reflection of his extensive real life experience in helping growing companies."

*Edward R. Uzialko, Jr., Founder/CEO, Lynk Systems, Inc.*

"A must-read reference guide for the financial and non-financial executive be they a lender, lawyer, entrepreneur or management executive. I have used this guide religiously since 1987 and I am sure you will too."

*Thomas S. Thornhill, Senior VP, Healthcare Finance Group, Inc.*

"This book is an invaluable resource and reference work for the entrepreneurial community. The inclusion of specific examples to illustrate concepts is of particular value."

*Edward C. McCarthy, Managing Director, River Cities Capital Fund*

"This book is no less than indispensable for the entrepreneurial manager. It clearly explains the special terms, concepts and jargon of the entrepreneur's world. Importantly, the author offers practical advice to help level the field on which small growth companies find themselves playing with venture capitalists, merchant bankers, shareholders, directors, consultants, underwriters and lawyers.

When I left the world of the large corporation to manage an entrepreneurial spin-off, I found myself confused by the special terms, concepts and jargon of the entrepreneur's world. Fortunately, I had this excellent book to help me. It proved to be indispensable during the initial spin-off negotiations, the first and second rounds of financing and the subsequent financial re-structuring of the company, as well as during the negotiation of license deals with large companies. The author offers practical advice in a clear and succinct fashion."
    *Adrian Hunter, M.D. Founder/President, BioCure, Inc.*

"This resource by regional author and attorney Clint Richardson shows how much depth and breadth of experience venture development exists in our area. The entries on deal structure and venture pricing should be particularly helpful to growth company managers."
    *Fred Sturgis, Managing Director, H.I.G. Ventures*

"Your *Guide* should be required reading for all aspiring entrepreneurs. Having this level of information so easily available would certainly have saved me significant time and dollars along the way and still may."
    *Frank W. Hulse, IV, Principal, River Capital*

"A careful read of the *Growth Company Guide* will enable entrepreneurs to fully comprehend the importance of the early decisions involved in financing and growing a new venture. It will help the first-time or repeat company builder make the right decisions from the very start, maximizing the venture's chances of success."
    *Timothy J. Patrick, President/CEO, Carticept Medical, Inc.*
    *Co-Founder/Former CEO, Proxima Therapeutics, Inc.*

"The *Growth Company Guide* is a terrific resource that I frequently recommend to the entrepreneurs we work with. It gives them an inside look at the mysterious world of angel and venture investing and arms them with important, practical insight as they negotiate through the capital raising process."

*Bonnie Herron, VP/CFO, Intelligent Systems Inc. (AMEX)*

"Whether seeking initial start-up capital or capital to grow a business, the *Growth Company Guide* is a "must read" for any entrepreneur. Just as the business plan enables prospective financial sources to gain an insight into the business, the *Growth Company Guide* provides a wealth of information that will allow the entrepreneur to gain an insight into the language and mindset of lenders and investors."

*Don Aronin, Founder/President, Tile Outlets of America*

"Extremely helpful resource for all entrepreneurs. Raising money is not easy and this resource will ease the process."

*I. Sigmund Mosley, Jr., President, Imlay Investments, Inc.*

"This is a first rate resource for growing companies. Full of practical guidance for company leaders facing the challenges brought on by rapid growth."

*Doug Tatum, Founding Chairman, Tatum, LLC*
*Author, No Man's Land (Penguin 2007)*

"A must read for all entrepreneurs, investors and business owners! Clint Richardson makes the confusing world of finance and law easy to understand and provides the reader with many sound, practical business and legal strategies."

*G. Huxley Nixon, Partner, Focus Enterprises, Inc.*

"I encounter many situations where an inventor or entrepreneur is not familiar with the terminology or typical structures of the "start-up" world. This book is a great navigational tool for them that is designed in an accessible manner. From now on I will make sure that they have it to refer to."

*Charles E. Larsen, Managing Director, Accuitive Medical Ventures*

"Understanding the concepts behind the jargon of venture deal-making advances discussions about deal structure and sets the stage for enduring relationships between venture investor and management team. The *Growth Company Guide* provides this background in an easily accessible and readily understandable way."

*Tench Coxe, Managing Director, Sutter Hill Ventures*

"Written by one of the leading growth company lawyers in the Southeast, this book levels the playing field for companies receiving venture capital financing. Read it before your VC Term Sheet, or wish that you had later."

*Jeff Stewart, Managing Director, HINRI Ventures LLC*

"An introduction to, reference for, and all comprehensive outline of venture capital for both adventure capitalist and entrepreneur."

*Roddy J. H. Clark, Managing Director, Redmont Venture Partners*

"A unique book from a veteran legal practitioner. Mr. Richardson represented us through six venture rounds and a $525 million exit. He knows his stuff. Full of practical strategies and insight."

*Douglas R. Sandberg, VP/General Counsel, RBS Direct USA*

"Some important VC investment concepts explained in easily understandable format. I have no doubt that the additional perspectives that especially first time CEO's would gain before concluding a deal with VC's will save them some painful future disappointments and translate into a positive financial return on their efforts."

*Laurie Olivier, Managing Director, Veritas Venture Partners LLC*

"The *Growth Company Guide* is not merely an indispensable handbook for entrepreneurs and investors. It surprises and delights with insider tips such as "The Seven Deadly Sins of Fundraising" and "How to Think Like a VC." It's a masterpiece!"

*Robert G. Cross, Chairman/CEO, Revenue Analytics, Inc.*
*Author, Revenue Management: Hard Core Tactics for Market Domination, (Broadway Books 1997)*

"We've worked with the author and appreciate the quality of his advice on structure and finance strategy. The book serves as a good reference guide to access information quickly."
*Kathy Lee-Sepsick, Founder/CEO, Femasys, Inc.*

"Venture capital investing is not generally well understood. As a result, many entrepreneurs find that both time and financial resources are misdirected in the search for funding. This book truly helps guide the individual through the process."
*John J. Huntz, Jr., Executive Director, Head of Venture Capital Arcapita Ventures*

"The *Guide 4.0* is a fantastic resource that is both comprehensive and imminently digestible. It should be treated as a de facto resource for entrepreneurs and investors, both neophyte and well-seasoned!"
*Nelson Chu, Managing Director, Kinetic Ventures*

"Interpretation of financial terms for entrepreneurs or seasoned business veterans can be confusing. The *Growth Company Guide* makes access to the terms straightforward, intelligent and useful."
*Robert T. McNally, Ph.D., Founder/CEO, Cell Dynamics, LLC*


*Praise for earlier editions:*

"Full of tips and strategies . . .. A real strength: short, to-the-point definitions of key concepts."
*Entrepreneur Magazine, April 2001*

"La bible du venture capital. Tres interessant . . .."
*Recherche de financements*

"Great for a financial officer whose strategy for raising capital requires regular review of expanding alternatives."
*David W. Howe, as CFO/VP, Lynk Systems, Inc.*

"Explain[s] just about every concept that should be known to you, the entrepreneur."
*EntreWorld.org, Kaufmann Center for Entrepreneurial Leadership*

"Your book will save me a lot of money! It's sometimes tough being an entrepreneur, but you made it a little more bearable."
  *Frank Hoen, President/CEO/Founder, Netpresenter*

"Nothing less than top notch. Direct, accurate, and straightforward. By far the high water mark in investment information offered on-line."
  *David W. Bruno, President and CEO, At the Bell, Inc.*

"A great resource for the uninitiated, an outstanding refresher for the experienced professional."
  *John N. Spencer, Jr., as Partner, Ernst & Young*

"*The Growth Company Guide* answers the key questions of my candidates. Sophisticated, to the point and covers the critical subjects."
  *Jerry Sears, Executive Recruiter, The Dunhill Agency, San Diego*

"Extremely useful, especially the methods for evaluating unlisted companies in which we are considering making investments. Very helpful by allowing us to structure our thought process and for communicating with our banking partners and investment committee."
  *Michael Carlton, Technolife 2010 , Luxembourg Life Science Fund*

"Heavy on content."
  *FinanceHub.com*

"Discusses business and legal strategies critical to growing companies and raising expansion capital."
  *BusinessCity.com*

"Important terms that companies should know when attempting to raise outside funding. How-to-advice . . .."
  *EdgeOnline*

"A concise and useful guide to venture capital. Reading this book is a must for new entrants to this close community."
  *Michael Easterly, as Founder/Partner, Legacy Investments*

"Excellent! An entire book on financing companies. Easy to use."
*ExpertsOn.com*

"Levels the playing field for the entrepreneur at the critical stage of raising capital. Required reading for an entrepreneur."
*David O. Ellis, as President, EGL Holdings*

"A highly valuable resource document which is used frequently by myself, by the professional staff of our premier ATDC technology incubator, and by the entrepreneurial companies of Georgia. It provides the entrepreneur with immediate knowledge of the basic principles and practices of the venture industry."
*Richard T. Meyer, Ph.D., Entrepreneur and former Director*
*Advance Technology Development Center*

"[A] Compendium of financial terms and their meanings that includes illustrative entries on various subjects, including business plans, going public, sample letters of intent and more. "
*Knowledgespace.com*

*Did you know?*

The first edition of the *Guide* series was published in 1987 as the *Venture Magazine Complete Guide to Venture Capital.*

The Soviet Union's Economic Ministry acquired case quantities of the *Guide* during Glasnost to train new entrepreneurs.

A complete online version of the *Growth Company Guide* was published on the Internet in 1996.

The *Guide* was adopted as the *Official Venture Guide* of IPO.com in 2000.

TechJournal South is publishing this 4th edition *Guide 4.0.*

# Growth Company Guide 4.0

### Investors
### Deal Structures
### Legal Strategies

## Clinton Richardson

Copyright © Clinton Richardson 1987-2007
All Worldwide Rights Reserved

Portions first published in

*The Venture Magazine Complete Guide to Venture Capital (1987),*
*The Growth Company Guide - Practical Advice for Growing Companies*
*and Private Company Investors (1993),* and
*The Growth Company Guide 2000 – Investors, Deal Structures and Legal*
*Strategies (2000)*

**Disclaimers**

The information contained in this book is provided for informational
purposes only and does not constitute legal, accounting, or other
professional advice. If you require such expert assistance, the services of
a competent professional person should be sought. *From a Declaration of*
*Principles jointly adopted by a Committee of the American Bar*
*Association and a Committee of Publishers.*

**Accuracy of Information**
While we endeavor to provide accurate and up-to-date information in this
book, no guarantee is made as to the accuracy or currency of the
information it contains.

A publication of TechJournal South
Research Triangle, North Carolina

ISBN: 978-0-6151-6409-0

*To the many entrepreneurs who have graced my life*
*and especially my entrepreneurial father*
*F. William Richardson*
*(1922-1983)*

# Contents

## Illustrative Entries

# *Preface*

Founding, funding and managing an entrepreneurial company are not for the faint of heart.

Federal and state regulations have set up a virtual minefield for the unsuspecting, inexperienced or over zealous entrepreneur. Venture capitalists, equity investors and investment bankers have their own language that company founders have to learn quickly, or risk paying the price for their naiveté.

Company founders have to learn to temper their dreams with an appreciation for the risks inherent in any new enterprise. Machiavelli said it best when he stated "There is nothing more difficult to take in hand, more perilous to conduct, or more uncertain in its success, than to take the lead in the introduction of a new order of things." - *The Prince* (1532).

Clint Richardson's *Growth Company Guide*, now in its fourth printing, is an excellent resource for entrepreneurs who are contemplating starting their own companies. Mr. Richardson offers keen insights into the identification and selection of venture investors; the various structures of investment transactions; and the development of creative strategies to accomplish the objectives of the budding entrepreneur.

Clint Richardson offers some observations on the ever-changing personal managerial skills entrepreneurs need to develop as their business grows and thrives. He offers some sage advice regarding how to deal with the volatile business environment that will confront the venture founder. He describes how to avoid some of the many pitfalls that confront every new business leader.

His insights and comments regarding the formation and development of a new enterprise are timely and cogent

**Steven G. Anderson, Founder and CEO**
**CryoLife, Inc. (NYSE:CRY)**

# *Foreword*

Womble Carlyle is proud to present the *Growth Company Guide 4.0* by Clint Richardson, a Member in our Atlanta office who has devoted more than a quarter-century to helping entrepreneurs launch, fund and expand their companies. Now in its fourth printing, the *Growth Company Guide* has helped thousands of successful companies and the investors who have helped those companies grow.

Clint is eminently qualified to write this valuable business reference. In addition to focusing his legal practice on emerging growth companies, Clint also helped found the Southeast's oldest venture and private equity trade association, the Atlanta Venture Forum. He understands firsthand the incredible effort and energy entrepreneurs devote to running their companies, and—on top of those responsibilities—the daunting challenge of raising money to grow the business. His *Guide 4.0* provides a roadmap to help business owners navigate the complex realm of fundraising.

When Clint wrote the first edition of the *Guide* back in 1987, it was one of the country's first books on venture capital. Through the years, the *Guide* has been a critically acclaimed primer on raising and structuring venture capital investments. In each edition, Clint has painstakingly researched and revised the content to give readers the most accurate, up-to-date information on this fast-changing field.

The *Growth Company Guide 4.0* epitomizes the type of innovative solutions that Womble Carlyle is committed to providing to help clients succeed, and Clint is the kind of dedicated, forward-thinking problem-solver who makes us proud to call him one of our own. We trust this guide will be a valuable resource to you and your company.

I wish you happy venturing and much success with all of your business endeavors!

**Keith W. Vaughan, Managing Member**
**Womble Carlyle Sandridge & Rice, PLLC**

xiv

# *Introduction*

Welcome to the fourth edition of a time-honored resource, the *Growth Company Guide 4.0.* In your hands is the latest, updated and expanded edition of a unique business resource. For two decades, prior editions of the *Growth Company Guide* have helped thousands of entrepreneurs and private company investors grow and finance successful companies.

### Authoritative, practical and accessible.

Presenting authoritative, practical content in an accessible format, the *Growth Company Guide* series helps business owners successfully navigate critical business challenges. Extensively updated and full of practical business and legal strategies, the *Growth Company Guide 4.0* contains counsel from an attorney and investor with 30 years experience with entrepreneurs and venture investors on the critical issues of fundraising, deal structuring, executive retention, and technology exploitation.

### Widely acclaimed by knowledgeable readers.

First published in 1987 as *The Venture Magazine Complete Guide to Venture Capital* and later updated and expanded as *The Growth Company Guide* and *Growth Company Guide 2000*, the *Guide* series has received critical acclaim from business managers, investors, business school professors, new business incubators and enterprise web sites.

Readers have hailed the series for its breadth of practical content, readability and ease of use. The series has been called everything from "highly valuable" to "top notch" to "full of tips and strategies" by leading enterprise resources and publishers. One French reviewer went so far as to declare the *Guide* to be "la bible du venture capital." The web resource of a leading enterprise leadership foundation declares that the *Guide* series "explains just about every concept that should be known to you, the entrepreneur."

Case quantities of the *Guide* have been purchased by prominent venture capital funds to train new associates and by a Moscow-based enterprise development agency to explain enterprise-building concepts to a new generation of Russian entrepreneurs. Business schools assign the text in their entrepreneurial business programs. Technology incubators use it to teach entrepreneurs.

Legal, accounting and business advisors use the book to help them advise their growing clients. Buyers of the *Guide* work around the world, from Silicon Valley to Boston to Moscow to Singapore.

**Practical business and legal strategies.**

The *Growth Company Guide 4.0* improves the odds of success for business owners and investors. It answers the questions most frequently asked by owners and operators of growing companies as they search for funding, negotiate for favorable financing terms, and address other critical growth company issues.

The *Guide* contains more than 250 strategy-packed entries arranged in alphabetical order. Each entry describes a word or phrase used by investors and entrepreneurs to describe an important growth company concept.

The book describes the types of investors who invest in private companies, methods companies use to attract these investors, and ways to evaluate funding proposals. It includes strategies for negotiating with investors and tools for valuing growing, private businesses. It addresses protecting and licensing technology as well as strategic partnerships and joint ventures. Using stock and other non-cash considerations to attract and keep key employees is discussed in detail.

xvi

**Unique, both-sides perspective.**

The *Guide* is different from other business books. It focuses exclusively on issues affecting growing companies. And, it does so from a unique perspective.

The *Guide* is not written by a venture capitalist, who may be biased toward protecting investors, or by an entrepreneur, whose experience may be limited to a few businesses. Rather, it is written by an attorney, one who grew up in the home of an entrepreneur and who has broad practical experience representing both growing companies and venture capital investors.

For more 30 years, the author, has represented growing companies, entrepreneurs, venture capitalists, individual investors, investment bankers, lenders, and executives in a wide array of legal and business issues faced by growing companies as they finance their expansion, deal with acquisitions and divestitures, survive shrinking equity markets, conduct securities offerings, borrow money, attract and retain key employees, structure equity and non-equity compensation packages, protect and exploit intellectual property, address company governance, and deal with contracts and other business matters.

**A real-time resource for busy entrepreneurs.**

The *Growth Company Guide 4.0* is designed to be a "real-time" resource for busy entrepreneurs and executives. Its A to Z, key-word format helps readers get directly to the information they want. For example, if a reader wants to know how venture capitalists price their investments, he can find out by simply turning to the entry entitled Pricing. There he will find a discussion of how investors evaluate and price investments in growing companies. The entry also suggests strategies for negotiating with investors and cross-references the reader to a discussion of the principal alternative pricing method contained in the Discounted Cash Flow entry.

If an investor offers funding but wants preferred stock and registration rights, the reader can quickly turn to the entries for those terms and learn the reasons behind the investor's request and the consequences the request may have on the company. In the <u>Business Plan</u>, <u>Business Plan Format</u> and <u>Summary</u> entries, the reader will find discussions of how business plans should be written to attract funding with detailed, tested outlines for producing a winning business plan and summary. In each case, the reader will also be directed to other entries in the book that treat related subjects.

The *Growth Company Guide 4.0's* key word entries make it easy to access practical experience and advice on issues of vital importance. Entries are not only extensively cross-referenced but organized by subject matter in a complete subject matter index.

**Good luck with your growing business.**

Use the book as a tool as you grow your business. Don't read it from cover to cover and put it away. Instead, keep it handy and refer to it often. And don't feel that you have to read the book from beginning to end. Start with an entry that interests you and proceed as you like through the others.

We hope the *Guide 4.0* will become as indispensable to you as it is to the serial entrepreneur who wrote us that his "dog-eared, underlined and highlighted copy is always within reach." We hope you will agree with the venture capitalist who wrote that the *Guide* "levels the playing field for the entrepreneur."

# Growth Company Guide 4.0

# A

**Adventure Capitalists** are entrepreneurs who invest money in private companies run by other entrepreneurs. Like the managers of venture capital funds, they invest to make money. But unlike those managers, they invest their own money instead of money others have placed in their care. Often, the money they invest is money they made by selling a company they started and grew.

Adventure capitalists fund new enterprises for a variety of reasons. They know that a wise investment can be very profitable. They believe their experience will help them identify attractive deals. Also, private company investing gives them something they cannot get in the public market: the chance to relive the experience of growing a business.

For many adventure capitalists, this last reason is the telling motivation. The exhilaration they experienced when growing their business may be waning. They may operate a public company that has become an institution or run a division of the large company that acquired their business. Many have retired from daily management. For each, there is something about making a new business succeed that draws them into adventure investing.

Like other investors, adventure capitalists expect to receive and study a business plan before they proceed. They usually require a seat on a company's board of directors and reports from management on the company's progress. Their active participation is important to them. They expect to be consulted by management and to have their advice heeded.

Adventure capitalists do not see as many deals as venture capital firms do. And, while most investigate companies before they invest, few have the know-how or resources to investigate an investment as thoroughly as a sophisticated venture capital firm. This, coupled with the fact that they do not have to consult with others before making an investment, often means a faster response on a deal.

The smaller deal flow and the part-time nature of their investment activity mean that entrepreneurs can sometimes get funding from an adventure capitalist they could not otherwise obtain from a venture capital firm. This is particularly true in smaller and earlier stage financings. Many venture capital firms, with their high administrative costs and large deal flows, will only invest in increments of $1 million or more. Others exclude the youngest companies from their investment profile.

Adventure capitalists are not so constrained. Many, however, lack the financial resources to do follow-on investments as a company grows. Practical experience also shows that the limited experience many adventure capitalists have in private company investing can make them less understanding when a company is delayed in meeting a milestone. Sometimes, they are less patient and more difficult to work with when things deviate from plan. This can lead to a refusal to provide follow-on investments or demands for repayment when additional funding is needed.

An investor's reluctance to provide agreed-upon future funding can be catastrophic when it forces management to divert attention to raising money when other aspects of the company's business need managing. Raising funds can be difficult with a disgruntled investor in a company. His refusal to meet a funding commitment can frighten away other investors.

Even binding contracts that require an investor to provide follow-on funding may not be enough to prevent problems. The expense and delay involved in enforcing those contracts against an unwilling investor may be too great for a company to afford. And the act of suing an investor can dampen the enthusiasm of other potential investors. The practical result can be an impoverished company forced to begin searching for money while struggling with a dissatisfied adventure capitalist.

To protect against this, entrepreneurs should investigate an adventure capitalist's reputation and ability to provide promised funding before they accept his money. If the investor offers to fund the company's needs in stages, management should ascertain how he intends to meet his funding commitments. If he must borrow or liquidate other promising investments to fund the company in later stages, he may become difficult to deal with when the money becomes due even if the company meets or surpasses its benchmarks.

By the same token, the adventure capitalist who does meet his commitments can provide a company with much more than money and he can do so when the company cannot attract traditional venture capitalists, either because its funding requirements are too low or its business is too new. The business savvy of a good adventure capitalist can often supplement management's experience in areas important to the company's growth and profitability. Those who have grown a company before, can often help management anticipate problems before they develop and counsel management on systems and organizational questions important to preparing a company to grow and attract future investors.

The advantages and disadvantages of seeking funding from an adventure capitalist can be summarized as follows:

*Advantages:*

- Actual, hands-on experience in managing a growing a company can help management anticipate company needs and manage growth more effectively.
- Willingness to make investments of less than $1 million.
- Willingness to spend time with management can translate into free or reduced-rate management assistance.
- Access to their personal network of business contacts can expand the company's non-financial resources.
- Willingness to sign guarantees or offer letters of credit can reduce company costs of lending or leasing.

*Disadvantages:*

- Because their financial resources are often more limited than traditional venture funds, they may do fewer deals and can be hard to find.
- Their lack of experience as investors may make them more difficult to deal with when the company falters or fails to meet its business objectives in a timely manner.
- They sometimes do not have the financial resources to provide agreed-upon future funding.
- As with any individual, if personalities clash they can become difficult to deal and unconstructive on the company's board of directors.

Where can you find adventure capitalists? Unlike traditional venture capital funds, there are few reliable and up-to-date compilations of adventure capitalists that are published. Sometimes groups of adventure capitalists form angel or private investor networks and these can be identified through regional entrepreneur support organizations. Networking in your local business and technology communities can help to identify those adventure capitalists who are actively looking for investments. Local bankers, accountants, and attorneys can often help identify adventure capitalists and provide introductions. *See: Angels, Deal Flow, Due Diligence, Ethics, Follow-On Fundings, Incubators, Seed Capital, Stage Financing, Venture Capitalists.*

**Affirmative Covenants** refer to the contractual provisions included in a venture funding that a company agrees to fulfill after the closing of a funding. The covenants typically appear in the financing or stock purchase agreement and are often accompanied by negative covenants that obligate the company to refrain from taking certain actions after the funding. Common affirmative covenants include:

- *Access to records.* The company will give the investor and its representatives reasonable access to company records and personnel.
- *Financial reports.* The company will furnish the investor with regular financial reports on the status of the company and its business. Balance sheets, profit and loss statements, and cash flow statements are usually provided monthly, quarterly, and annually. Audited annual statements are often required. Sometimes a short "state of the company" statement is also required from the company president on a monthly basis.
- *Budgets.* The company will prepare annual budgets approved by the board of directors and, sometimes, by the investor.
- *Existence and maintenance of property.* The company will preserve its corporate existence and all rights necessary to conducts its business and own its properties. The company will keep its properties in good repair.

- *Insurance*. The company will maintain adequate insurance. Often, the company also agrees to purchase key-person life insurance on the lives of management.
- *Payment of debts and taxes*. The company will pay its debts and taxes in the normal course of its business.
- *Compliance with laws and agreements*. The company will comply with all laws applicable to it and perform its obligations under its agreements.
- *Litigation and other notices*. The investor will be promptly notified of any lawsuit, default under a major agreement, or other event that could have a material adverse effect on the company or its operations.
- *Proprietary rights protection*. The company will take reasonable steps to protect its patents, trade secrets and copyrights. These steps may include securing secrecy or non-competition agreements from company employees and consultants.
- *Use of proceeds*. The company will use the funds provided by the investor in the manner described in the investment agreements.
- *Accounting system*. The company will maintain its current accounting system.
- *Board of directors*. Management shareholders will vote their shares to elect a representative of the investor to the company's board of directors.

Affirmative covenants can also relate to specific deal points that are to be performed after the closing of a funding such as management's undertaking to identify an additional board member or hire a suitable chief financial officer or other designated officer to round out the management team. Sometimes investors also require management agreements that engage them as paid consultants to the company after funding. *See: Consulting Agreements, Financing Agreements, Key Man Insurance, Management Agreements, Negative*

*Covenants, Operating Covenants, Reps & Warranties, Take Away Provisions.*

**Angels** are people who provide funding for very young companies to help get them started. The term comes from Broadway, where show backers have traditionally been referred to as angels. In venture capital, the term refers to an entrepreneur's first investors who put their money in before there is a product or a viable business.

Angels are most often friends, relatives, or business acquaintances who, because of their belief in an entrepreneur's abilities or in the value of his idea, are willing to invest significant sums of money in the entrepreneur long before his business is established. Most invest only a few times during their lifetime and are unsophisticated about investing in small companies. Many invest once, lose their money, and never do it again.

More often than not, an angel's investment is poorly documented, poorly structured and not particularly well considered. Because they lack familiarity with the types of problems young companies face and the difficulty of getting money out of a young company, angels often invest without obtaining an adequate method for cashing out. Entrepreneurs who value the friendship and commitment of their angels, however, will take pains to discuss how the angel can get his investment out so that both the entrepreneur and the investor share realistic expectations. *See: Adventure Capitalists, Cashing Out (or In), Seed Capital, Venture Capitalists.*

**Antidilution Provisions** are agreements that entitle an investor to obtain additional equity in a company without additional cost when a later investor purchases equity at a lower cost per share. Many investors insist on some sort of antidilution protection to protect themselves against the dilutive effects of future sales of stock at lower prices. Because these provisions can result in protected investors receiving free shares of stock when a future funding is at a lower price, antidilution provisions disproportionately reduce the percentage ownership of shareholders who are not protected. These unprotected shareholders usually include the company's founders and management.

Antidilution protections can appear as provisions of a financing agreement, in the conversion terms of a convertible preferred stock, in a warrant or option, in an investors rights agreement, in a shareholders' agreement, or in any other agreement between an investor and a company. One form of antidilution provision provides that the percentage of a company owned by an investor will not be reduced until some future event occurs. The event could be the passage of time, the funding of an additional sum of money or some other occurrence. Any stock issued by the company before the future event occurs would entitle the protected investor to receive more shares, either for free or for some agreed-upon price.

Another more common form of antidilution provision requires a company to give an investor "free" stock if it sells shares to a later investor at a lower price. For example, an investor who purchased 100,000 shares for $2 a share would be given more shares at no charge if the company later sold stock to another investor for $1 per share. If the earlier investor receives enough free shares to reduce his average cost per share to the price paid by the new investor (100,000 shares in this example), his antidilution right would be called a "ratchet." If he receives fewer shares, he probably has a "weighted average" antidilution provision.

Another type of antidilution provision allows an investor to purchase additional stock if later share prices are lower or if more than a certain number of shares are sold. These antidilution provisions are called preemptive rights. Provisions that entitle investors to obtain a percentage of outstanding stock in the future instead of a fixed number of shares, are also antidilutive. There are many other variations of antidilution provisions. Any agreement that tends to insure an investor his relative price advantage or percentage ownership is an antidilution provision.

Issues to consider when negotiating an antidilution provision include:

- *Type.* Is it a ratchet, a weighted average provision, or something different all together? Ratchets dilute unprotected shareholders more than weighted average provisions. Some weighted average provisions are more dilutive than others.
- *Term.* How long does the provision apply? When and under what circumstances does it expire? Does it terminate with the conversion of the investor's security or with a sale or public offering of the business? Will it expire after a fixed period of time or the accomplishment of some agreed upon goal?
- *Exceptions.* Does the provision apply to all sales of stock, all sales of stock at lower prices or only some future sales of stock? Are shares granted under the company's stock option plan included or excluded?
- *Impact.* Who will be impacted? Is it just management or does it impact other owners of common stock? If the provision guarantees a fixed percentage for a period of time, the other shareholders will bear all the risk of dilution.
- *Control.* Who will be in control of the decision to issue future shares than might trigger an antidilution provision? If it is not the shareholders who bear the brunt of the dilution, is the provision fair?

To protect management, all antidilution provisions should stipulate an expiration date. Under no circumstances should antidilution provisions be allowed to survive a public offering of the company's stock or the sale or merger of the company.

The survival of these provisions can hamper the ability of management to raise funds in the public market or to close a favorable merger or sale of the company. Also, whenever possible, investor antidilution rights should exclude the issuance by management of a number of shares for use in an incentive stock option plan or other employee incentive plan to help the company attract and retain key personnel. *See: Convertible Preferred Stock, Dilution (Percentage), Equity Penalties, Financing Agreements, First Refusal Rights (Shareholder), ISOs (Incentive Stock Options), Preemptive Rights, Ratchets, Weighted Average Antidilution.*

**Articles of Incorporations** are the documents that create a corporation and establish its charter. They are filed with the Secretary of State's office in the state of incorporation and enfranchise the company to conduct business. Articles of incorporation create the stock that investors purchase, establish the number and types of securities it may sell to generate capital, and articulate the company's purpose. When an investor purchases convertible preferred stock while funding a company, the Articles of Incorporation are routinely amended to create the convertible preferred stock used to make the investment. *See: Charter, Convertible Preferred Stock. See also Sample Charter.*

**Auctions** refer to a practice investment bankers use to maximize the potential sale price of client company. The practice involves completing a descriptive memorandum, or book, about the company that is then distributed to potential buyers. The community of potential buyers can be determined in a variety of ways. In a formal auction, the investment banker frequently specifies the proposed terms of a sale and invites bids to purchase the company. Interested buyers are invited to submit bids for purchasing the Company. *See: Book, Exits, Investment Bankers.*

**Audits** are methodical reviews by a disinterested third party of a company's accounts or, more generally, its financial situation. Most later-stage venture backed companies have audits of their financial books and records conducted annually by independent certified public accounting firms.

Few venture capitalists, however, expect a new company to have audited financial statements. Audits are expensive, and some early stage investors believe a young company's money is better spent in other areas. This is not to say, however, that investors do not expect a company's books to be complete and accurate. They do. They also expect companies to have financial reporting systems that report regularly on those business matters that are important to the company's success.

Venture capital investors usually examine a company's books and records thoroughly before they invest. Most of them also interview a company's internal accountants and outside accounting firm. They also routinely check behind a company's books by calling suppliers and creditors. In their financial statement reviews, they look for accurate and timely information they can use to evaluate the company's prospects. Often, working with an outside accountant can help a company improve its reporting and enhance management's ability to run the business and attract capital.

When a company anticipates going public in the future, it is wise for it to have audits conducted or, at least, to have independent certified public accountants verify the company's yearly inventories. This is because companies are usually required to disclose three years of audited financial statements in their initial public offerings. Sometimes only two years are required for limited offerings and, of course, a company that has been in existence for less than three years can only provide financial statements for the period it has been in business.

The audits required by initial public offerings can sometimes be performed just beforehand, but this can delay the offering and result in unexpected changes to the offering documents when the independent accountants apply their procedures to make the company's statements comply with the requirements of the Securities and Exchange Commission. This is particularly true with the advent of Sarbanes-Oxley and the many reporting and internal management controls it imposes on public companies. These requirements make early preparation and routine audits important for companies who have a public offering in their future.

When a company plans to go public, the safer, and often cheaper, course of action is to engage an independent accountant to conduct audits on a regular basis. Most accountants will take this opportunity to get to know the company better and suggest reporting mechanisms that can help management run the company more effectively. With company legal counsel, they can also help the company adopt reporting and management control systems required by Sarbanes-Oxley. At the same time, they can help management organize other records, such as reports on industry segments, to fit the disclosure requirements of initial public offerings. While audits may seem expensive for a young company, having an independent CPA oversee and review the company's books may reduce the time and cost of having the audit done at a later date. *See: CPAs (Certified Public Accountants), Due Diligence, Going Public, IPOs (Initial Public Offerings), Reports and Records, Sarbanes-Oxley.*

# B

**Bargain Stock** refers to stock that is acquired at low cost, usually in the early history of a company. Often referred to as "sweat equity," bargain stock is inexpensive because it represents an ownership interest in a company that is acquired before the company's business has proven its value. Sometimes called "cheap stock" or "founders' stock," this early-purchase stock almost always includes the original stock issued to the company's founders. Bargain stock only becomes a bargain when later events, resulting from managements' hard work and business acumen, create higher values for the stock that significantly exceed the value paid for its purchase. *See: Cheap Stock, Sweat Equity.*

**BDCs** refer to business development companies that are organized under special state statutes for the purpose of providing funds to small businesses in their state. Most can provide debt and equity financing.

Business development corporations often borrow the money they provide to businesses. When they do, they tend to finance later stage companies that can generate enough cash to enable them to make their interest and principal payments to the BDC. To support their own debt service, BDCs often lend money instead of making pure equity investments. This way, the portfolio companies support the BDC's obligation to repay its lenders by making regular payments of principal and interest to the BDC.

When this type of BDC acquires stock in a company, it usually requires warrants to purchase company stock in the future as a condition to their making the loan. The economic justification for requiring the warrant is the reduction in fees or interest rate or the willingness to make a loan others will not make.

Because BDCs that borrow their investment capital need to make regular debt service payments to their lenders, they (unlike equity backed investors) tend to be more interested in a company's ability to support and repay debt in the short term than in the company's prospects for rapid, profitable growth. As a result, BDCs are often precluded from investing in early stage companies or companies that cannot demonstrate the ability to generate sufficient cash flow to support the debt. *See: CDCs (Community Development Corporations), Debt Service, Personal Guarantees, SBICs (Small Business Investment Companies), Venture Capitalists.*

**Benchmarks** are performance goals used to measure or determine success. They often define a performance condition a company must fulfill to receive additional funding from an investor. Sometimes benchmarks are used to determine whether management will receive extra stock. Sometimes companies agree to issue more stock to an investor if the company does not meet its benchmarks, thus compensating the investor for the  company's failure to perform.

Benchmarks are also common in product development and sales performance agreements. In these cases, they may be used to determine when a payment becomes due to the developer or when the agreements may be terminated.

When used in financing agreements, unmet benchmarks almost always penalize the company and management for failure by postponing or canceling obligations to provide additional capital or by increasing the cost of capital. Consequently, management should always try to negotiate conservative benchmarks that are easily measured. Whenever possible, benchmarks should be at levels that management and the investor believe are realistic.

For example, a benchmark could be stated as "the sale of at least 500 product units during any single month before the first anniversary of the funding date." Failure to sell 500 product units in a month before that time would indicate to management and investors that the forecast was too optimistic or that the sales department was inadequately staffed.

As a rule, the financial projections contained in a business plan make poor benchmarks because they are usually prepared long before unforeseen, but inevitable, problems arise. Since many business plans are prepared to attract investors, they tend to be optimistic in their assumptions. In fact, venture capitalists discount most company projections when they price a deal and do not really expect a company to meet all of the goals stated in their financial projections. Few companies, even the best, meet all of their projections.

Nonetheless, business plan projections frequently provide the starting place for discussions about potential benchmarks. Some investors even try to impose benchmarks that are the same as the performance estimates contained in a company's projections. When this happens and the projections are not met, the unfortunate entrepreneur may find his investor released from future funding obligations, entitled to more company shares, or vested with greater control over company operations. To avoid these consequences, management should vigorously oppose attempts to use business plan projections as benchmarks. Conservative benchmarks should be used whenever possible. *See: Projections, Stage Financing.*

**Blank Check Preferred** refers to a method used to simplify the process of creating new classes of preferred and convertible preferred stock for a company. The method enables a company to use newly created classes of preferred stock to raise additional funds from sophisticated investors without obtaining separate shareholder approval for each new class of stock.

Blank check preferred stock is created by amending a company's articles of incorporation or charter to create a class of unissued shares of preferred stock whose terms and conditions may be expressly determined by the company's board of directors. The adoption of the blank check provision requires the approval of the company's board of directors and shareholders.

Once the provision is approved and incorporated into the company's charter, the board of directors can, within the limits contained in the provision, create new classes of preferred and convertible preferred stock and authorize their issuance to new investors without seeking additional approval from the company's shareholders.

A blank check preferred provision for a company that has already issued 2,000,000 shares of Series A convertible preferred stock might read as follows:

> The corporation is authorized to issue 10,000,000 shares of preferred stock, 2,000,000 of which shall be designated as "Series A Convertible Preferred Stock" having the rights, preferences, privileges and restrictions provided in Article II(b). The remaining shares of preferred stock may be issued from time to time in one or more series as determined by the corporation's Board of Directors, which is authorized to designate all rights, preferences, privileges and restrictions attendant to each series as well as the number of shares authorized for issuance in each series, which matters shall be expressed in resolutions

adopted by the Board of Directors and filed with the Secretary of State as required by the General Corporation law of the State.

Blank check preferred provisions must be prepared in compliance with the laws of the state in which the company is incorporated and so should be adopted only after consultation with a qualified attorney. Because these provisions authorize a company's board of directors to create securities that have preferences over existing shareholders without first obtaining the approval of affected shareholders, they may not be appropriate for every company. *See: Board of Directors, Control, Convertible Preferred Stock, Preferred Stock.*

**Blue Sky Laws** refer to state statutes that govern how stocks and other securities may be sold or offered for sale within their state. As with the federal securities laws, these statutes generally prohibit companies and shareholders from selling (or offering to sell) stocks and securities unless the sale is registered with the state's securities commission or fits into one of the exemptions from registration provided by the state's blue sky statute.

In most states, these exemptions parallel or complement many of the federal exemptions. Nevertheless, management should be certain, before offering or selling any securities, that the offer and sale will comply with the securities laws of the state in which the company is incorporated and in the states of residence (or formation) of each person to whom the shares are offered or sold. Failure to comply with the requirements of applicable blue sky laws can subject a company and its principals to substantial liability. *See: Legend Stock, Private Placements, Reg D, Restricted Securities, Safe Harbors, SEC (Securities and Exchange Commission), 33 Act.*

**Board Committees** are groups assembled by a company board of directors who are assigned responsibilities to oversee or duties to fulfill. Committees typically include only directors as members but may engage the assistance of company officers or others to fulfill their responsibilities. In many companies, significant responsibilities, such as review and approval of company financial reporting systems or executive compensation, are delegated to committees. Public companies in the U.S. are required to establish certain committees and to staff them with directors who meet certain designated qualifications.

Committees are usually established under authority of the company's bylaws and the laws of company's state of incorporation. They improve efficiency by giving management smaller groups of directors to work with on particular issues and by reducing the number of full-member board meetings that must be called.

Committees can be ad hoc committees established to address an pressing issue that will be resolved over time or standing committees established to deal with reoccurring issues over an extended period of time. Ad hoc committees might oversee a company's response to a governmental inspection or review. Or one might be established to assist management with a fundraising campaign, analysis of borrowing opportunities, or the hiring of someone to fill a key executive position.

The most common standing committees are audit committees, compensation committees, and stock committees. Audit committees typically establish and oversee auditing and accounting standards for a company and, thereby, establish the mechanisms by which management and the board monitor the operations of the company. Their review may include critical evaluation of the types of material the company's financial reporting systems tracks and the methods and timing for reporting to the board.

Compensation and stock committees are often combined into one committee that establishes salaries for company executives, recommends the issuance of stock options and other equity grants to executives, and oversees operation of any company incentive plans. Those plans could include qualified or nonqualified stock or stock option plans, phantom stock plans, or other benefits plans. Sometimes, separate benefits committees are established to deal exclusively with employee benefit plans.

Often the power of the stock committee includes the power to issue options to employees within guidelines established by the board of directors. When this is the case, the committee should be thoughtfully constituted to avoid inadvertent issuances of company stock. If the committee consists of one person, as is sometimes the case in younger companies, the company can find itself in difficulty when it later prepares to go public or merge with another company.

This is because a one-person committee can inadvertently leave the impression the company has made a stock or option grant when, in fact, no such grant has been made. When the committee and the individual are one in the same, later claims from employees based on conversations or writings from the individual about the prospect of future grants can fuel disputes that can be costly to settle. Often, these unintended "grants" do not come to light until the company has inked a deal to go public or merge with another company, making the value of the stock measurable and creating pressure for the company to resolve the dispute quickly.

In their early years, companies often find themselves short of cash and desperate to hire and keep qualified people. To bridge this gap, many companies issue shares or options to new and senior employees. The stock and options attract key people by giving them the opportunity to participate as owners in the company's future growth.

Given the intense pressures faced by new companies and their employees, discussions of more stock and more options can become commonplace. If the company president participates in these discussions and is the only person on a one-man stock committee, these discussions can easily lead to expectations of binding stock grants that come back later to haunt the business.

To reduce this risk, companies should avoid single-member stock committees so that stock and option grants require the approval of two or more persons before they become binding on the company. It is also helpful for the company's bylaws or board minutes to require options to be in writing and signed by all committee members. If company employees know this is the case, casual conversations are less likely to lead to misunderstandings. *See: Board of Directors, Going Public, ISOs (Incentive Stock Options), Stock Committee, Vesting Schedules.*

## *Revolution in Public Company Governance*

*Public and Congressional reaction to accounting and business governance scandals at Enron, ImClone Systems and WorldCom brought about a revolution in public company governance rules in 2002 with the adoption by the U.S. Congress of the Sarbanes-Oxley Act. Many consider the Act to be the most sweeping and dramatic change in securities regulation since the Depression era adoption of the Securities Exchange Act of 1934.*

*In addition to changing public companies relationships with their auditors, requiring CEO and CFO certification of financial statements and adoption of codes of ethics, Sarbanes-Oxley increased the role and independence of public company directors and board committees. Major stock exchanges followed suit using their listing rules to impose additional governance requirements on the companies listed on their exchanges.*

*The net effect of these changes has been to create more duties and require more time of public company directors. The additional standards and requirements adopted have also increased the exposure of public company directors and management to liability from shareholder suits. Companies have had to adopt costly new reporting systems. They have also had to reconfigure and expand the size of their boards to meet new standards for independence.*

*The cost of incorporating these changes into the company's operations has been steep. The average cost to companies in remuneration, increased professional fees, and redirection of management time required to comply with the new governance standards have been estimated to average more than $500,000 per year. Not surprisingly, many smaller public companies have reevaluated the benefits of being public against this additional cost and hassle and have chosen to take their companies private to avoid the added expense. See: Going Private, Going Public, Sarbanes-Oxley Act.*

**Board of Directors** is the governing body of a corporation. It is elected by the shareholders and, in turn, elects the company's officers. The board of directors sets company policy and direction and oversees the activities of its of officers. Boards of directors are also vested with the power to approve and issue stock and options. Their majority approval is required to approve major transactions such as significant acquisitions or borrowings. Creating a new class of stock, such as a new series of convertible stock to be sold to venture investors, is not among the board's powers, however, unless the company's charter authorizes blank check preferred stock. When blank check authority does not exist, boards can recommend new securities but the shareholders must approve their creation and inclusion in the company's articles of incorporation.

Most boards convene on a regular schedule that may meet quarterly or monthly. Special meetings are also sometimes called to deal with a specific issue, such as formally approving a new borrowing arrangement with a bank or addressing some unexpected event. For the most part, board meetings include presentations by management on the financial status and plans for the company as well as reports on significant matters occurring within the company. Plans for the future are a regular item at board meetings. To make them more useful, many management teams provide board members with agendas and financial reports ahead of the meeting.

Boards are configured differently from company to company. Some consist of as few as one individual or as many persons as the company's bylaws permit the shareholders to elect. Many entrepreneurial companies have small boards consisting of the company's president or the president and one or two key shareholders. Others contain many members and include general business advisors, industry experts, and others with skills to lend to the company. The size and configuration of a company's board of directors usually depends in large part upon management's method of operation and the concessions that have been made to raise money. Investors routinely require board representation as a condition to their investment.

Company boards also differ in how involved in they are in company management. Some consult regularly with the officers and set specific directions for company operations. Others may function more as sounding boards for management, becoming involved only at the request of management and then usually only to approve a specific action. As with the size and configuration of a board, the method of its operation usually reflects the personalities of the individuals involved. If the company has a strong chief executive officer and profitable operations, the board may be relatively quiet. However, if the board members have a significant stake in the company's success, they may stay very active with the company even when it is doing well.

What's the best configuration for a growing company's board of directors? The answer depends in part upon the talents of the company's officers and its success in attracting outside board members who can add significantly to the company's prospects. As a general rule, however, smaller boards are easier to work with than larger ones and also tend to be more actively involved in their companies. Too many members on a board can create inertia, making it difficult to call a board meeting and difficult for the board to arrive at a consensus when it does meet. As a result, entrepreneurs should try to keep their boards small, inviting only those people to serve as directors who have the interest and the time needed to devote to the company's affairs. Members should only be added to the board if they are required to complete a substantial funding or important contract, or if their contributions can add significantly to the strength of the company. *See: Board Committees, Bylaws, Charter, Control, Cumulative Voting, Stock Committee.*

## *Private Company Board Room Etiquette*

*Both private and public company boards of directors meet periodically to provide oversight to company management. Creating effective boards and interacting efficiently with directors can help management improve business operations. Here are some observations on board oversight and director management.*

- *Meeting Content. Meetings should include reviews by management of company financial results and business activities. Oftentimes, boards can be most effective when they help management focus on developing and monitoring meaningful metrics for measuring company progress. Financial projections and plans for future expansion are regular topics in venture-backed businesses. Providing copies of financial information and other presentations to be presented at the meeting in advance will help board members absorb the information and prepare them for constructive dialog.*

- *Minutes. Most board minutes summarize general discussions and provide detailed resolutions on matters formally acted upon by the board of directors. They also routinely reflect who attended, the location and place of the meeting, and whether a quorum was present. Draft copies of the minutes are often presented to board members for their comment and sometimes read at future meetings and formally approved by the Board.*

- *Meeting Frequency. While there is no standing rule on how frequently a board should meet, most boards meet quarterly. Some, particularly younger companies, meet more frequently. Meetings can be conducted in person or by telephonic conference.*

- *Committees. Boards are not required to have committees but may appoint committees to carry out board functions as needed. Private companies frequently use committees to manage qualified stock option plans or other equity grants to employees. As companies approach a going public decision, most formalize their committee structures and add independent directors to meet the increased corporate governance requirements for public companies.*

- *Number of directors. It is usually best to have an odd number of directors to avoid deadlocks. The most appropriate size for the board depends on the company's circumstances. As a general rule, smaller boards are easier to work with but may lack experience that might be available from additional members with specific qualifications.*

- *Attracting board members. Board members who have a significant stock ownership may receive reimbursement of their expenses for attending meetings but are usually not paid separately for their attendance. Attracting and retaining other non-employee board members may require compensation in the form of monetary payments, options, or stock grants. Another key feature to attracting and protecting directors against liability is the obtaining of reasonable amounts of directors and officers insurance to protect directors from suits by disgruntled shareholders. Indemnification agreements for directors and key man insurance can also make it easier to attract qualified candidates.*

- *Appointing directors. Directors are usually elected once a year by the company's voting shareholders. Shareholder agreements and special voting terms of different classes of stock need to be considered in conducting director elections. Boards often have the authority to appoint directors until subsequent shareholder elections in order to fill vacant positions.*

*See: Board Committees, Board of Directors, Corporate Governance, Sarbanes-Oxley, Stock Committee. See also: Revolution in Corporate Governance.*

**Boilerplate** refers to "standard" terms and conditions contained in an agreement that deal with routine matters common to contracts in general. Sometimes because of their routine nature, they are only lightly negotiated when the major terms of a deal are discussed. Common issues addressed in the boilerplate of a venture capital financing include:

- *Entire Agreement.* The contract contains all the agreements of the parties respecting the fundraising.
- *Accurate Plan.* The business plan provided by the company's management does not contain any intentionally misleading information.
- *Survival.* The parties' agreements and representations remain in effect after the agreement is signed.
- *Governing Law.* Specifies what jurisdiction's law will be applied to resolve a dispute involving the contract.
- *Counterparts.* The parties can sign different copies of the agreement and it will still be effective.
- *Notices.* Identifies how the parties deliver notices to one another.
- *Finder's Fees.* Provides whether a finder or broker was involved in the transaction and who is responsible for paying the broker's fees.
- *Expenses.* Describes who pays expenses incurred in completing the financing. Often specifies who pays the investor's attorney's fees.
- *Amendments.* The agreement may be amended or a requirement may be waived in the manner described in this provision.
- *Severability.* If one provision in the agreement is unenforceable for some reason the parties, nonetheless, agree that the other provisions will remain enforceable.
- *Specific Performance.* Each party agrees if they breach certain provisions that they will not object to a court granting the other party the legal right to force them to perform.
- *Construction.* The agreement will not be construed to favor the party who had the least to do with its drafting if a provision is imprecise or vague.

While they can be numerous, boilerplate provisions are not as standard or innocuous as some people believe (or would lead others to believe). In fact, boilerplate often contains important promises and representations made by a company and its principals. These promises and representations should be reviewed carefully.

One boilerplate provision that appears in many financing agreements is the "accurate business plan" boilerplate. Its purpose is to assure the investor that management has not misrepresented its existing business or its plans for growth. The provision frequently appears as a warranty of both the company and its management. It is a legitimate provision that can have very different effects depending on whose boilerplate is used. An investor friendly provision might appear as a representation that:

> The business plan of the company is accurate and complete and does not contain any untrue statement or omit to state any fact that is necessary in order to make the statements contained therein not misleading.

A literal reading of this particular boilerplate can make company management a guarantor of the facts, assumptions, and conclusions contained in the business plan. If future events prove any of those facts, assumptions or conclusions to be untrue, the company and its management could wind up liable to the investor for damages.

Since much of a business plan is based on soft information instead of hard, verifiable facts, and since much of it is judgmental and prospective, business plans almost always turn out to be untrue in some respect. When they do, a management group making this representation may find itself surprised by the liability it has assumed.

A friendlier and more forgiving boilerplate provision about the company's business plan, at least from management's perspective, would read:

To their knowledge, the business plan does not contain any untrue statement of a material fact or omit to state a material fact that is necessary in order to make the statements contained therein not misleading in light of the circumstances under which they are made. To their knowledge, the financial projections contained in the business plan were prepared accurately based on the assumptions described therein.

This boilerplate gives reasonable assurances about the plan but with less exposure to the company and its officers. It talks in terms of knowledge instead of absolute facts and acknowledges that the projections are merely estimates based on disclosed assumptions. These differences can be important as a company's progress varies from its projected plans. For management, they can mean the difference between business-as-usual and defending a lawsuit brought by an investor.

The key point to remember with boilerplate is that there is no fixed standard for the wording of these provisions. They need to be carefully considered with all the other provisions in an agreement before it is signed. Management should never sign an agreement until it is comfortable with the boilerplate it contains. *See: Financing Agreements, Investment Reps, Reps and Warranties, We Always Do It This Way, We Never Exercise Our Rights Under This Section.*

**Books** refer to descriptive memoranda prepared by investment bankers or company management for use in attracting prospective purchasers, investors, or partners. The books identify the company's purpose in preparing the book and describe its business and management. The term 'book' is most often used to refer to descriptive company memoranda prepared by professional investment bankers who have been hired to complete a company sale, fundraising, or other business transaction. *See: Auctions, Business Plan, Exits, Investment Bankers, Offering Memos, Prospectus.*

**Bridge Loans** refer to short-term borrowings that fund a company's operations for a fixed period of time. The purpose of most bridge loans is to provide a company with funds to continue operation until longer-term financing can be secured. That funding may come in the form of a loan, the sale of company securities, or receipt of a large payment. The need for a bridge loan can arise when a company runs out of cash before it succeeds in obtaining more capital investment through an offering of long-term debt or equity. Existing investors frequently provide the funding for bridge loans.

The short-term nature of a bridge loan creates pressure to complete the long-term financing package within the bridge loan term. Failure to find replacement funding within the term can result in penalties. Depending on the conditions in the bridge loan agreement, a default can give the lender substantial rights to company assets or additional influence over management. Negotiating an extension to a bridge loan agreement can be costly. If the bridge loan came with options granted to the lender, additional options may be required or the cost of the loan my increase. By the same token, management's eagerness to liquidate a bridge loan by finding replacement financing can cause it to conceded points in the permanent financing it would not otherwise concede.

The most important terms to consider when negotiating a bridge loan include the following:

- *Term.* The longer the term is the better. In any event, the term should be long enough to give management a reasonable opportunity to find and close a long term funding to replace the bridge loan.
- *Interim Payments.* From management's perspective, a loan without interim payments is preferable.

- *Interest Rate.* The cost of the loan should always be considered carefully. If options or warrants are granted to the bridge lender with the loan, the value of those options or warrants should be included in the cost.
- *Conversion.* Will the lender agree to convert its bridge loan into the security sold in the permanent financing that replaces it? A conversion commitment can make it easier to find replacement funding because it demonstrates the bridge lender's long-term commitment to the company.
- *Security.* Is the loan secured by company assets or stock? While less protective of the investor, an unsecured loan would be preferable to management and easier to document and complete.

When accepting bridge financing, management should be careful to understand the consequences if the long-term financing does not come through on time. It helps to negotiate as long a term as possible on a bridge loan and to borrow enough money to carry the company through the loan's term. If the bridge financing is with an outside investor, management should explore the possibility of converting it into longer-term financing if the need arises, even if the terms of converting the bridge are less favorable than the anticipated terms of the "take-out" financing. *See: Financing Agreements, Investment Memorandums, Letters of Intent, Leverage, Negotiation.*

**Brokers** are intermediaries who help companies and investors find one another. Brokers, who are licensed by the federal Securities and Exchange Commission, are sometimes confused with "finders" who provide similar functions but are not so registered. Many entrepreneurs hire brokers or finders to help them raise money. They do so hoping the broker will increase the likelihood of finding interested investors, get them a better price for their company stock, and reduce the amount of time they will have to spend in looking for investors. For a busy entrepreneur, the last reason may be the most telling. Time spent raising money takes time away from running the business.

Brokers can sometimes provide companies with valuable introductions that lead to financing. For the right company, they can sometimes create an auction atmosphere that can increase the negotiating power of the company in its discussions with investors. Some brokers can explain alternative sources of funding and help structure viable financing packages.

Few brokers, however, can completely replace management in the fundraising process. Usually, the most they can do is provide management with introductions and a chance to "pitch" the company. Potential investors invariably want to deal directly with management. As a result, most entrepreneurs stay involved in the fundraising process and continue to look for investors on their own, even when they hire a broker.

Brokers also help companies buy and sell businesses and look for joint venture or licensing opportunities. They also help with recaps, where one or more investors sell their company stock to a third party. Brokers also provide transaction fairness opinions and business valuations to support company sales.

Entrepreneurs should be careful when dealing with a broker. They should make their agreements explicit and put them in writing. The agreements should define what the broker's responsibilities are, when the broker is entitled to a commission (usually when an investor he introduced to the company funds the company's needs), how much the commission will be, and when his assignment expires.

To the extent possible, entrepreneurs should investigate the broker's reputation by talking with his present and former clients. They should also have explicit written understandings about the limits on the broker's authority to commit the company to any funding proposal and the conditions under which the broker may disclose confidential company information.

Common issues management needs to address carefully in any brokerage agreement include:

- *Scope of engagement.* When is the broker entitled to compensation? In addition to a retainer to cover operating costs, most brokers ask for a success fee computed as a percentage of the funds actually raised or the transaction value of a company sold. Under what conditions is the success fee payable? What, if anything, does the broker have to do besides identify the prospective funding source or buyer to get paid? Is the broker paid if the company is funded or bought by a source identified by the company or someone other than the broker? If so, is the success fee reduced because of the prior contact?

- *Size of the success fee.* Is the amount of the fee reasonable? How does it compare with rates charged by other money finders?

- *Success fee payment.* When and under what conditions does the success fee become payable? If portions of funds raised or sale price to be received are delayed or contingent on future activities, are corresponding portions of the success fee also delayed?

- *Broker's duties.* What does the broker have to do in addition to making introductions? Is the broker being engaged to prepare a plan or perform other specific tasks? If so, they should be specified.

- *Company rights.* How involved will the company be in the process of contacting funding sources? What controls does the company retain over the process? The company is ultimately responsible for the securities sold. Does the company have the right to control who the broker shows company information to? Does the company have approval rights over travel and other expenses incurred by the broker.

- *Termination of company obligations.* When does the engagement expire? When and under what conditions can the company terminate the agreement before the expiration date? What is the effect of termination on the company's obligations to pay fees? Most brokers insist on being paid a success fee if the company receives funding from a source introduced by the broker after the agreement has been terminated. They do this to remove the company's incentive to terminate the brokerage agreement just before funding in order to escape the success fee payment obligation. Even so, there needs to be some reasonable limit to the time after the engagement during which the company is required to pay a success fee. At some point the connection between the broker's activities and the funding become too tenuous to support paying a success fee.

- *Broker's license status.* Is the broker a registered broker-dealer? While the securities laws do not require all money finders to be registered, the structure of the company's engagement may require the broker to be registered. If he is not, it may cause difficulties with state securities laws when funds are raised.

Most brokers will work on a contingency fee or other prearranged fee basis. Whatever arrangements are made, however, management should understand that the broker's fee for raising money may end up coming out of management's pocket. Although rare, some investors insist that money they put into a company go toward developing the company's product, not toward paying a broker.

Other professionals who can provide introductions and advice about finding money and structuring financing packages include bankers, accountants, lawyers, and - probably the best source - other entrepreneurs. Some of the planning and document preparation can be developed with the help of qualified business planners. *See: Consultants, CPAs (Certified Public Accountants), Due Diligence, Finders, Investment Bankers, Lawyers, Packages.*

**Burn Rate** refers to negative cash flow and how fast a company goes through its cash. It is describes the rate at which a company uses up its capital base. A company with a burn rate of $1 million per month would exhaust a capital base of $6 million in six months. The burn rate can exceed forecasts whenever expenses exceed expectations or revenues fail to meet plan. As a measure of negative cash flow, burn rate is of intense interest to investors and management. *See: Cash Flow, Debt Service, Leverage*

**Business Plan** is a concise document, usually written by management, that describes a company, its products, business methods, financial condition, and need for funding. Business plans are written to clarify company purposes, to plan new directions, and to raise capital from private investors. Often, business plans are written exclusively to raise money.

A good business plan should be concise, complete, and easy to understand. It should introduce a company and its objectives in a positive way that makes investors want to learn more. The content of a plan should show that management knows what it is doing. It should show that the company's management has the experience and talent necessary to make the company succeed.

Most venture capitalists insist on seeing a company's business plan before they will even consider an investment. The document's content gives them a basis upon which to evaluate their interest. If the plan interests them, they will investigate further. If it does not, they will reject the company as a potential investment. Most venture capitalists see too many deals to spend time with companies whose business plans fail to excite them.

It is important, therefore, to prepare a business plan carefully and to make it easy to understand. Enough time should be allocated to writing and rewriting the plan so that it articulates clearly the excitement the company presents. At the same time, it must be well organized and carefully researched. Its discussion of the company and its industry should be based on thorough analysis. It should be thoughtful and realistic. After reviewing it, an investor should be excited about the company's prospects and impressed with management's preparation and candor.

There are many sources of help available to entrepreneurs who are preparing their first business plan. For example, accounting firms will often help prepare financial statements and projections. Some have professionals who will review a business plan and provide constructive criticism. Consultants can be used to conduct market research, assist at arriving at reasonable assumptions for projections, or help prepare parts of the plan. Other businessmen and lawyers will sometimes critique a business plan if asked.

For more information about business plans, entrepreneurs can check with accountants, lawyers, and other entrepreneurs. Many accounting firms have detailed brochures on how to prepare business plans that are available for the asking. Local bookstores, libraries, and the Internet also have valuable materials on business plans. *See: Brokers, Business Plan Format, Deal Flow, Downside, Due Diligence, Finders, Summary, Three Questions.*

# Writing the Business Plan

*Everyone talks about the importance of the business plan and they are correct to do so. Whether the plan is read by potential investors, friendly business associates or magazine editors, it represents the first opportunity to make an impression upon them. It will take lots of fancy footwork to overcome the bad impression created by a poor one.*

*Therefore, when all else is said and done, your plan's key points should be abundantly clear. [Clear means easy to read, easy to understand, complete and accurate.] The authors of books on plan writing are right to point out all the details one should remember when constructing a plan, and the importance of a well-rehearsed presentation to accompany it.*

*However, no book on plan writing I have read focuses on one particular benefit that I have learned from several attempts at writing business plans: to write a clear plan, one must have a clear idea of the business being planned. And it is the process of writing that clarifies.*

*Long ago, in journalism school, I learned two axioms that kept occurring to me as I wrote the business plan for this publication: If You Can't Explain It, You Don't Understand It; and, Muddy Writing Reflects Muddy Thinking. As I wrote the plan for VCCM [Venture's Capital Club Monthly], all the areas that I thought I could "fudge" became so apparent that the plan started to become farcical. At that point, I knew the only way the plan would get funded was for me to stop writing a plan and start planning a business. After that realization, the hard work really began, as I had no choice but to answer the questions I knew others would ask. Sure enough, readers asked questions about exactly what I knew was weak in the plan.*

*The process of writing itself benefits the business plan. Through the process of writing, the business becomes defined, its weaknesses become evident and demand to be* rectified. As the plan goes through subsequent drafts, the thoughts of new readers can be included, so that the plan becomes consensual. By following the outline in many of the "How To" books, the gaps in your own thinking should emerge. As you gather the information necessary to respond to the suggested outline, your plan becomes denser, containing more of the stuff it is supposed to contain and you become more confident of the quality of the business.

Sales and financial projections were the hardest part for me. I resisted making projections in which I had no confidence, and yet I knew the plan was supposed to contain them. I resolved this dilemma three ways: (1) I did a lot of research to find "comparable" information; (2) I assigned probabilities to the projections, thus indicating those numbers where I had great certainty and those where I did not; and (3) I went ahead and made projections based on nothing but "feel," and when the time came, I admitted to "making the numbers up" where no data were available. I asked the readers to suggest sources of data I may have over looked. When no one could suggest a source, they were more understanding of the necessity to "plug" a number in.

My point is to appreciate the writing of the plan as a necessary thinking exercise, totally separate from the necessary fund-raising exercise. While you may hate to write at all, in this case it is unavoidable and you had better plunge in. Show your work around, don't be defensive about the criticism, re-draft to include good suggestions and anticipate the questions others will ask and include the answers.

One last thing; once you've written it, start updating it.
By Steven Marshall Cohen

**Business Plan Format** refers to the organization and content of a business plan. A well formatted plan for a good business should reflect management's thorough understanding of its company, its products, and its market.

The organization of the plan should be apparent so that investors can find what they want quickly, without getting distracted by material that does not interest them. At the same time, it should present management's plan clearly and forcefully.

There are many general formats available to follow when writing a business plan. Plan formats can be found in business books, software programs, and on the Internet. Accountants, lawyers, and consultants can often provide outlines or guidance. The key in evaluating a format to use in connection with a fundraising effort is to choose one that allows management to present the company's opportunity well while addressing the questions investors expect to see treated. Here is an example of an acceptable format to use with a plan that will be the basis for a fundraising effort. It outlines many of the questions prospective investors need to see addressed to enable them to evaluate their interest in investing.

### *Sample Business Plan Format*
### *Table of Contents*

1. Summary
2. Company and industry
3. Products (or services)
4. The market
5. Sales and marketing
6. Management
7. Development plan
8. Overall schedule
9. Risks
10. Financial statements and projections
11. Appendix

# Contents

*1. Summary.* Investors expect a short summary of the important aspects of the company's proposal at the beginning of the plan. The summary should highlight the company's opportunity in a way that leaves no doubt in the reader's mind what the company does, the key qualities of its management and what it looks to achieve. If the summary is confusing or poorly presented, the venture capitalist will probably read no further.

The summary should identify concisely:

- The company's name, address, and telephone number.
- Who the investor should contact and how that person can be reached.
- The company's offering and what distinguishes it in the market.
- Key members of the management team.
- Why the company's market is attractive.
- How much money the company needs and when it will need it.
- How the company will use the money.
- How the investor will get his money back.

The summary should also contain abbreviated historical financial statements and projections to highlight where the company is and what it hopes to achieve.

It pays to write the summary first and to revise it several times. Have friends and business associates review this portion of the plan and ask them: Did it hold their interest? Did they understand what the company is making and why its product is unique? Was it clear how much outside capital management needs and how management intends to use it? Revise the summary if any of these points are missing or unclear.

*2. Company and industry.* This is the background section of the business plan. It should contain a concise history of the company, when it was formed, how management decided on its product, and what operations have been conducted. A brief description of the product and who its customers are should also appear here.

This section should give management's analysis of the company's industry and the opportunity it provides to the company and its product. The company's competition in the market should be described. What are competitors doing and how will the company's strategy be different and better? If there are economic, technological, or social trends that management believes will affect the company and its market, they should be mentioned.

It is important for this section to be well researched. Venture investors will conduct a thorough review of the industry and of management's analysis of it. If the company's analysis appears shallow or unsophisticated, they will not invest.

Most investors will have their own view of the company's industry. They will not, however, know the industry from management's point of view or why management thinks the industry holds a special opportunity for their company. If this section does not express the company's opportunity clearly, management should not be surprised if no one invests.

*3. Products (or services).* This section should describe the company's product. The description should emphasize what distinguishes the company's product from other offerings in the marketplace. Diagrams and pictures can be used if they will help investors understand the product and what makes it distinctive.

The plan should be candid about the product's shortcomings as well as its strengths. Is it ready for market? Can it be easily copied? Will competitors bring out the next generation of the company's product soon? A venture capitalist will not expect the product to be perfect. If management pretends that it is, it will only make him suspicious. In being candid, however, it is also important to describe the product enthusiastically.

This section should also describe the types of protection the product has from competition. If it is patented, the nature and importance of the patent should be explained. This may involve explaining why a particular patent claim is important to the distinctive features of the product, or why it would be difficult, costly, or time-consuming to engineer around the patent claim. If the protection of the product depends upon trade secrets or copyright protection, that should be explained.

Finally, the company's plans for future products should also be discussed. Few products dominate a market for long. Venture capitalists realize this and like to know that management has given some thought to what comes next.

*4. The market.* This is an important and difficult part of the business plan. Here management must describe in detail why the market for the company's product is such that the company can expect to achieve its sales goals despite the existing competition. It is here that management must explain and justify its choice of marketing strategy.

In describing the market, management should identify the major buyers for the company's product. Are they more interested in price, quality, or features? How does the company's product meet these interests? The results of any research conducted with customers should be described. Are customers interested in the product at the company's price? If so, how concrete is their interest? If not, why not, and how does their lack of interest affect the company's plans?

Give the magnitude of the market the company is going after in whatever measurements are appropriate - units, revenues, etc. Who are the players? How much will the market expand, and how much of the market must the company capture to succeed? Describe in detail the factors that are moving the market and the direction in which it is going. Is the company's product positioned to take advantage of the trends?

Avoid overestimating the size and growth rate of the market. Base the company's estimates of market size and projections of market growth on discussions with potential customers, distributors, and competitors. Also, review the available market surveys, but do so critically. Markets change quickly, and the most respected market survey is often considered outdated by insiders. Be careful to describe the market for the company's offering instead of some larger market that includes the company's market. For example, don't describe the market for all cardiac care products when your company sells only pacemakers.

Finally, evaluate the competition realistically. Evaluate competitors' products and their histories in the marketplace. Consider the market share and reputation for aggressiveness of each of the company's main competitors. Explain why potential customers buy from the company's competitors and why some of them will switch to a new supplier.

*5. Sales and marketing.* This section should contain an analysis of the company's sales and marketing strategy with projections of the unit sales management believes the company can achieve.

The company's strategy should be explained in detail. The company's sales techniques and pricing policies should be described in relation to the distribution channels it will employ. How did management arrive at its pricing? How does that method compare with the pricing practices of the company's competitors?

What part will advertising play in the company's marketing? What type of advertising will be employed, and who will direct the effort? How will the company sell and distribute its product? Will it use a direct sales force, independent agents or distributors? Discuss why management chose the sales and distribution channel it selected. Explain how management will organize the company's sales effort and how that effort will compare with that of its competitors.

*6. Management.* This section should describe the relevant qualifications of the important members of the company's management team and the function each person performs. The descriptions should emphasize relevant experience, training, and education. Business accomplishments that illustrate the ability of management to make the company successful, such as having grown a company or division in a similar market, should be highlighted.

If the company's management team has weaknesses, as all do, discuss them candidly and describe what plans management has for overcoming these weaknesses. If you choose to describe the company's accounting, legal, advertising, banking, and other professional relationships, do so briefly.

*7. Development plan.* In this is the section, management should explain how it plans to achieve the company's objectives. What is the current status of the company's product? If it requires further development before it is ready for the market, who will do the work and on what schedule? Will the company use outside experts for some of the work? If company employees will do the work, are they all on board, or does management still have to locate key people?

The development plan should describe the company's requirements for space, facilities, equipment, and personnel. Will the company begin manufacturing immediately or contract out manufacturing at first? If the company will do some assembly work or testing, explain why and how. Describe who the company's suppliers will be and how management will control quality, production, and inventory.

*8. Overall schedule.* This schedule should show when management plans to accomplish each of the milestones that are critical to the company's success. A well-considered and realistic schedule demonstrates management's ability to plan the company's growth. It also displays management's ability to identify the critical tasks to be achieved by the company and how they interrelate.

This section should contain a flow chart analysis that shows the timing of the company's product development and operational activities and when the company plans to meet the important thresholds in its marketing plans. Some of the events management might cover include:

- When the company was incorporated.
- When the management team will be completed.
- When the company's product prototype will be finished.
- When the company will complete product testing.
- When the company will begin producing products for sale.
- When products will be offered for sale.
- When the company will begin receiving orders.
- When the company will make its first deliveries.
- When the company will begin receiving payments for products shipped.

The schedule might also show:

- When the company will need money and in what amounts.
- When trade shows or exhibitions are scheduled.
- When and what additional people will need to be hired.
- When the company will need to add new facilities or significant amounts of equipment.

Be realistic in the schedule. Follow it with a narrative discussion of those events that are most likely to be delayed and how those delays could affect the company's overall schedule. Also, explain what management can do to make up for any schedule slippage that occurs.

*9. Risks.* Every venture capitalist knows that new businesses are risky. They may not, however, understand which risks are most dangerous to the company or how management intends to neutralize them. This section enables management to discuss those risks and how it plans to overcome them. By doing this thoroughly, management increases its credibility with investors and demonstrates its foresight.

Some risks that might be discussed include:

- Risks that relate to the industry.
- Risks associated with not obtaining financing on schedule.
- Risks of not meeting the development schedule or the product cost estimates.
- Risks that competitors may develop new, more competitive products.
- Risks that key personnel cannot be located or retained.

Every major risk should be addressed. Nothing is gained by omitting important items from the list of risk factors. Many managers find it useful when preparing this section to first set down in a separate writing the five risks most likely to hurt the company is a material way followed by a practical discussion of what management can do to minimize those risks.

*10. Financial statements and projections.* This section should contain historical financial statements of the company's operations and projections of future operations. The projections should be for a period of three to five years. They should include profit-and-loss forecasts, cash flow projections, and pro forma balance sheets broken out on a monthly basis.

Narrative explanations should accompany the financial projections, highlighting important facts and assumptions contained in the projections as well as conclusions management wants the investor to draw.

*11. Appendix.* The appendix should supplement the business plan and support management's conclusions. Use the appendix to attach full resumes of key management members when those resumes elaborate on relevant experiences. Copies of key contracts or commitments from suppliers and customers that demonstrate the viability of the company's product or concept can be included. If there are any surveys or studies that emphasize the company's good prospects or explain a key concept, photocopies of relevant portions of those surveys can help an investor understand the company better. *See: Brokers, Business Plan, Downside, Due Diligence, Exits, Market Research, Packages, Projections, Summary, Three Questions.*

## Buy-Sell Agreements

**Buy-Sell Agreements** are the Russian roulette contracts of private company finance. They enable one shareholder to force another shareholder to sell his ownership but only by giving the other shareholder the option, instead, to purchase the initiating shareholder's ownership. They appear most frequently in situations where two dominant shareholders own control of a privately held company. In these cases, they can provide a last-resort method of breaking a deadlock between owners who disagree over the management of a company. When they are used, they frequently appear in standalone buy-sell agreements or as part of other financing or shareholders agreements.

Buy-sell agreements typically work like this: Two shareholders agree that under certain agreed upon conditions, either may buy all of the other's stock in the company. By the terms of the agreement, whichever shareholder exercises this option must also offer to sell his stock to the other shareholder. The purchase price per share is usually the same for both shareholders but undetermined when the contract is signed. The initiating shareholder selects the price per share and makes his offer to buy. The other shareholder can then sell his stock or buy the other party's stock at the tendered price. In this way, either shareholder can force the other out of the company but only by risking having his interest bought out instead.

Sometimes outside investors insist on buy-sell agreements with the owner-managers of companies they fund. They do so to provide a last-resort mechanism to withdraw from a company at a later date. With a buy-sell, an investor knows that if the owner-manager is unwilling to sell the company or assist them in obtaining liquidation, they can use the buy-sell agreement to either get their money out or get management's shares. With management's shares, they can replace management or have enough shares to sell a controlling interest in the company to others.

The risk-of-sale feature, leads many to assume these agreements are fair allocations of risk inasmuch as both parties face the same risk of being forced to sell it they try to force a sale. In practice, however, buy-sell agreements often tend to favor the investor and result in the removal of the owner-manager. This is because the agreements are usually exercised when a company is not living up to expectations. In these circumstances, it can be hard for an owner-manager to raise enough money to buy out the investor. Even when the owner-manager succeeds in raising the money, he may have to welcome a new investor into the company to raise the funds. This can reduce the manager's ownership in the company.

When management cannot raise the money it loses its stock and its control of the company. If management has given personal guarantees to secure company borrowings, not only does management lose its interest in the company, it also remains bound on its guarantees. Because many new company borrowings require guarantees, management should be sure that any buy-sell agreement it signs requires the investor to get management released from any personal guarantees it has made for the company. Otherwise, management may remain liable on its guarantees while the company's ability to repay its loans is determined by how well others manage the company.

With any buy-sell agreement, management should try to structure the agreement in ways that reduce the investor's ability to exercise the buy-sell and increase the chance that the investor, and not management, will be the party that sells. The best way to keep a buy-sell silent is to make its exercise contingent on the company failing to meet goals that are easily attainable. As long as these goals are met, the investor has no right to force a buy-sell on management. Making the purchase price lower for management can make it easier for management to buy out the investor and stay in control.

Giving management the right to use promissory notes for part of the purchase price helps too, by making it easier for management to pay for the investor's shares. So does giving management a long time in which to respond to the investor's offer. It is much easier to raise $5 million in 180 days than in 30 days. Finally, buy-sells should expire after a fixed period of time.

Factors to consider when faced with a buy-sell proposal include:

- *Relative ownership.* If the parties to the buy-sell do not own approximately the same number of shares, the party with the fewer shares will have to buy more shares. If the share prices are equal, this translates into a higher purchase price for the smaller party.
- *Relative resources.* If one party has more financial resources than the other it may prove easier for him to buy than the other party.
- *Exercise prices.* Should each party have to pay the same per share price? If not, what kind of discount is appropriate and for which party?
- *Response time.* How long does the party receiving the offer have to reply? Is the period long enough to enable him to obtain necessary funding?

- *Payment method.* How and when does the buying party have to pay the purchase price? Do both parties have to pay in the same way or can management pay a portion by promissory note?
- *Conditions to exercise.* Should there be conditions that must be met before either party can exercise their rights under the agreement. For example, should a predefined period of time expire or should their be a failure to meet a defined goal.
- *Guarantees.* If one party has guaranteed company notes or leases, he may want to provide for his release in case his interest is bought out.
- *Substitution.* Can the company substitute for management as a buyer? If it can, company resources may be used instead of management's to buy out the investor.
- *Termination.* When does the agreement terminate?

Buy-sell agreements are also sometimes used for estate planning purposes in privately held companies. When funded by insurance, they can provide for orderly succession of ownership and liquidity for the estates of company owners when one owner dies. These buy-sell agreements, because the buy-out is funded by insurance and because the sale is triggered only by an owner's death, provide none of the potential inequities described above. Care must be taken with these agreements to provide assurances of continuing insurance coverage and mechanisms for adjusting price to reflect future values. *See: Co-Sale Agreements, Exits, First Refusal Rights (Shareholder), Liquidity Agreements, Puts, Shareholders' Agreements, Unlocking Provisions.*

**Bylaws** refer to one of the core operating documents of a corporation. The other core document is the charter or articles of incorporation. Bylaws generally provide direction for the general operation of a company while the charter establishes the company's franchise and provides for its capital structure and ownership rights.

Bylaws are adopted when the company is formed and govern such things as the election of directors, the size of the board of directors, and the election and function of each of the company's officers. Bylaws also specify how meetings of directors and shareholders may be called and held. They identify quorum and voting requirements for meetings. Most bylaws authorize directors and shareholders to take action by unanimous or majority consent in lieu of formal meetings. Most also provide for indemnification of company directors provided their actions are not reckless.

When there are classes of stock with specific rights to appoint a representative to the board of directors, these rights are sometimes reflected in the bylaws. Sometimes they can also appear in a company's charter or a shareholders agreement. Bylaws can be amended by the company's shareholders. They can frequently also be amended by the company's directors. *See: Charter, Directors' Indemnities.*

**Calls** refer to a company's right to require a shareholder to surrender shares of company stock in return for payment of an agreed-upon sum of money. Calls are created by contract or charter provision and are usually contingent upon the happening of some event, such as the passage of time or the accomplishment of some goal by the company. Most calls are optional and give the company the right but not the obligation to redeem stock. Calls can be also made mandatory, in which case the company is required to redeem when the triggering event occurs.

Company management might use a call to redeem an investor's stock when another investor is willing to pay a higher price for shares. Even without a ready investor, management might call an investor's stock if it believed the market value of the company's stock had risen to more than the call price. In each case, redeeming stock at a below-market call price can increase the value of the stock held by the remaining shareholders.

The cost of exercising a call is the cash required to pay the investor for his shares. In deciding to exercise a call, management must weigh the potential benefit of redeeming shares against the company's need for the cash used to exercise the call and its ability to replace that cash when needed.

Calls can also be used to end stock preferences. In some financings calls are used to force a purchaser of convertible preferred stock to chose, after a predetermined period of time has elapsed or after the company has met an agreed-upon milestone, between converting his preferred stock into common stock or accepting the call payment in redemption of his stock interest. When used for this purpose, the call provisions are frequently included in the convertible preferred stock terms that appear in a company's charter. They empower the company to purchase the convertible preferred stock at a fixed price after a designated date or event. The holder of the stock can avoid the company's purchase only by using the convertible preferred stock's conversion feature to turn the stock into common stock before the call. When used in this way, the call mechanism sets a time limit on the preferences granted in the preferred stock.

As with a put or any other stock redemption, management must be careful when exercising a call to comply with corporate law requirements when funding the stock purchase. Corporate codes routinely limit the types of funds a company can legally use to redeem shares. *See: Cash Flow, Convertible Preferred Stock, Convertible Securities, Exits, Puts.*

**Cash Flow** refers to the money coming into (actually received) and going out of (actually disbursed) a business. Cash comes into companies from product sales, service fees, royalties, stock sales, and borrowing. Cash goes out to pay operating expenses like payroll, make capital expenditures like equipment purchases, and to service debt.

Planning for future cash needs, with regularly updated cash flow projections, is important to running a successful business and to attracting outside capital to fund growth.

Venture capital investors are very interested in whether a company will have sufficient cash flow to meet its needs and very sophisticated in analyzing a company's need for cash. Most investors will study a company's monthly cash flow projections carefully before making an investment decision.

Inadequate cash flow can cause acute problems for any business. A shortage of cash can divert management from the crucial business of running the company to the business of searching for funds. It makes it harder to pay bills and finance operations. Cash flow problems quickly become visible to suppliers and can be used by customers to suggest to customers that the cash strapped company is unstable. The damage from such suggestions can be considerable.

Fast growth, even with growing profits, can put extreme pressures on a company's available cash. Growing sales are usually accompanied by demands for cash that grow faster than the growth in cash receipts. This is due, in part, to the fact that more sales create more receivables before they create more cash receipts. At the same time, demands for payment from suppliers grow, and other new expenditures must be made to support the growth. Many of these expenditures cannot be delayed.

This mistiming between the receipt of funds and their disbursement can become so severe that operations are interrupted and profitable expansions must be postponed. Because of this possibility, companies should thoroughly analyze and review their anticipated cash flow needs on a regular basis, even when they are not searching for capital. *See: Debentures, Debt Service, Equity, Leverage.*

**Cashing Out (or In)** refers to when an investor exchanges his investment for cash. A shareholder who sells his company stock for cash can be said to have "cashed out." The term is near and dear to the hearts of private company investors, who have limited opportunities for turning their investments into cash. Even cashing out at a loss can be preferable to holding stock in a declining company, particularly when the stock is illiquid because of restrictions on resale. Cashing out can be accomplished in a variety of ways, including selling shares in a public offering, receiving cash from the sale or merger of the company, selling shares to the company through a put or call exercise, or selling shares to a new investor. *See: Buy-Sell Agreements, Calls, Convertible Securities, Co-Sale Agreements, Demand Rights, Exits, Going Public, Liquidity Agreements, Piggyback Rights, Puts, Registration Rights.*

**CDCs** refer to community development corporations. These governmental or quasi-governmental agencies provide debt or equity funding to companies that locate in their communities. They are often affiliated with local municipalities or economic development agencies.

CDC managers review investments and conduct due diligence as other investors do. But because of their interest in community development, they often consider factors that do not interest traditional venture capitalists, such as the employment opportunities and tax revenues the proposed business will generate for the community. Businesses that meet a community need can sometimes secure funding from a CDC when other investors might not be interested. And the funding they secure is sometimes at lower rates and for longer terms than other sources will provide. This is because of many CDCs consider the generation of new jobs and tax revenues by the portfolio company to be part of their investment return, which enables them to justify lower monetary returns on investment and longer-term investments. *See: BDCs (Business Development Corporations), Corporate Venture Capital, Due Diligence, ROI (Return on Investment), Venture Capitalists.*

**Charter** is the formal document filed with the incorporating authority that creates and enfranchises a corporation. It is sometimes called the articles of incorporation and is usually filed with the Secretary of State in the State in which the company is formed or in Delaware, where an extensive body of corporate law has been developed. Charters typically spell out what activities the corporation may undertake, the number and type of shares of capital stock it is authorized to issue, and the names of the company's founding members. Charters often include indemnification language to protect the company's officers and directors.

Charters for companies that have venture capital investors routinely authorize more than one class of capital stock, with the venture investors purchasing shares of convertible preferred stock whose terms are specified in the charter. Typically, the charter is amended to create the venture investors class of stock at the time of funding. As a general rule, charters may only be amended by a vote of the shareholders. Charters with blank check preferred provisions, however, enable the company's board of directors to create the new class of stock, within limits, without shareholder approval. *See: Blank Check Preferred, Bylaws, Convertible Preferred Stock.*

# Basic Charter for a Company With No Venture Capital Investors

### NEWCO INC. ARTICLES OF INCORPORATION

The undersigned, being a natural person of the age of at least 18 years and acting as sole incorporator to organize a corporation (the "Corporation") under the provisions of the Georgia Business Corporation Code, does hereby adopt and sign the following Articles of Incorporation:

#### I. NAME

The name of the Corporation is: Newco Inc.

#### II. AUTHORITY

The Corporation is organized pursuant to the provisions of the Georgia Business Corporation Code.

#### III. DURATION

The Corporation's duration shall be perpetual.

#### IV. PURPOSE

The nature of the Corporation's business is to engage in any lawful act or activity for which corporations may be incorporated under the Georgia Business Corporation Code and to exercise all the rights, privileges, immunities, and authority granted to or exercised by business corporations under the laws of the state of Georgia now in effect or that will become effective during the existence of this Corporation.

#### V. CAPITALIZATION

The aggregate number of shares of stock that the Corporation shall have authority to issue is 100,000, all of the par value of $.001 each. All such shares are of one class and are designated as Common Stock.

#### VI. MINIMUM CONSIDERATION

The Corporation will not commence business until it has received consideration of at least $500.00 for the issuance of shares.

## VII. DENIAL OF PREEMPTIVE RIGHTS

*No holder of any shares of any class of the Corporation shall be entitled as a right to subscribe for, purchase, or otherwise acquire any shares of any class of the Corporation which the corporation proposes to issue, any rights or options which the Corporation proposes to grant for the purchase of any shares of any class of the Corporation, or any bonds, securities or obligations of the Corporation which the Corporation proposes to issue or grant which are convertible into or exchangeable for, or which carry any right to subscribe for, purchase, or otherwise acquire any shares of any class of the Corporation.*

## VIII. CAPITAL SURPLUS

*The Corporation may make distributions to its shareholders out of its capital surplus and purchase its own shares out of its unreserved and unrestricted capital surplus upon such terms and conditions, as the Board of Directors shall deem appropriate.*

## IX. REGISTERED AGENT AND OFFICE

*The address of the initial registered office of the Corporation is 2800 Peachtree Street, Atlanta, Georgia 30303, and the name of the initial registered agent at such address is Clinton Richardson.*

## X. DIRECTORS

*The number of directors constituting the initial Board of Directors of the Corporation shall be one and the name and address of such director is:Ann Arthur, Imagination Lane, Atlanta, Georgia 30335*

## XI. INCORPORATOR

*The name and address of the incorporator is: William Francis, 1201 West Peachtree, Suite 3500, Atlanta, Georgia 30309*

*IN WITNESS WHEREOF, the undersigned executes these Articles of Incorporation this 1st day of September, 2007.*

**Cheap Stock** refers to company shares that were issued prior to a public offering at prices lower than the fair market value. The term is also used to refer to stock issued to founders and others at low prices that may, in fact, have reflected fair market value at the time but which, in the context of much higher public offering prices, later appear to have been sold at a discount.

A number of states impose restrictions on cheap stock issued to company promoters when the company conducts a public offering. The securities commissions in these states generally review stock issuances to company insiders during the three years prior to the public offering for the purpose of determining whether the stock was issued at less than its fair market value when it was sold. If the stock was issued at a steep discount to the proposed public offering price, one or more state securities commissioner may determine the stock to be cheap stock and impose conditions on the company's ability to conduct its offering in their state. The most common condition is to require holders of the cheap stock to escrow their shares for a period of time. The net effect is often to reduce the number of states in which a company chooses to qualify its offering, thereby depriving the residents of states that are excluded of the opportunity to invest in the new company's offering.

A different cheap stock issue can arise with the federal securities commissioners. At the federal level, the SEC can determine that options issued to company employees under a company's incentive stock option plan were issued at exercise prices that were lower than fair market value at the time of issuance. In this case, a cheap stock determination can result in reclassification of qualified options as non-qualified. This can result in a charge to earnings for the company and a loss for the employee of the beneficial tax treatment afforded to qualified stock options. *See: Bargain Stock, Blue Sky Laws, Going Public, IPOs (Initial Public Offerings), ISOs*

*(Incentive Stock Options), Qualified Stock Option Plans. See also, The Language of Going Public.*

**Closing** is when all of the agreements between two or more parties are completed, the documents are signed, and the deal is consummated. In a venture funding, the closing is when the company formally issues new shares to the investors and the investors provide their first funding. The financing agreements signed at the closing identify the closing obligations of all parties, designate the rights and privileges of the investment security sold, and contain agreements to govern the ongoing relationship between the investors and the company.

Closings are a time of high expectations and emotional release. They often follow a long and involved process of negotiation, document preparation, and revision. Due diligence investigations typically continue right up to closing through the preparation of extensive disclosures by company management that are included as written representations in the closing documents. When the disclosures contain surprises, terms of the deal can change. If the surprises are significant enough, the deal can be upended. A successful closing brings the uncertainty of the process to an end and accomplishes the parties' objectives. *See: Due Diligence, Financing Agreements, Reps and Warranties.*

# How to Care for an Entrepreneurial Investor

*Intelligent information transfer and timely communication are my prescriptions for a continuing happy (or at least satisfactory), healthy and nondestructive investor-entrepreneur relationship. What I mean is very simple. The entrepreneur should prepare the investor for realism, frequently spelled the same as disappointment.*

*Specifically, the entrepreneur should establish a regularly scheduled series of communication elements with the investor(s). These communication elements should be both written and personal. I am a strong believer that monthly newsletters with charts should be sent to investors. The charts should be the reflections of a living business plan. The charts display previously achieved results, current period results, and projected results as well as new or amended projections.*

*The entrepreneur should meet with the investor at least quarterly, and probably monthly, for the purpose of keeping the investor within the family and delaying, for as long as possible, the development of the "we v. they" syndrome. Once the we/they thinking has developed and the camps become established, the problems begin. The entrepreneur should do everything possible to have the investor play a role that keeps him feeling that he is on the entrepreneur's team and is in fact making a contribution. If the problems of the company in achieving objectives are fully and fairly understood by the investor and he feels that he is on the team, he will possibly be available for additional funding and certainly not be resentful of the need for it.*

*Entrepreneurs can ask their investors to help: Help to gain information, help to gain customers, help with public relations and, on occasion, help with personnel matters. The entrepreneur should recognize that in most cases the investor had to have been competent in some areas of activity that are, or can be, useful to the entrepreneur's company to have made the money that he has invested.*

*By Arthur Lipper III, author of The Guide to Venture Investing Angels.*

**Clubbing** refers to the practice of investors joining together and making a joint offer to purchase a company. The practice can be used to gather together enough investors to make an offer or as a means for sharing a deal among investors. Because it has the potential to reduce competition among investors for a given deal, the practice can sometimes result in lower prices to the selling company's owners. *See: Syndications.*

**Collateral** is any asset pledged as security for a loan. If a collateralized loan is not repaid as agreed, the creditor can foreclose upon the collateral to secure repayment. By reducing the lender's risk, collateral makes it easier for a company to borrow or to borrow on more favorable terms. In contrast to bank loans, which are often collateralized, most venture capital investments are made with little or no collateral.

Typical assets used for collateral include land, buildings, equipment, vehicles, inventory, accounts receivables, cash balances in accounts, and furnishings. Patents, trademarks, intellectual property, computer software, contract rights, stocks, bonds, and certificates of deposit are also used as collateral.

Available collateral should not be ignored. When borrowing from traditional lenders, it can decrease the lender's risk and thereby increase the principal amount lent to the company. It can also reduce the interest rate charged for the loan. By making more borrowed funds available to a company, collateral can delay the need for expensive venture capital and the dilution of management's stock ownership that occurs when equity securities are sold. Collateral can sometimes be used to secure portions of a venture capital investment as debt and thereby make the capital easier to attract and less dilutive to management. *See: Dilution (Percentage), Equity, Factoring, Inventory Financing, Nonrecourse Debt.*

## Commitment

**Commitment** is what venture capitalists look for in entrepreneurs. They prefer to invest in companies whose management is fully committed to the company's success. They want management's passion, attention to detail, and full-time attention.

Starting a new business is an exhausting and all-consuming endeavor. Entrepreneurs often work more than twelve hours a day, day after day, seeing to all the details that make a company succeed. Weekend and late night work is common. In the process, family relationships can suffer. Investors understand this. They want to invest in management teams whose families know this as well and who are prepared to make the sacrifices required.

Investors also prefer management teams who show their commitment by investing their own financial resources. Entrepreneurs who have a significant financial stake to lose if the business fails, the logic goes, are more likely to put in the extra effort it can take to succeed. By the same token, many investors do not like entrepreneurs who hedge their financial bet on the company. Entrepreneurs who retain an unreasonably large safety net of personal assets outside the company make some investors nervous and reduce the potential pool of likely investors fro their company. *See: Angels, Entrepreneur, Ethics, Zeal.*

## Commitment Letters

**Commitment Letters** are documents issued by lenders to companies after they have decided to make a loan but before they are ready to complete the formal loan documents. Commitment letters vary in complexity and length but are usually much shorter than the eventual loan agreements. They typically describe the business terms of the proposed loan and the key terms under which the lender is willing to advance funds.

The terms of a commitment letter routinely include the type, amount, term, and interest rate for the loan as well as any separate fees being charged by the lender. Repayment terms and type of security interests granted, if any, to secure the loan are also usually specified. Loan covenants the borrower must meet on an ongoing basis to retain the loan, such as an undertaking to maintain a specified current ratio. If there are company affiliates or individuals who are required to guarantee the loan, their identities and the nature of their obligation will be specified.

Most commitment letters specify conditions the borrower must meet to qualify for the proposed loan and contain a time limit, after which the commitment expires. Once the conditions are met, the commitment is further documented with the more complete and detailed  loan, security, and guarantee agreements that contain additional terms and conditions not specified in the commitment letter.

By setting out the general terms of a loan, a commitment letter helps to move the lending process forward by articulating the key terms of the deal and confirming that the parties have, in fact, come to terms. Commitment letters should be reviewed as carefully as the final, formal loan documents they precede. Even though many of their provisions may not be legally binding (at least until all the conditions are met), both parties will expect the loan to be completed on the business terms set out in the letter and changing those terms can be very difficult once the term sheet has been accepted. *See: Bridge Loans, Investment Memorandums, Letter Agreements, Letters of Intent.*

**Common Stock** is the security most frequently issued by companies to their owners. Companies create common stock shares by authorizing them in their charter documents. Once purchased, the shares represent an ownership interest in the company. In most cases, common stock carries the right to vote for directors and to vote on other matters presented to the shareholders by the company's board of directors. Some actions, such as a proposed sale of the company itself, require shareholder approval before they may be consummated. Common stock shareholders are also entitled to attend and receive notice of shareholder meetings. As is true with other stock issuances, certificates are usually issued to holders of common stock to evidence the stock's existence.

Common stockholders can receive cash dividends based on company earnings but, usually, only after such dividends are approved by the company's board of directors and, if preferred shares are also outstanding, only after preferred stockholders receive their dividends. Dividends are the exception, not the rule, with most fast growing, privately held companies. Holders of common stock participate last in company liquidations. Company creditors, debenture holders, and preferred stockholders get paid in that order, before holders of common stock.

Common stock can be issued in one or more classes. One common company structure authorizes the issuance of two classes of common stock, which differ only in the number of directors each class is entitled to elect. This arrangement can be used to insure an investor a seat on a company's board of directors while, at the same time, insuring that control of the board will remain with management.

For example, Class A stock might be issued to management and give its holders the right to elect three directors while Class B stock is issued to the investor and gives its holders the right to elect one director. Even if the investor holds twice as many shares of stock as do the Class A stockholders, he can still elect only one director. In this way, even if management holds less than half of the company's stock it can still control the company and its board of directors. Common stock can also be structured so that a class of stock has no right to vote for directors. *See: Board of Directors, Control, Cumulative Voting, Debentures, Equity, Junior Common Stock, Options, Preferred Stock, S Corporations, Voting Agreements.*

## Compensation and Bonus Plans refer to company adopted plans that provide money or other benefits to an identified class of company officers or selected employees that is in addition to their base salaries.

Many companies seeking venture capital cannot afford compensation and bonus plans that require them to use cash. At the same time, however, they need incentives to attract and keep valuable employees. In many instances, younger venture-backed companies need their key employees more than their established competitors need theirs. This is because with fewer employees, each employee is important. Unfortunately, the entrepreneurial status of the company also frequently means less job security and lower salaries.

To offset these disadvantages, many privately held growth companies use their stock to attract key employees. They do so by offering important employees the opportunity to acquire equity in the company. The attraction for the employee is the chance to purchase quantities of stock at current prices in anticipation of the company growing and the stock increasing in value.

Young companies take advantage of their inexpensive stock by fashioning compensation and bonus plans around the right to acquire shares of company stock. The most widely used plans are ones that allow key employees to purchase company stock or acquire options to purchase stock at current prices in the future.

Often, the grants of stock or options are conditioned in ways that encourage the employee to remain with the company after the stock is purchased. For instance, shares of stock purchased pursuant to a plan may not vest immediately. Instead, they may vest over a period of years. During the vesting period, the company may have the right to repurchase the unvested shares from the employee at cost if he leaves the company for any reason. The company may even have rights to repurchase a departing employee's vested shares for some other predetermined price. All of these conditions are designed to reward the employee who stays by increasing his ownership in the company and to penalize those who leave.

With stock option grants, the company may make them exercisable at today's low prices but contingent upon some future event. The employee's right to purchase shares may be restricted until he has been with the company for a year or until the company attains certain sales goals. Once the exercise conditions are met, the employee can purchase the stock until the option's expiration date. If the conditions are not met, the option expires before the employee can qualify to purchase the stock.

Options are commonly made to become exercisable in increments over a period of several years. For example, an option to purchase 10,000 shares of company stock might be structured to become exercisable as to 2,500 shares on each of the first four anniversary dates of the option grant. In this way, the employee would have to remain for four years before he could purchase the full 10,000 shares. If he left during the third year, he would be entitled to purchase only 5,000 shares.

Other common plans include issuing "phantom stock" and granting options to purchase special classes of stock. Grants of stock bonuses to employees from a pool of shares set aside for that purpose are used also. The variety of plans available to attract important employees is limited only by the imaginations of management and its advisers. A good adviser can help management select an incentive plan (or plans) that reward employees in ways that secure their attention, enthusiasm, and tenure with the firm.

Careful consideration of potential tax consequences is essential to selecting an effective incentive plan. To minimize unwanted tax consequences to the employee and the company when stock is granted or options are exercised, many growing companies fashion their initial incentives from qualified incentive stock options or vesting stock plans or a combination of both. The tax laws governing stock and option grants to employees are complex. Qualified tax advisers should always be consulted before granting stock or options to employees. *See: ISO's (Incentive Stock Options), Qualified Stock Option Plans, Vesting Stock Grants. See also: Golden Handcuffs, Phantom Stock Plans, Stock Committee, Vesting Schedules.*

## Confidentiality Agreements are contracts used to
protect trade secrets and know-how from being misused or misappropriated by those who have access to them. When they are used, they can help companies prevent competitors from learning valuable secrets. For many start-up and technology-based companies, the secrets these agreements help protect are among the most valuable properties they own. Often, those secrets constitute the essential difference between them and their competitors. Having written contracts that obligate employees to maintain the secrecy of a company's techniques, processes, or know-how can mean the difference between maintaining a competitive advantage or losing it to competitors.

Confidentiality agreements can even cover "negative know-how." That is, they can prohibit the transfer of information about mistakes the company made while it perfected its technology or project, information many would not normally think of as secret or important. Restricting negative know-how, however, can help insure that a company's competitors will have the opportunity to make the same time-consuming mistakes the company made, and thereby delay the introduction of competitive products.

State laws generally permit companies to prevent others from using their secrets only as long as they treat the secrets as confidential and take reasonable precautions to prevent them from being disclosed to others. Depending upon the nature of the secrets, these necessary precautions might include restricting access to confidential data or setting aside a safe or room for storage of secret documents. For material accessed through computers, limiting access using available technology is essential.

In most cases, written confidentiality agreements should be required from everyone who has access to company secrets. These agreements and the secrecy procedures enforced by a company create the legal basis for using the courts to prevent others from misappropriating important company information. The importance of these agreements and of complying with the company's secrecy procedures should be impressed upon new employees and consultants. Departing employees should be reminded of their secrecy agreements upon departure. No one should be given access to a company secret before he signs a confidentiality agreement.

No venture capitalist wants to invest in a company that has not taken reasonable steps to protect its valuable secrets. Most will carefully review a company's arrangements to protect its secrets. And most will expect management and other company employees to be bound by written confidentiality agreements. Many will engage local counsel to be sure the agreements are enforceable. Because of this and the fact that the state laws that govern the enforceability of these agreements vary widely and are quite specific in their requirements, care should be taken when drafting confidentiality agreements. To be sure of enforceability, they should be prepared or reviewed by experienced legal counsel.

*See: Employment Contracts, Patents, Software Protection, Think Capital, Trade Secrets.*

**Consultants** refer to company and individual specialists who are contracted by companies to perform specific services. Many early stage companies hire consultants to obtain specific expertise and to delay the expense of hiring additional full-time employees. Later stage growth companies often engage consultants who have specific training or expertise not available from the company's employees. Consultants do not earn fringe benefits, as employees do, and thus can be less expensive in the short run. They can also be hired by task and thereby may be used when a full-time employee would not be economical.

Companies commonly use consultants to assist in the preparation of their business plans. Consultants also commonly assist in conducting market research or provide advice in developing product, manufacturing, or marketing strategies.

Sometimes, companies engage individuals to consult, in part, to determine their interest in hiring them as full-time employees. This allows the company to get services it needs and evaluate the person for staff employment at the same time. (As with company employees, consultants should always be required to sign confidentiality and work for hire agreements when they are given access to company secrets.) Consultants' services can be paid for in a variety of ways.

Consultants hired to help raise money should be engaged with clear expectations about their responsibilities, the limits to the scope of their authority, and the term of their engagement. Regardless of their claims, consultants should never be expected to replace management entirely in the fundraising process. Even with the best consultant or broker, investors will want to meet and measure management's knowledge of its business plan and its ability to make the company succeed. They can only do this if management participates actively in the preparation of the business plan and in discussions with investors. See the entry on *Brokers* for more information about contracting with consultants to assist in fund raising. *See: Consulting Agreements, Work for Hire Agreements. See also: Mistakes Made at a Business Plan Forum, Writing the Business Plan.*

## Consulting Agreements refer to contracts between companies and their non-employee advisors. Whenever practical, these agreements should be in writing.

Good consulting agreements should specify the consultant's obligations, the company's payment obligations, and identify any deliverables the consultant is obliged to produce. They should also specify who owns the consultant's work product. If the consultant has access to company secrets, the agreement should contain secrecy provisions. If his duties require him to interact with company customers or suppliers, the limitations on his authority should be carefully delineated.

Investors sometimes condition their investments on obtaining consulting agreements that provide them with access to management and a source of continuing cash flow. These contracts usually require the company to pay a monthly or quarterly fee to the investor for advice management might obtain anyway from the investor.

The real purpose of many of these consulting agreements is to increase the investor's return and to help cover its cost of monitoring its investment. Some investors believe consulting agreements improve their communication with management. They argue that managements feel fewer reservations about asking for investor advice when they are paying for it.

The fee paid for investor-consulting services increases the company's cost of capital and decreases its available cash. Whenever possible, these consulting agreements, and their fees, should be avoided. When avoiding them is not possible, the consulting fee should be included in the company's calculation of its true cost of capital. *See also: Brokers, Cash Flow, Consultants, Financing Agreements, Management Agreements, Pricing.*

**Control** refers the ability to direct the actions of a company. It includes the power to determine company strategy and to select the people who will carry out that strategy. In a corporation, control resides in two places: with the shareholders, who elect the company's board of directors and with the board of directors, who set company strategy and elect company officers. The ability to elect or persuade a majority of a company's board of directors is usually considered the deciding factor with respect to who controls a company.

Company control can be assured through ownership of enough shares of stock to elect more than half of the company's directors. In most cases, this means owning more than 50 percent of the company's voting stock. When more than one class of stock has been issued, control may, instead, require owning enough shares of the different classes of stock to elect a majority of the board of directors.

Raising capital affects management's control in several ways. When enough stock to elect a majority of a company's board of directors is sold, management continues to direct the company only as long as the investors consent. Even when less stock is sold, contractual provisions required by an investor as a condition to funding can also change control by reducing management's unrestricted freedom to run the company. These provisions usually entitle the investor to participate in certain management decisions and to receive detailed and regular financial reports. Some contractual rights affect control by giving investors the right to manage the company if performance standards are not achieved. Often, these contractual rights appear as conditions or rights written into the description of preferred classes of stock issued to outside investors.

Even when an investor acquires the ability to elect a majority of a company's board, there are ways management can retain operating control. A shareholders agreement requiring the investor to vote his stock for a slate of directors that is controlled by management is one example. Management contracts are another. These can be used to insure management of at least minimum representation on the company's board of directors or the right to direct the company's activities as long as it does so within agreed-upon parameters.

Classes of common stock can also be created to insure that control stays with management. By issuing to investors a second class of common stock that only has the right to elect a minority of the company's directors, management can retain majority control of the company's board of directors even when it sells a majority of the company's outstanding capital. A combination of these devices can be used to keep control in management's hands.

As a rule, venture capitalists are more interested in obtaining a high rate of return on their investment than in obtaining control of a company. Most want control only to the extent that they believe is necessary to protect their investment. Few are interested in running the day-to-day affairs of a company. Even so, the right to control company actions is often jealously guarded by management for as long as possible.

Most venture investors insist on some influence over a company's affairs as a condition to funding, often requiring a seat on the company's board of directors as a condition to their investment. Few will want to control the board unless they lack confidence in management's abilities. Most will expect to receive regular financial reports from company management.

Investors may not be interested in control as long as management runs the company successfully. Nonetheless, management's definition of success may differ significantly from that of its investors. And investors may develop independent reasons for moving a company in a direction that does not interest management. The only way for management to assure its control is through ownership of enough stock to elect a majority of the company's board of directors or through a binding written agreement with the investors. *See: Affirmative Covenants, Board of Directors, Common Stock, Cumulative Voting, Management Agreements, Negative Covenants, Operating Covenants, Shareholders' Agreements, Take Away Provisions, Venture Capital Deal Structures, Voting Agreements, Voting Trusts. See also, Maintaining Control in Business.*

## Maintaining Control in Business

*For growing businesses, operational control rarely exists as an absolute in one individual or group and maintaining control is not a simple matter of controlling a company's board of directors. Instead, a variety of factors influence who really decides a company's fate. Consider the following real world examples:*

*Director Deadlock Brings About a Company Dissolution. This entrepreneur built his business from the ground up with groundbreaking technical innovations in the computer industry. When his golfing buddy offered to provide $2 million to fund his start up, the entrepreneur readily accepted his offer and his condition of equal representation on the Board. A few years later when his investor passed away, his heirs, not interested in growing the business further, used the investor's equal Board representation to block the entrepreneur's attempts to borrow funds and expand his business. They insisted, instead, that the company liquidate* *its assets and distribute the proceeds to the shareholders. Faced with the inability to take affirmative actions that required majority Board approval, the entrepreneur conceded to their wishes and dissolved his company.*

*Maintaining Management Control Through Deadlock. After multiple rounds of venture capital financing and reduction of his percentage stock ownership below 30%, this successful entrepreneur managed to leverage his company's operational success to limit the outside investors to two representatives on the Board of Directors while he retained, by contract, the right to elect the other two Board members. Remaining in control of the company's operations until it was later acquired to the significant profit of all shareholders, this founder was able to leverage a deadlocked Board with operational success to retain day-to-day operating control of the company and to determine when and under what circumstances the company would finally be sold. Eventually the desires of executive option holders for an exit event combined with an attractive offer from an acquirer convinced the founder it was time to sell in a transaction that suited all of the company's investors.*

*Veto Rights Wrest Control From Management. This successful medical technology business grew rapidly after securing its first round of venture capital financing from a group of sophisticated individual investors who acquired Series A convertible preferred stock for their investment dollars. When management went to the market and secured a favorable offer for Series B funding, the Series A investors exercised their contractual veto right to prevent the company from accepting the funding offer, announcing to the management team that they were more interested in selling the company. Faced with the inability to raise additional capital, management succumbed to the investor's wishes and sold the company at a valuation lower than the one offered to them by the Series B investor candidate.*

_Board Management and Operational Success Leave Management in Control._  Operational success and shrewd management of the Board configuration helped this successful entrepreneur survive as CEO of his company for decades from its founding to long after its listing as a New York Stock Exchange company.  Never conceding Board control to outside venture investors, management managed to string together regular growth and profitability through its public offering and stock exchange listings to maintain control of the business even after it owned less than 20% of the company's outstanding stock.

_Operational Realities Shift Control to Outsiders._  Many companies have suffered through this scenario. After months or years of toil, management finds itself unable for any number of reasons to generate sufficient cash flow to support company operations or, by reason of a down market or lack of sufficient measurable success, unable to find outside investors willing to provide the funding needed to continue operations. Not willing to concede total defeat, one or more existing venture capital investors agree to fund continued operations of the company for a time but, being the only available investors, dictate terms in a "down round" that wipes out the value of other investors' holdings and firmly secures operational control of the business in their hands.

As the examples illustrate, operational success is the biggest, but not always sufficient, factor in retaining control. Other factors impacting control include majority ownership of voting securities, majority representation on the Board of Directors, contractual terms, and specialized voting or veto rights. See: Venture Capitalists, Angels, Control, Convertible Preferred Stock, Down Round, Liquidation Preferences. See also, How to Care for the Entrepreneurial Investor.

**Convertible Debentures** are debt instruments that entitle lenders to exchange the right to receive principal and interest payments into stock of the borrowing company. Subordinated convertible debentures are sometimes used in lieu of convertible preferred stock to fund a portion or all of a company's funding needs. These convertible debentures are usually less attractive to growing companies than preferred stock because they accrue interest and require scheduled repayments unless and until they are converted. They are preferable to non-subordinated convertible securities, however, because their terms make it easier for companies to obtain debt financing from other sources. *See: Convertible Preferred Stock, Convertible Securities, Debentures, Subordinated Convertible Debentures, Subordinated Debt, Venture Capital Deal Structures.*

**Convertible Preferred Stock** is an investment vehicle frequently used by sophisticated private company investors and a staple deal structure term of most venture capitalists.

The preferred aspect of the stock gives the investor a preference in the event of a company liquidation or sale. In growing companies, this preference usually entitles the investor to receive back its investment and an agreed upon return, before other investors receive any proceeds from a liquidation or qualifying sale of the business.

The conversion feature enables the investor to exchange the convertible preferred shares for common stock at his option at an exchange rate specified in the stock description. Most of the conversion provisions also provide a mechanism for sheltering the security holder from the full dilutive effects of a later sale of stock by the company at lower prices. An adjustment mechanism in the conversion formula, called an antidilution provision, entitles the investor to receive additional shares of common stock upon conversion if the company sells stock at prices lower than his purchase price.

These rights to additional shares reduce the dilutive effect of a company sale of cheaper stock but also cause the company's common shareholders to suffer a larger reduction in their percentage ownership when the company sells stock at prices below the purchase price of the convertible preferred stock.

A typical convertible preferred stock also entitles the investor to vote the preferred stock on issues presented for shareholder vote as if it were common stock. Voting rights conferred on the convertible preferred stock often include the additional right to elect one or more directors to the company's board of directors and to approve certain specified major decisions. Common major decisions the class of preferred shareholders must separately approve include the issuance of new shares of stock to others, the sale of the business, the creation of new stock with preferential rights, and the change of the company's core business activity.

Some convertible preferred stocks permit the investor to require the company to redeem the preferred stock after a predetermined time for an amount that gives the investor a modest profit. Some contain provisions that entitle the company to force redemption of the stock or its conversion from preferred to common stock after a period of years. *See: Antidilution Provisions, Calls, Convertible Debentures, Convertible Securities, Dilution (Percentage), Dilution (Value), Preferred Stock Umbrellas, Puts, Ratchets, Structure, Subordinated Convertible Debentures, Venture Capital Deal Structures, Weighted Average Antidilution.*

**Convertible Securities** are equity or debt investments that can be exchanged, at the holder's option, for something else of value upon the happening of some future event. The most common convertible securities are debentures and preferred stock that can be converted into common stock. The election of the holder is usually all that is required to convert. Sometimes, however, the right to convert is made contingent upon the happening of a future event, such as the passage of time, the occurrence of an specified event, or the failure of the company to meet an identified goal.

Convertible securities provide investors with extra value and a hedge against risk. They allow them to acquire a debt instrument, for example, with its rights to interest and principal payments, without sacrificing the chance to participate in the company's capital appreciation. When a company does well, the investor can convert his debenture into stock that is more valuable. When a company is less successful, he can retain his debenture and receive his interest and principal payments.

Most venture capitalists use convertible securities as their principal investment vehicle. As between convertible preferred stock and convertible debentures, convertible preferred stock is more commonly used. *See: Convertible Debentures, Convertible Preferred Stock, Debentures, Subordinated Convertible Debentures, Venture Capital Deal Structures.*

**Copyrights** are protections afforded to written expressions by federal law. They prevent unauthorized copying or duplicating of protected works. The protections are available to writings of all kinds, including computer software.

Copyrights protect the expression of ideas and are often contrasted with trade secrets, which protect ideas themselves but not their expression. The distinctions are important.

Companies cannot publish their secret processes in a magazine with a copyright notice and expect to keep others from using the process. The copyright will prevent only the duplication of the way in which those ideas were expressed in the magazine. By the same token, there are things such as mass-marketed video games and monitor displays for which copyrights provide valuable protections that trade secrets cannot. And, where the use of a secret process requires copying of the expression of that process, as with many computer software programs, copyrights can, for many practical purposes, protect the process itself.

Copyrights can be obtained for computer software in object code or source code. They can also be obtained for documentation, manuals, and display screen configurations. Copyrights are available to software that is mass-marketed or sold under restrictive license.

Securing copyright protection requires careful compliance with the federal copyright rules. Whenever copyrights are used to protect a valuable asset, companies should engage qualified counsel to assist them in making the application. Particularly when the asset is software, management should understand the advantages and disadvantages to copyrights and the best application procedure to follow before sending a program printout or a portion of a program printout to Washington.

Qualified lawyers can help management determine whether copyrights, trade secrets, or patents, or a combination of the three, provide the best protection for a company's asset. They can also plot a strategy for obtaining those protections. *See: Patents, Software Protection, Trade Secrets.*

**Corporate Governance** refers to the manner in which corporations manage their operations and distribute information and authority among its officers, directors, and shareholders. The systems by which corporations are directed and controlled, as well as the quality of information reported by public companies to the investing public, has come under close scrutiny in recent years. The corporate governance requirements that apply to public companies are significantly more extensive than those that apply to privately held companies.

The rules and procedures by which public corporations make decisions and report on their operations became more extensive and exacting with the adoption of Sarbanes-Oxley and new governance requirements by the major stock exchanges.

Public company officers now have to personally certify the accuracy of financial reports and face the prospect of personal liability for misstatements. Boards must include directors who meet independence standards established by the act and the trading exchanges that list their securities. Whistleblower policies, executive session board meetings, and additional emphasis on oversight by audit and other board committees are all now part of public company governance. *See: Board Committees, Board of Directors, Bylaws, Charter, Control, Sarbanes-Oxley, Stock Committee. See also: Board Room Etiquette – Private Companies, Revolution in Public Company Governance, Sarbanes-Oxley.*

## Corporate Venture Capital refers to operating

companies, as distinguished from venture capital firms, that invest money in growing companies. Many companies that make venture investments do so through separate subsidiaries that control a budget dedicated to making investments. Others invest through divisions without a committed capital budget. Whatever the form, these companies typically focus their investments, like specialty funds, on businesses within their industry or on technologies that are complimentary to their business.

Corporate venture investors use many of the same methods venture capital firms use to evaluate investment proposals. They conduct extensive due diligence and look for a high rate of return from their investment. In addition, corporate venture capital funds frequently look for companies and products that can benefit from the firm's expertise or distribution capabilities.

Corporate venture capitalists can make good partners for growing companies, especially for those who need the kind of assistance a good corporate partner can provide. Often, the corporate investor can lend its marketing or technical expertise or partner with the portfolio company to provide distribution channels that accelerate its growth. Because they are often able to provide some specific strategic assistance, managements should explore the additional value-added the corporate investor can bring to the table and contract in the financing agreement for those investor services the company needs.

While there are advantages to working with a corporate investor, there can be disadvantages as well. Some will request an option or first refusal right to purchase the company in the future as a condition to providing funding. This can depress the company's future value. The investors access to information about the company through a board or advisor's seat can put company secrets at risk if the investor is in the same industry. A veto over future fundraisings, a feature that is common in convertible preferred stock terms, can be more dangerous if future acquisition by the investor is a possibility. Having an industry insider as an investor with a director representative can make it harder to partner with other companies in the industry.

These and other potential disadvantages can be mitigated with careful negotiation and contracting. For example, limits can be placed on access to company secrets. Vetoes over future fundings can be limited and information about partnering with other industry sources can be restricted. As with any fundraising, counsel from and experienced legal counsel is important to avoid foreseeable pitfalls. *See: Joint Ventures, Specialty Funds, Value Added, Venture Capitalists.*

**Corporations** are a favorite form of business entity used extensively by small and large companies. Chartered by any one of the 50 states, corporations afford their owners and operators with limited liability in most situations and provide clear mechanisms for business management. Owned by shareholders who elect a board of directors to direct management, corporations are operated day-to-day by officers who are appointed by the board.The most common form of corporation is the C corporation which is taxed as a separate entity and whose shareholders are not taxed until they receive distributions, commonly called dividends, from the company. Since the C corporation is separately taxed on its earnings, any dividend paid to shareholders is effectively taxed twice. For example, $1.00 of earnings would be taxed to the corporation at its rate, say 25%, leaving $.75 in after-tax earnings. If that $.75 is distributed to shareholders, it will be taxed again to the shareholder at his rate, say 33%, leaving $.50 of the original $1.00 in earnings after-tax.

S corporations are taxed differently. They are not taxed as separate entities but their shareholders are taxed on their pro rata portion of company earnings regardless of whether distributions are made. One dollar of earnings from an S corporation would generate no tax to the corporation but would create a tax liability for the shareholders whether or not any funds are distributed to the shareholders. To address this issue, many Scorporations routinely distribute enough cash to shareholders to enable them to pay the tax generated by their shareholdings. Many specific requirements must be met to qualify as an S Corporation.

Ownership in corporations can take many forms. The most common ownership form, common stock, provides its holder with pro rata ownership interests in the company together with the right to one vote per share. Common stock can also be issued without voting rights or in classes with specially defined voting rights.

Preferred stock and preferred stock that is convertible into common stock can also be used confer ownership rights in a corporation. Options, warrants, and debentures that are convertible into stock are also frequently used to afford varying rights to acquire ownership in a company. *See: Common Stock, Control, Convertible Debentures, Convertible Preferred Stock, Convertible Securities, Joint Ventures, LLC's (Limited Liability Companies), Limited Partnerships, Options, S Corporations, Strategic Partnerships, Warrants.*

**Co-Sale Agreements** are contracts between investors and company management that entitle investors to participate in any future sale of stock held by management. Sometimes referred to as tag-along provisions, these agreements are usually imposed on management as part of the funding terms and are included in the financing agreements.

The purpose of a co-sale agreement is to prevent important management members from selling out their interest in the company while the investors are still shareholders. The investor fear they address is that management will be able to negotiate a profitable sale of their personal shares in the company, abandon the company, and leave the investors "holding the bag." While co-sale agreements do not prevent management shareholders from selling their shares at a profit, they do force them to share the benefit of their sale with the investors by allowing the investors to include their shares. In so doing, they motivate managements who desire to sell their shares to look for a sale transaction large enough to also buy out the other shareholders.

In practice, co-sale agreements work like this: Whenever a management shareholder is approached and has the opportunity to sell his shares of company stock, he must notify the investors and tell them the terms that have been proposed. Then the outside investors have an opportunity to sell some of their shares to the purchaser. If the outside investors elect to include some of their shares in the sale, the management shareholder will reduce the number of his shares being sold so that the purchaser acquires the number of shares he originally offered to buy.

The number of shares the outside investors are entitled to include is usually a predetermined percentage of the total number of shares being sold. Typically, that percentage reflects the relative number of shares held by the investors and the selling management shareholder. For example, if an investor owns 30% of the company's outstanding shares to management's 70%, the investors would be entitled to sell 30% of the shares to the buyer. If management finds a buyer for 100,000 shares at $10 per share, the investor can require management to include 30,000 of the investors' shares in the sale, generating a $300,000 sale for the investor. Management would sell 70,000 shares and receive $700,000.

While they are a staple element of many venture capital deal structures, co-sale agreements raise some interesting securities law questions. For instance, does the participation by outside investors in the management shareholder's sale of shares create an obligation on the management shareholder to provide more formal disclosure to the buyer of the shares than he would otherwise have had to make? Certainly, it creates an obligation on the part of the participating outside shareholders to be as candid with the buyer as the management shareholder is required to be. Just as certainly, the management shareholder has a separate responsibility to the participating outside shareholders to make full and accurate disclosure to them about the offer and the condition of the company.

Because they restrict management freedom, co-sale agreements are often resisted by company managements. Because they are so commonly used, however, managements seldom succeed in avoiding co-sale agreements.

When co-sale agreements cannot be avoided, cross-indemnification agreements can be used with them to make each party responsible for potential liabilities created by their misrepresentations or failure to comply with securities laws.

When possible, managements should negotiate for short terms and automatic termination when the company goes public. Management shareholders can also try to limit co-sale rights by making them nontransferable and requiring participating sellers to bear a share of the cost of consummating a sale. These costs could be significant if the sale requires the preparation of an offering circular or other significant disclosure document.

Managements frequently succeed in  negotiating carve outs from co-sale agreements that permit them to sell a limited  number of shares during any twelve-month period without triggering the co-sale rights. After all, the rationale for the co-sale provision is to prevent management from selling out wholesale and leaving the investor with an unmanaged company. Sales of small numbers of shares should not diminish management's interest in the company. Sometimes gifts or limited transfers of shares for estate planning purposes are also permitted. On occasion, even the use of the shares to secure debt can be excluded from a co-sale obligation.

In all events, any sale made under a co-sale agreement should be made only on the advice and with the assistance of counsel. Otherwise, management and the outside investors participating in the sale may find themselves exposed to unexpected liabilities. *See: Blue Sky Laws, Exits, First Refusal Rights (Company), First Refusal Rights (Shareholder), Reg D, SEC (Securities and Exchange Commission), 10b5, 33 Act.*

**CPAs**, or certified public accountants, are professionals who, by training and certification, are qualified to audit a company's financial statements. These audits provide outsiders with a higher level of comfort with the accuracy and completeness of company financial statements and, in so doing, can help attract investors. Audits from independent CPA's are required before a company can go going public.

Companies that lack experienced in-house accounting expertise should consult with an outside accountant to establish a company accounting system that is appropriate to their business. Even a company with a good accountant can usually benefit from the counsel of an experienced accounting firm. Such firms can help management decide what types of books and records the company should keep and what types of regular reports management should receive to help it manage its business and attract investment. These firms can also help management design a bookkeeping system that anticipates rapid growth and provides mechanisms to make it easier to manage the problems such growth inevitably brings.

Many accounting firms also help companies prepare projections and draft business plans. Many have contacts in the business community and can provide introductions to potential investors. Some even assist start-up companies on a reduced or deferred fee or delayed-billing basis. *See: Audits, Reports and Records.*


**Cram Down** refers to a negotiation where one party has so much leverage over the other that it is able to dictate deal terms that are extremely favorable to dictating party. Although often civil, the negotiation sessions in a cram down are characterized by the lack of meaningful give-and-take on the substantive issues. They occur most often in situations where one party knows that the other party has no viable alternative to accepting the offered deal.

In fundraising situations, growing companies can subject themselves to an unwanted cram down by waiting too long to begin raising funds and by having no viable alternative to raising capital (often because of acute cash shortages and an inability to generate sufficient cash from operations) from the investor who is dictating his terms. Cram downs are common in down round financings where the acute need for cash forces company management to raise money on unfavorable terms. Because of the acute cash need, bridge loans made to keep the company afloat often mark the first step in a cram down negotiation for a down round financing. *See: Bridge Loans Down Round, Leverage, Negotiation.*

**Credit Lines** refer to commercial loans that establish a maximum amount of money a company may borrow and then permits the company to draw down against that amount to fund its operations. Also referred to as lines of credit, these financial instruments differ from term loans where the company draws down the total available credit at the beginning of the loan and pays it back over time.

Credit lines give the borrower the ability to draw against the line from time to time so long as the company remains in compliance with the loan covenants included within the loan documents. The company can also make payments to pay down the outstanding balance and then draw again on the line when it has the need. Credit lines may be secured or unsecured and have a fixed term during which they remain effective. At the end of the term, the borrowed amount plus accrued but unpaid interest must be paid.

Often, the borrower pays a commitment fee on the portion of the loan that is not being drawn against as well as interest on the portion borrowed. The commitment fee compensates the bank for making the credit facility available. *See: Commitment Letters, Loan Covenants, Secured Loans, Security Agreements, Term Loans.*

**Cumulative Voting** refers to a special method of voting shares of stock that can be provided for in a company's governing documents. It allows a shareholder to cast all of his votes in elections for company directors - determined by multiplying the number of his shares by the number of director positions being filled - for just one director. Cumulative voting can be used to insure a minority shareholder that he will have a seat on a company's board of directors.

In a normal voting arrangement, a shareholder with 30 percent of the voting stock can never be assured of any representation on a company's board of directors. This is because each director position is voted on separately. As each position is voted on, the 70 percent shareholder can outvote the 30 percent shareholder and, thereby, elect all of the directors.

Cumulative voting can change this result. Instead of electing each director separately, all the director positions are voted on at once with the top vote getters taking seats on the board. If three positions are being filled, each shareholder gets three votes for each of his shares. He can vote them in any fashion he wants.

With three positions open, a shareholder with 30 shares gets 90 votes (three times 30 votes), while a shareholder with 70 shares gets 210 votes (three times 70 votes). If the 30 percent shareholder votes all of his 90 votes for one candidate, that candidate is guaranteed to be one of the top three vote getters because the remaining 210 votes can only give two other candidates more than 90 votes. Since the three candidates receiving the most votes are elected to the board, the 30 percent shareholder is assured of being represented on the board. *See: Common Stock, Control, Management Agreements, Minority Shareholder, Shareholders' Agreements, Voting Agreements, Voting Trusts.*

**Cure Periods** refer to provisions in agreements that allow a defaulting party to avoid the consequences of a default by "fixing" the cause of the default. In a financing agreement, a cure (or sometimes "grace") period provision might state that if the company fails to perform a required task, such as meeting goals that are a condition to obtaining more funding from the investor, the company will, nonetheless, be given an extra 30 days in which to perform that task before it is held to be in default of the agreement. If the company meets the goal within the cure period, the default will be "cured" and the investor will remain contractually bound to provide the next round of funding. *See: Benchmarks, Default, Stage Financing.*

# D

**Deal** refers any joint undertaking agreed to by at least two parties. In a fundraising, the deal refers to the terms for the financing that are contained in the final investment agreements between the investors and the company. In a joint venture, the deal refers to the terms contained in the joint venture agreements.

A deal is different from an offer, a counter offer, or any kind of proposal because a deal does not exist until all the parties involved have agreed to the terms. Deals involving a significant commitment of resources frequently involve extensive negotiation and investigation by the parties. The final deal reached is often quite different from what either party originally envisioned, with both parties learning from the negotiation process and compromising where appropriate.

The time it takes to complete a joint venture, license, or venture capital funding can vary from weeks to months. The number and types of documents involved in any given deal can vary depending on the terms and number of parties involved.

A typical fundraising deal with a venture capital investor might involve most or all of the following agreements:

- Term sheet or letter of intent,
- Bridge loan promissory note,
- Stock purchase agreement,
- Amended company charter,
- Investors rights agreement,
- Shareholder agreements,
- Subscription agreements,
- Noncompete agreements,
- Employee confidentiality/inventors rights agreements,
- Information rights agreements,
- Promissory notes or debentures,
- Director indemnification agreements,
- Preemptive rights waivers from earlier shareholders,
- Stock certificates, and
- Investor check or wire transfer.

Each of the documents contains agreements or commitments that are required to complete the deal. All of them must be considered in their entirety to fully understand all of the implications of the deal. The purpose of each of these agreements are summarized below:

- *Term Sheet.* This preliminary document sets out the basic business terms of the proposed deal, typically in a form that is not intended to be binding or enforceable as to either party. It's purpose is to fix the main deal terms while the parties continue due diligence and prepare the final, more detailed, transaction agreements.

- *Bridge Loan Promissory Note.* Sometimes an investor will advance funds to a company pending completion of the formal financing agreements. When this occurs, the loan is documented first in a short promissory note. If assets are give to secure the note, security agreements and UCC financing statements will also be prepared.

- *Stock Purchase Agreement.* This agreement sets forth the number and type of securities being sold, the sale price, the conditions to the sale, and the timing of the sale. It also contains representations from the company about its business and assets and from the investor about its ability to purchase the securities.

- *Amended Company Charter.* If the investor is purchasing an equity security, the rights and preferences of those securities are typically described in an amendment to the company's existing articles of incorporation. The amendment creates the new security being purchased.

- *Investor Rights Agreements.* Negotiated rights of the investor to force or participate in a registered public offering of company securities, to require future action by the company such as providing periodic reports of activities and financial performance, and to participate on the company's board are typically contained in one or more separate agreements.

- *Shareholder Agreements.* Investor rights of first refusal to purchase stock sold by management or to participate with management in sales of stock to outside parties are contained in agreements typically called cosale or shareholder agreements.

- *Subscription Agreements.* Often contained within the stock purchase agreement, these agreements contain representations by the investor that enable the company to qualify the sale of stock as a private placement.

- *Noncompete Agreements.* Often contained in an investor rights agreement, these contracts restrict the ability of management to leave and compete with the company and also protect company technology from unauthorized use or disclosure.

- *Employee Confidentiality and Inventor Rights Agreements.* Most companies already have these in place at the time of funding. These are agreements between the company and its employees and consultants that protect the confidentiality of the company's proprietary information and assign inventor rights from the employee or consultant to the company

- *Information Rights Agreements.* Commonly entitled confidentiality agreements or non-competition agreements, these are contracts between the company and its employees protecting the confidentiality of company technology and information and the company's rights to inventions developed by employees. These agreements commonly contain employee noncompetition agreements and covenants prohibiting attempts to hire away other company employees.

- *Promissory Notes or Debentures.* If a portion of the funding is provided by debt, they will be documented with promissory notes or debentures.

- *Director Indemnification Agreements.* A common practice with sophisticated investors if for them to insist that their director nominees be protected by separate indemnification agreements from the company. These agreements supplement protections afforded in most company bylaws or charters and give the director the ability to look to the assets of the company to help defend himself from shareholder claims.

- *Preemptive Rights Waivers.* Earlier investors in growing companies are often protected by contractual or statutory preemptive rights that entitle them to participate in later financings of the company. If these exist they will need to be waived as part of the new financing.

- *Stock Certificates.* These are issued to the investor against payment to evidence the investor's ownership in the company. In these private company financings, these certificates routinely contain extensive legends describing the limitations on their transferability.
- *Investor Check or Wire Transfer.* Typically the investors money is sent by a fed wire of same day funds to an account designated by the company.

The best deals are ones between capable and well-intentioned partners that clearly define the rights and obligations of both parties. Successful deals usually work best when they equitably combine the contributions of both parties and provide both parties with real opportunities to benefit. In venture fundings, as with joint ventures and licenses, it is important to remember that the parties are establishing the framework for an ongoing cooperation that will work best if both parties see continuing benefit in the relationship defined in the deal documents. *See: Closing, Deal Breakers, Deal Flow, Financing Agreements, Joint Ventures, Letters of Intent, Negotiation, Structure, Term Sheet, Venture Capital Deal Structures.*

# Deal Breakers are substantive or non-substantive points of disagreement that prevent a deal from closing. Deal breakers can also refer to individuals who intentionally or unintentionally impede the normal progress of a deal.

Some parties impede deal closings because they are so interested in something other than closing a deal that they hinder or stop a financing without good reason. Others cover lack of experience or judgment with strategies that keep parties apart. Some negotiate in apparent good faith but with private agendas inconsistent with completing the deal or with unrealistic expectations of dramatic concessions from the other party. No one wants a deal breaker near an important negotiation.

Individual deal breakers can be hard to distinguish from friends and counselors who try to help management get a good deal. They come in assorted varieties:

- *The novice* may be well intentioned but lacks the experience and skill to negotiate constructively through the process. He may become obsessed with a detail that is relatively unimportant in the larger context of the deal or be unyielding on points routinely compromised in the type of transaction being negotiated. Even when he succeeds in completing the deal, his party may be poorly served with an agreement that is dangerously flawed.

- *The hard-liner* believes that the best way to negotiate is to take firm positions and not discuss the issues. He presents a proposal on a take-it-or-leave-it basis and acts annoyed when the other side raises a legitimate issue. The hard-liner's intransigence results in a dead deal even when the parties' respective interests could have resulted in a good deal for both sides. The best deals are usually made between parties who discuss their concerns intelligently and search creatively for common ground on which a deal can be based.

- *The minutiae master* wears everyone out with his obsessive concern for detail. He wants to document every detail regardless of its practical importance to the deal. This sometimes disguises the fact that he does not understand its economics. He is often heard repeating phrases such as "we did it this way on the last deal" or "this is our standard language, we always insist on it."

- *The best dealer* is obsessed with getting the best deal. Instead of working to get the best deal available, he insists on a deal that is so good for him and so bad for the other party that it cannot be made. This person often appears as an adviser to a businessman who is unsure of himself and does not completely understand the economics of the proposed transaction.

- *The last dealer* wants the current deal to be exactly like the last one he worked on. It doesn't matter to him that this deal is different: He understood the last deal and will do everything he can to force this one into a format with which he is familiar. Since his last deal is different from the present deal, the other side will object. If he goes unchecked, the deal will die.

Individual deal breakers can be hard to distinguish from advisors who have the parties' best interests at heart. This is particularly true when their approach is related to some hidden agenda, such as fulfilling their personal idea of what a tough negotiator is or hiding their inexperience with the substance of the deal or the process for completing the deal. By contrast, good negotiators are not constrained by personal agendas that are unrelated to the goals of the negotiation. They are able to keep the goals of their party clearly in focus throughout the negotiations and work diligently, using all their creativity and experience, to obtain the best deal. For the entrepreneur, distinguishing between an advisor who is a deal breaker and one who is a good negotiator can mean the difference between success and failure. *See: Deal, Deal Flow, Negotiation, Shopping.*

**Deal Flow** refers to the never-ending stream of business proposals that come to most venture capitalists for review. It is common, in active markets, for a venture capital firm to receive more than 100 business proposals each month. Therefore, it is not unusual for a venture capitalist to invest in less than one percent of the deals arriving at his doorstep.

This deal flow helps explain why it can be so important to have an outstanding business plan and a personal introduction to an investor. The intense competition for venture capital funds also explains why investors can often impose their deal structures and pricing on a funding.

Before even approaching a venture capital fund for investment, management should explore the various financing alternatives available to it and determine that venture capital is the right funding source for the company at the time. Reviewing alternative sources with professional advisors like accountants, attorneys, and investment bankers can help management understand what funding sources are most appropriate and available for their situation.

Private capital from friends and family may be the best source for an early stage company. Debt financing from banks or other lenders may make more sense, particularly if a company generates a lot of cash but does not expect to grow rapidly. Private placements of company stock where several interested individual investors are approached may be the best fit, especially if a qualified underwriter is interested.

If venture capital is the appropriate choice for the company, it is almost always best to approach more than one venture fund at a time. Few sophisticated investors will lose interest in a company's proposal when it is selectively shopped to potential investors. Approaching more than one institutional investor can even create competition among investors and enhance a company's bargaining position. In the best case, several investors will bid against each other to fund an attractive deal. This is not to say, however, that companies should shop their business plans indiscriminately to a large number of investors. To do so shows a lack of sophistication on management's part and can discourage interest from investors. *See: Business Plan, Business Plan Format, Shopping, Summary.*

**Deal Structure** refers to the terms and conditions of a deal. When people refer to a deal's structure, they often mean the broad business terms of the transaction. In a joint venture, for example, the deal's terms might describe each party's contribution to the venture, their respective duties, how the venture will be managed, and how the profits of the venture will be divided. A venture capital deal structure might describe the main elements of price, company valuation, investment vehicle (security type), and control concessions.

Term sheets and letters of intent, completed before formal closing documents are prepared, typically contain a summary of the important business terms, or structure, of a deal. Attorneys and accountants are frequently included in the discussions of term sheets and are routinely included when the formal financing agreements are completed. Their expertise on the tax, accounting, and legal ramifications of the proposed deal structure can be invaluable. At a minimum, their involvement can help avoid unpleasant tax, accounting, or liability surprises for all parties.

A more detailed discussion of the structural elements of a common venture capital deal structure appears in the *Venture Capital Deal Structures* entry of this book. The *Deal* entry provides a summary of deal documents for a typically equity venture funding. *See: Deal, Preferred Stock Umbrella, Venture Capital Deal Structures.*

**Debentures** are debt instruments or bonds issued by companies to borrow money from individuals and institutions. Like promissory notes, they are typically structured with a definite term and bear interest until paid. Debentures are usually not secured by company assets but, instead, are issued based on the general credit worthiness of the company.

Debentures are common in private company financings. Investors who desire to split their investment between debt and equity frequently use debentures for the debt portion of their investments.

Investors can use debentures to increase their return on investment. This happens when an investor characterizes a portion of his equity investment as a debenture while computing the amount of stock he requires for his equity investment based on the total equity and debt dollars invested, instead of just on the equity dollars invested. When this is done, the investor receives money as a debt repayment without reducing his potential return from the stock purchase. If the investment is only moderately successful, the debenture also helps the investor reclaim a portion of his money for investment in another company.

How can characterizing a portion of an investment as a debenture benefit investors at the expense of management? Assume, for example, that an investor agrees to provide $600,000 in return for 30,000 shares of company stock. The investor wants to pay $100,000 for the stock and $500,000 for a debenture. The debenture proposed will have a term of ten years and the company will not have to repay any principal or interest until then. In the meantime, if the company generates enough profits to pay off some of the debenture without hurting cash flow, then the company will begin to do so.

The investor improves his potential return dramatically by shifting a portion of his investment into the debenture if he does not reduce the number of shares he receives. If he invests all $600,000 in the stock and the company succeeds, his initial investment may pay back $2 million, for example, making his profit $1.4 million. If, instead, he invests $100,000 for the 30,000 shares of stock and diverts $500,000 to a debenture, his profit will be more than $1.9 million because in addition to the $2 million he also gets paid back his $500,000, with interest. In the first case his return on his stock investment is 2.3 to 1; in the second case it is more than 19 to 1!

Some investors will argue that shifting some equity dollars into long-term debentures will not hurt the company or disadvantage other shareholders. The company, they will point out, still gets $600,000. If it does well and meets its projections, the company can pay back the debenture early. If the company does not do well enough by the tenth year to pay back the debenture, the argument goes, it probably will not matter because management will have abandoned the project by then anyway. It is a corporate debt, after all, and if the company cannot make the payment, it will not be doing well enough to keep the entrepreneur's loyalty. There's no personal liability, so management should not care.

The proposed structure does allow the company to use the $500,000 without making interest payments during the start-up years of its operations. It may even help the company to borrow other funds as long as the debenture holder's rights are subordinated to another lender's. It will not, however, improve the company's balance sheet to the same extent or give a lender as much comfort as an equity investment will.

The terms of a typical debenture require a company to start repayment after three or four years of operations (if the company is generating enough cash). If the company is expanding at that point, as everyone hopes it will be, management may need cash to support larger inventories or more ambitious marketing efforts. Therefore, if management agrees to the proposed structure, the company may incur the expense of further borrowing earlier than it would have had to if the original investment had been all for stock.

A debt and equity investment is clearly not as valuable as an all equity investment of the same size. The deferral of a portion of the investment into debt may not reduce the value of the investment below what the company needs, but it does reduce it in a measurable way. As a result, when companies cannot avoid a mixed investment they should, nonetheless, try to structure the debenture portion of the investment in ways that reduce and delay the disadvantages of the debenture. Here are some ways to accomplish this:

- *Make the term as long as possible.* The longer the company has the money to use before it has to repay the loan, the more like equity it is to the company. This also applies to interest payments and early principal payments required by the terms of the debenture. These principal "prepayments" may become due when the company exceeds its projected profits.

- *Reduce the portion of the investment made as a debenture and make required prepayments small.* Ideally, any prepayment obligation should be small, start late, and be at management's option. If the investor wants interest on optional prepayments that the company chooses not to make, payment of that interest should not be required until late in the term of the debenture. The financing agreements should make it clear that any failure to make prepayments or interest payments before the end of the term will not give the investor any rights to require earlier payments under the debenture.

- *Persuade investors to subordinate their debentures to other debt of the company.* This will make it easier for the company to borrow additional cash, which, in turn, makes it easier for the company to succeed. Success of the company, after all, is the primary goal of management and its investors.

- *Negotiate a right for the company to force the investor to convert the debenture if certain events occur.* For example, if the company meets its performance goals, give management the option to force conversion of the debenture into equity and thereby improve the company's debt-to-equity ratio and make it easier for the company to borrow from outside lenders.

Management can also try to convince investors to make the company's payments on the debentures contingent on company success and not require a fixed term repayment obligation. But do not expect an investor to be sympathetic to this suggestion. Without a definite repayment obligation, the IRS may treat principal repayments under a debenture as dividends to the investor. This means unwanted taxable income to the investor and reduces the debenture's after-tax value. As long as the IRS recognizes the debenture as a legitimate debt, repayments of principal create no income and no taxes to the investor.

The use of a long-term debenture does not decrease the risk to the investor that he will lose his money if the company fails. It does, however, increase the size of his reward if the company succeeds and makes it easier to withdraw part of his investment if the company is modestly successful. At the same time, the debenture decreases the value of what the company receives. Because of this, investors who split their investments between equity and debt should expect to receive fewer shares of company stock than those who invest exclusively in equity.

Do not confuse debentures with convertible debentures. Straight debentures do not give investors any option to convert their debt into stock. Convertible debentures do. If an investor requests convertible debentures, be sure the number of shares the company is willing to sell equals the number he buys outright plus the number his convertible debenture entitles him to buy. *See: Convertible Debentures, Convertible Securities, Debt Service, Leverage, Participating Preferred Stock, Structure, Subordinated Convertible Debentures, Subordinated Debt.*

**Debt Service** is the amount of money a borrower must pay to his lender in order to keep his loans out of default. It consists of the interest and principal payments that are required to pay off the loan.

Debt service payments reduce cash flow, which explains why equity investments, which do not require repayments, are often preferable. Debt service also explains why certain types of investment companies, such as SBICs, SSBICs, and BDCs, usually structure their investment as loans with warrants instead of as straight equity purchases. These types of companies rely on borrowed funds to provide all or most of their capital. By using loans when they invest, these venture firms are able to use the debt service payments from their portfolio companies to repay their loans and stay out of default. *See: BDCs (Business Development Corporations), Cash Flow, Default, Debentures, Leverage, SBICs (Small Business Investment Companies), SSBICs (Specialized Small Business Investment Companies).*

**Default** refers to the failure of one party to fulfill its obligations to another party under an agreement. Company defaults on financing agreements usually give substantial rights to the investor. Depending on the nature of the default and terms of the contract, those rights could empower an investor to withhold funding, to take over management of the company, or to accelerate the company's obligation to pay off debt.

Whenever possible, management should try to limit an investor's default rights to circumstances that involve material defaults so that inconsequential, technical defaults do not cause the company to be penalized. Rights to remedy or cure defaults can often be obtained and written into an agreement. These cure rights permit a company to correct defaults and avoid the severe penalties they can involve. *See: Benchmarks, Cure Periods, Projections, Take Away Provisions.*

**Demand Rights** are contractual agreements that entitle an investor to force a company to register his shares of company stock so that he can sell them to the public. Demand rights are often contrasted with piggyback rights, which allow an investor to include his shares of stock in a public offering that the company voluntarily conducts for its own benefit.

Most venture capitalists require companies to grant them demand rights as a condition to their investing. Demand rights enable the investor to liquidate his investment by forcing the company to register his shares for sale to the public. This registration process, however, is expensive and time-consuming. And a public sale at the wrong time can reduce the future value of a company's shares. Because this can increase a company's cost of raising equity in the future, the number of demand rights granted and the conditions under which they can be exercised are usually heavily negotiated issues.

The outcome of those negotiations can seriously affect the future success of a company. Among the points management frequently seeks to obtain in negotiations over demand rights are:

- *Limitations on the number of demand rights.* One demand right is preferred. The fewer demand rights the better for management.

- *Control over when the demand right may be first exercised.* Typically, managements seek to delay a demand registration until at least 12 months after the company has conducted a company initiated initial pubic offering. Alternatively, managements negotiate for a fixed period of time, such as three years, during which the demand right may not be exercised.

- *Minimum requirements to exercise a demand right.* Usually, this translates into a requirement that a fixed minimum number of shares be offered for sale and that the proposed offering be of at least a certain minimum dollar size.

- *Rights to delay or convert a demand registration.* Managements routinely request the right to delay a demand offering for a period of time if the company's directors have commenced preparations for a public offering or believe a delay would benefit an offering because of market or other conditions. They also frequently request the right to convert a demand offering into a company initiated offering to give the company preference and control over the number of shares offered.

*See: Piggyback Rights, Private Placements, Registration Rights. See also: Going Public, IPO's (Initial Public Offerings), Public Offering.*

## Dilution (Percentage) is a decrease in the percentage of a company's outstanding stock represented by a fixed number of shares. Percentage dilution occurs to existing shareholders whenever a company issues shares of stock to a new shareholder. It results from the increase in the total number of company shares outstanding caused by the sale of new shares. This increase reduces the percentage ownership each share represents in the company. As a result, existing shareholders who do not purchase new shares find themselves owning a smaller percentage of the outstanding equity.

For example, if management owns all 80,000 shares of a company's stock and the company issues 20,000 new shares to another investor, management's percentage ownership in the company will be reduced from 100 percent of 80,000 shares to 80 percent of 100,000 shares. Its 80 percent of the stock may be worth more than the 100 percent it owned before the new investor bought 20,000 shares, but, nonetheless, management's percentage stock ownership has been diluted.

Percentage dilution is inevitable in venture capital financings. In fact, few entrepreneurs manage to retain a majority of the stock in their company by the time it has grown sufficiently to go public. Still, 25 percent of a $50 million company with publicly traded stock is worth a lot more than 100 percent of a privately held company worth $5 million. Not only is it more than twice as many dollars, but the stock is also in a more liquid form, which adds to its value.

Percentage dilution does not occur in stock splits. This is because the percentage increase in outstanding shares caused by the split results from an equal percentage increase in each shareholder's holdings. *See: Antidilution Provisions, Dilution*

*(Value), Fully Diluted, Going Public, Pricing, Restricted Securities.*

**Dilution (Value)** is an accounting concept. It refers to the difference between what an investor pays for his shares of company stock and their book value immediately after the transaction. Whenever an investor pays more than book value for his shares he suffers value dilution.

Assume, for example, that an investor buys 20,000 shares at $10 per share when 80,000 shares are already outstanding and the book value of the company is $50,000. The investor's $200,000 investment will be added to the $50,000 to increase the company's book value to $250,000. Dividing the company's new book value by the number of outstanding company shares gives the per-share book value. In this case, the $250,000 book value divided by one hundred thousand shares (the investor's 20,000 plus management's 80,000) gives a per share book value of $2.50. The investor who paid $10 per share suffers a $7.50 per share value dilution. At the same time, management's shares experience an increase in book value from $.62 per share ($50,000 divided by 80,000 shares) to $2.50 per share.

Venture investors expect value dilution. They know that book value is conservative measure of company value that infrequently approximates market value. Knowledgeable investors are more interested in the fair market value of the shares they purchase and the company's prospects for success. *See: Antidilution Provisions, Dilution (Percentage), Fully Diluted, ROI (Return on Investment).*

## Percentage and Value Dilution Comparison

| | |
|---|---:|
| Management share ownership | 80,000 |
| Investor share purchase | 20,000 |
| Total shares after purchase | 100,000 |
| Investor price per share | $10 |
| Company book value before investment | $50,000 |
| Company book value after investment | $250,000 |
| Company per share book value after investment | $2.50 |
| Percentage dilution of management (100% to 80%) | 20% |
| Per share value dilution of investor ($10.00 to $2.50) | $7.50 |

**Director Indemnities** refers to a common practice among private and public companies to provides protection to members of their boards of directors by pledging the companies' credit to protect them against liabilities they might incur when acting on behalf of their companies. Most states permit corporations to provide these indemnities for their directors. The indemnities typically apply only when the directors act in good faith on company related activities. Most states exclude from protection actions taken by directors that are willfully fraudulent or grossly negligent.

Venture capitalists routinely require these indemnities to be included in a company's bylaws before they invest in a company or join its board of directors. Some also require written indemnification agreements between the company and their director nominees. A common bylaw indemnity provision reads like this:

*Investors, Deal Structures, Legal Strategies - 107*

*Indemnification of Officers and Directors.* The corporation shall indemnify any current or former director, officer, employee or agent of the corporation, or any persons who are or were serving at its request as a director, officer, employee, trustee or similar functionary of another foreign or domestic corporation, trust, partnership, joint venture, employee benefit plan or other enterprise, against any and all liabilities and expenses actually and necessarily incurred by such person in connection with or resulting from (a) any threatened, pending or complete action, suit or proceeding, whether civil, criminal, administrative, arbitrative or investigative, (b) an appeal in such an action, suit or proceeding, or (c) an inquiry or investigation that could lead to such an action, suit or proceeding, all to the full extent permitted by law. Such indemnification shall not be deemed exclusive of any other rights to which such person may be entitled, under any bylaw, agreement, insurance policy or vote of shareholders, or otherwise.

*See: Board of Directors, Board Committees, Bylaws.*


## The Director's Duties

*Individuals who sit on company boards owe fiduciary duties to the shareholders of the company. The duty is owed to all owners. When a company is not in financial distress this generally refers to the company's shareholders. When bankruptcy is a possibility, the duty may also be owed to company creditors.*

*Individuals who are elected directors as representatives of a class of preferred investors, such as a venture capital fund manager, owe fiduciary duties to all of the company's shareholders and not just the class of shareholders responsible for their appointment. Directors elected by a 90% owner owe the same fiduciary duties to the 10% shareholder as they do the 90% owner who elected them. Individuals, when acting as directors, must act for the benefit of the company as a whole and all of its owners.*

*Director fiduciary duties fall into two general categories, duties of care and duties of loyalty. The duty of care requires directors to be reasonably well informed, diligent and careful when acting for the company. The duty of loyalty requires directors to act in good faith with the honest belief they are acting in the best interests of the company.*

*In most states, courts will not second guess an action taken by a company board when the directors acted in good faith with the honest belief that their action was taken in the best interests of the company. This general deference to board decisions is often referred to as the business judgment rule. It applies only when actions are taken, when the directors have considered all relevant material reasonably available to them, and when they have acted in the good faith belief that their action was in the best interests of the company.*

*To meet the requirements of care and loyalty, directors are well advised to do the following:*

- *Prepare for and attend board meetings regularly. Preparation should include review of financial and other information provided by company management before director meetings. Be active in meetings. Raise questions and probe issues. Offer constructive counsel.*

- *Work to understand the company's business and industry. Keep apprised of the company's activities and developments within its industry.*

- *Give meaningful deliberation and attention to issues. When appropriate, meet with company advisors or solicit advice from qualified professionals.*

- *Take care to avoid conflicts of interest. When potential conflicts exist, disclose those conflicts and avoid involvement in decisions that involve the potential conflict. Advice of counsel is often useful when potential conflicts arise.*
- *Develop and maintain good oversight of company management so that they can be in a position to make informed decisions about officer retention and replacement.*
- *Make sure regular minutes of board and board committees meetings are kept and approved. This documents the board's exercise of care in its deliberations.*

*Directors who violate their fiduciary duties can become liable to company shareholders who can show they were damaged by the directors' actions. This potential personal liability can have severe consequences for directors who act without regard to their fiduciary duties. Growing companies routinely indemnify directors from the risk of shareholder suits but state statutes limit the activities for which directors may be indemnified. Directors and officers insurance is also routinely obtained to help reduce this risk for company directors.*

*Fulfilling the loyalty duty creates the most problems for directors in growing companies. The risk of violating the duty arises whenever a director has a potential interest in a company transaction other than his interest as a director of the company. Such an interest can exist when a director sits on the board or owns an interest in a business the company transacts business with, when the director has an interest in a competitive company, or when the director negotiates his compensation with the company. A director representing preferred shares held by a venture capitalist has potential conflicts when a company sale generates a return to his preferred investors but not to others.*

*States generally provide safe harbors for directors in conflict situations that are designed to protect shareholders and directors from the potential for conflict of interest. The safe harbors vary from jurisdiction to jurisdiction but generally apply in two scenarios. The first is when the director fully discloses the conflict to the board, removes himself from deliberations and the transaction is nonetheless approved by the disinterested directors. The second is when the director fully discloses the conflict to the shareholders, the transaction is submitted to the shareholders for approval, and is approved by the shareholders in good faith. When a safe harbor is obtained, the business judgment rule applies to create the presumption that the company acted on an informed basis in good faith for the best interests of the company.*

*Because of the personal risks involved it is always wise for a director with a potential conflict of interest to fully disclose his potential interest in a proposed transaction to the other directors, remove himself from the deliberations, and permit the disinterested directors to decide about the activity that creates the potential conflict. When disinterested directors do not exist, making a full disclosure and submitting the question to the company shareholders for decision can also help avoid the conflict. Whenever possible these actions should be taken with advice of counsel so that the benefits of a safe harbor may be obtained.*

*See: Board of Directors, Corporate Governance, Golden Rule. See also: Revolution in Corporate Governance, Board Room Etiquette – Private Companies, Real World Conflicts in Fundraising.*

**Discounted Cash Flow** refers to a method of valuing a company that is commonly used by private company investors. Unlike the market valuation method described in the *Pricing* entry, the discounted cash flow method estimates company value without resort to the price-earnings ratios of similar publicly held companies.

The premise of the method is that company value can be estimated by forecasting the future performance of the business and measuring the surplus cash flow it generates. The surplus cash flows and cash flow shortfalls are discounted back to a present value and added together to arrive at a valuation. The discount factor used is adjusted for the financial risk of investing in the company. The mechanics of the method focus investors on the internal operations of the company and its future.

Like any other valuation method, the discounted cash flow method has its shortcomings. Since it focuses only on the generation of cash flow it ignores outside factors that affect company value, such as price-earnings ratios. It also ignores asset values and other internal factors that can reduce or increase company value.

Nonetheless, it is a commonly used method in venture capital financings because it focuses on what the venture investor is actually buying, a piece of the future operations of the company. Its focus on future cash flows also coincides nicely with a critical concern of all investors - the company's ability to sustain its future operations through internally generated cash flow.

The discounted cash flow method can be applied in six distinct steps. Since the method is based on forecasts, a good understanding of the business, its market, and its past operations is a must. The steps in the discounted cash flow method are as follows:

- *Develop accurate, debt free projections of the company's future operations.* This is clearly the critical element in the valuation. The more closely the projections reflect a good understanding of the business and its realistic prospects, the more confident investors will be with the valuation its supports.

- *Quantify positive and negative cash flow in each year of the projections.* The cash flow being measured is the surplus cash generated by the business each year. In years when the company does not generate surplus cash, the cash shortfall is measured. So that borrowings will not distort the valuation, cash flow is calculated as if the company had no debt. In other words, interest charges are backed out of the projections before cash flows are measured.
- *Estimate a terminal value for the last year of the projections.* Since it is impractical to project company operations out beyond three to five years in most cases, some assumptions must be made to estimate how much value will be contributed to the company by the cash flows generated after the last year in the projections. Without making such assumptions, the value generated by the discounted cash flow method would approximate the value of the company as if it ceased operations at the end of the projection period. One common and conservative assumption is the perpetuity assumption. This assumption assumes that the cash flow of the last projected year will continue forever and then discounts that cash flow back to the last year of the projections.
- *Determine the discount factor to be applied to the cash flows.* One of the key elements affecting the valuation generated by this method is the discount factor chosen. The larger the factor is, the lower the valuation it will generate. This discount factor should reflect the business and investment risk involved. The less likely the company is to meet its projections, the higher the factor should be. Discount factors used most often are a compromise between the cost of borrowing and the cost of equity investment. If the cost of borrowed money is 10% and equity investors

want 30% for their funds, the discount factor would be somewhere in between.

- *Apply the discount factor to the cash flow surplus and short-fall of each year and to the terminal value.* The amount generated by each of these calculations will estimate the present value contribution of each year's future cash flow. Adding these values together estimates the company's present value assuming it is debt free.

- *Subtract present long term and short-term borrowings from the present value of future cash flows to estimate the company's present value.*

The chart on the following page illustrates the computations made in the discounted cash flow method. The chart assumes a discount factor of 13% and uses the perpetuity assumption to generate a residual value for the cash flows after the fifth year. The numbers contained in the Discount column represent the present value of 1.00 discounted back at 13% per year.

The perpetuity assumption is used to determine the residual value. In this case, the fifth year's cash flow ($310,000) was divided by the discount factor (13%) to get a residual value of $2,384,615. This resulting value represents the value of the company at the end of the fifth year and must be further discounted back to present value, as shown in the chart.

Since the discounted cash flow method can only estimate value using agreed upon assumptions, it is always wise to compare the valuation generated using this method with valuations generated using other methods, such as the market valuation method described in the *Pricing* section of this book. Also, changing the assumptions in the calculations can create large swings in "value." Because of this it is wise to test the assumptions used carefully. *See: Cash Flow, Market Price Method, Pricing.*

# Discounted Cash Flow Chart

| | Year | Cash Flow | Discount | Present Value |
|---|---|---|---|---|
| | 1 | $ -50,000 | 0.885 | $ -44,250 |
| | 2 | 10,000 | 0.783 | 7,830 |
| | 3 | 60,000 | 0.693 | 41,580 |
| | 4 | 150,000 | 0.613 | 91,950 |
| | 5 | 310,000 | 0.543 | 168,330 |
| Residual value | | 2,384,615 | 0.543 | 1,294,846 |
| Present value of projected cash flow | | | | 1,560,286 |
| Subtract: Outstanding debt | | | | -150,000 |
| Present Value | | | | $1,410,286 |

**Down Round** refers to an equity financing that raises money at share prices lower than the previous equity funding. For example, a sale of one million shares of Series B Convertible Preferred Stock at $2.50 per share after an earlier sale of Series A Convertible Preferred Stock at $3.00 per share would be a down round. While any sale of voting securities reduces the percentage ownership and relative voting power of existing shares, down rounds do so more dramatically than rounds at higher prices. They can also depress ownership and voting power of management shareholders more than earlier venture investors. This is because antidilution protections contained in the terms of most convertible preferred stock entitle their venture investors to receive extra shares of common stock when they later convert their shares of convertible preferred stock into common stock. These rights are not typically provided to management or other holders of common stock. The result is that holders of common stock, like management, are usually disproportionately diluted in a down round.

In difficult fundraising environments, such as the period after the bust of the dot-com bubble, and in situations where fundraising has been particularly difficult, creative down round investors have employed other mechanisms to enhance their ownership rights and reduce the value of the shareholdings of existing investors even more. The combined use of some or all of these mechanisms can reduce the ownership and voting power of existing shareholders, including earlier venture investors, to next to nothing. These mechanisms include:

- Pay-to-play provisions
- Liquidation preferences
- Participating preferred stock
- Adjustments to existing shareholder rights

*Pay-to-play provisions.* These are requirements imposed by the investors of new money on prior investors, as a condition to making the new investment, that require the prior investors to invest with the new investor to avoid being penalized. One example of a pay-to-play provision is an amendment to the company's charter that enables existing shareholders who invest in the down round to convert their existing convertible preferred stock into a more valuable amended series of convertible preferred stock that allows conversion into a greater number of shares of common stock. Existing venture investors who do not reinvest are left with their original, now devalued, convertible preferred stock.

For example, participating investors might be allowed as a part of their investment of new Series B stock to convert their Series A into a preferential Series A-1 stock. The preference might be a revised conversion formula that increases the number of shares of common stock they are entitled to receive on conversion by a factor of five to make the new conversion more closely resemble the value afforded in the subsequent Series B down round. Nonparticipating investors are left with the original Series A stock.

Another pay-to-play strategy might issue a highly dilutive new Series B stock, say at one-tenth the price of the Series A stock, and provide existing shareholders who invest their pro rata portion in the Series B stock to also receive additional shares of another class of stock that enables them to retain some of the value diluted out of the Series A stock.

A third approach is to build the pay-to-play requirement into the original Series A stock when it is first issued. Then the stock terms themselves can provide for different treatment of Series A shareholders who invest in the later round and those who do not.

*Liquidation preferences.* Many venture capital investment vehicles, such as convertible preferred stock, contain provisions that give the investor the right to receive back its investment amount before other shareholders receive proceeds from a liquidation. These preferences can be used to reserve first value to new investors and decrease the value of other shareholdings when a later liquidation event occurs, such as a sale of the business. In down rounds the value of this liquidation preference is often increased to exaggerate this reduction in value to existing shareholders.

For example, a down round liquidation provision might provide the Series B shareholders with three dollars for every dollar they invested out of the first funds distributed from a liquidation event and before any funds are made available to other shareholders. By defining liquidation to include a sale or merger of the business, the Series B investor of $5 million assures himself of receiving the first $15 million dollars generated by a qualifying liquidation event and reduces the value of the company to other shareholders.

*Participating preferred stock.* Down round investors sometimes couple participation features with their liquidation preferences to enhance the prospective value of their securities even further. The participation feature entitles them to receive a liquidation preference before distribution of proceeds to other shareholders and then to participate with the other shareholders in the proceeds remaining after payment of the preference.

*Adjustments to existing shareholder rights.* Antidilution protections afforded to existing shareholders, either as incorporated into the description of their stock or by separate contractual negotiation, may increase the shareholdings of existing shareholders after a down round. Liquidation preferences or participating preferred rights might also exist in earlier series of convertible preferred stock. Because of this, another condition sometimes imposed in a down round is that existing holders of preferential rights agree to terminate or reduce those rights. This could take the form of cancellation of antidilution rights, reduction of a liquidation preference or amendment to remove a participating right. It could also take the form of a forced conversion from a preferred security into common stock or a new form of convertible preferred stock with reduced rights. *See: Antidilution Provisions, Dilution (Percentage), Dilution (Value), Equity Penalties, Follow-on Fundings, Liquidation Preferences, Liquidity Event, Participating Preferred Stock,*

*Pay-to-Play Provisions, Ratchets, Weighted Average Antidilution.*

**Downside** is the investor's risk that he will lose the money he invests in a company. While the downside in almost every venture investment includes some possibility that the investor will lose all of his money, most investors use the term in a more limited sense. They use it to describe a realistic appraisal of the probable risk in the situation.

Venture investors use a number of deal-structuring devices to reduce their downside risks. Often, they delay part of their funding obligation and make it contingent upon the company meeting a predetermined benchmark. This allows the investor to postpone risking some of his money until the company has proven its ability to meet a goal. The later rounds of funding are put in at less risk when the company is more established. Taking collateral and guarantees also reduces the downside by increasing the probability that the investor can salvage something if the company goes under. Preferred stock and debentures do the same thing by giving the investor a preference over common stockholders when a company is liquidated.

Other investor practices also reduce the downside. Rigorous due diligence investigations into the business of prospective portfolio companies before investments are made helps investors pick good companies and avoid losers. Board participation and regular reports from management help investors identify and address problems early. Puts, buy-sells, redemptions, and registration rights can liquidate an investment before all is lost or help an investor get his money out of a modestly successful company and into something else.

Management can reduce the downside too. When they do, they increase the chance of getting funding at a reasonable price. The best way to reduce the downside is to anticipate strategic and operating problems and address them realistically in the business plan. This will not eliminate the downside entirely, but it will increase the investor's comfort and help management deal better with problems as they arise. Since most of the deal structuring devices that reduce the investor's downside also tend to increase the risks of management shareholders (by delaying needed funding, making it contingent on future events and giving preferences to the investor when the company fails to live up to expectations), precautions that reduce everyone's risk (such as good planning) not only help attract new investors but also enhance the value of the management's shareholdings. *See: Business Plan, Business Plan Format, Collateral, Convertible Securities, Co-Sale Agreements, Debentures, Due Diligence, Exits, Liquidity Agreements, Negotiation, Pricing, Puts, Stage Financing, Structure, Upside.*

**Drag Along Agreements** are agreements that entitle one party, usually an outside investor, to require other parties, often founders or management, to sell their stock in the company to a third party when the investor desires to sell its shares. Under the agreement, the party being "dragged along" receives the same consideration per share as the selling investor but does not control the timing or terms of the purchase.

Sometimes referred to as bring along agreements, these contracts enable their holders to deliver more than just their shares to a potential buyer. If the agreement includes all shareholders, the holder can deliver the entire company. Even if the agreement does not include all shareholders, it may enable the holder to sell a controlling interest in the company. In either case, the drag along provision increases the holder's liquidity by providing it with the ability to deliver more than just its shares to an interested buyer.

The essential element of every drag along agreement is the extraordinary ability it gives one party to force another party to sell its company shares at a time and on terms and conditions determined by the holder. Time limits and price limits are often added as conditions to exercise in drag along agreements, when they are agreed to at all. Because these agreements take from the "dragged" shareholder the basic right to determine when and under what conditions it will sell its stock, they are infrequently agreed to. When they are, careful consideration should be given to the terms and conditions under which they may be exercised. *See: Co-Sale Agreements, Exits, First Refusal Rights, Liquidity Agreements, Tag Along Provisions.*

**Due Diligence** is any investigation by one party of another party. When used in a fund raising context, it usually refers to the investigation conducted by a prospective investor into the background of a company, its management team, and the statements and assumptions contained in it business plan. It is usually intensive, time consuming, and thorough. It is not unusual for the investigation to take weeks or months to complete.

Due diligence customarily includes background checks on the management team, independent verifications of statements made in the business plan, and studies of the company's product and market. It includes extensive questioning of management and other company personnel. Most venture capitalists will talk with company suppliers, customers, competitors, and others who know the company and its industry.

Entrepreneurs should conduct due diligence too. They should investigate their industry and their partners thoroughly to gauge their company's prospects and the depth of experience and commitment of each of its principals. Business plans should not be completed without giving careful attention to the assumptions and facts that support the company's profits and cash flow projections.

Just as important, entrepreneurs should conduct due diligence investigations about the company's potential investors. Selecting the right investor for a company can mean the difference between success and failure. A disreputable or reluctant investor can slow and even prevent company success. Conversely, an honorable investor can help management by giving it the benefit of his experience with growing companies and his contacts with financial institutions. This can be as valuable as cash.

One way to learn about a particular investor is to ask bankers, lawyers, and accountants about his reputation. If a publicly held venture capital fund is considering investing, a good deal of information about it can be obtained from the Securities and Exchange Commission. If it is privately held, as most are, management can usually obtain a copy of the offering circular it used to raise funds by simply asking the investor for one. The National Venture Capital Association and the National Association of Small Business Investment Corporations (NASBIC) are also good resources. There are also several commercially available compilations of venture capital firms and their investment preferences.

Once it has begun investigating a company, most venture firms will give an entrepreneur a list of the companies in which it has invested. These companies can provide valuable insights into the personality of the fund and its desirability as a business partner. Appropriate questions to ask the founders of these companies are:

- Was the firm easy or difficult to work with?
- Was it prompt in making investment decisions?
- What type of participation in management did it require?
- Are its managers honest and candid?
- Were they reasonable in their negotiations?
- Have they provided services promised to the company?
- Have they helped or hindered company success?
- Are they responsive to company needs?
- How has the firm reacted to company problems?

- Is it flexible?
- Has the firm participated in later rounds of financing?
- Did it help identify further investors?
- Did its performance live up to its promises?

The more specific the questions are the more valuable will be the information obtained. Questions to and about the venture capital firm are appropriate and demonstrate management's concern for the future. Questions about how long it will take the investor to make a decision and whether it has the funds and freedom to make an investment are particularly appropriate. *See: Audits, Business Plan, Downside, Ethics, NASBIC (National Association of Small Business Investment Companies), National Venture Capital Association, Venture Capitalists.*

# E

**Earnouts** refer to a contingent form of purchase price or performance bonus that becomes payable only if the purchased company meets agreed upon targets after the closing. The term can also refer to any payout obligation that is contingent upon future results. A loan repayable only from company profits would also be a kind of earnout.

Earnouts are frequently used to bridge the gap between seller price expectations and buyer willingness to pay. For example, a buyer may be willing to pay $10 million dollars for a company the seller thinks is worth $15 million. In the course of the negotiations, the buyer may sweeten his offer to $12 million and the seller may compromise to $12 million if the buyer agrees to pay an additional $1 million in the future. The buyer may agree to this if the additional payment is structured as an earnout that becomes payable only if the company exceeds agreed-upon goals after the sale.

The goal could be completion of an important technology development, attainment of a sales or profit goal, completion of a desired transaction, or an advantageous settlement of an outstanding claim. Whatever the goal, it is in the best interest of both parties that the goal be clearly described and that mechanisms be put in place to assure that the goal is fairly measured.

For the seller, it is critical that sufficient resources of the company be made available to enable the goal to be met. Consequently, when they are used, earnouts are usually painstakingly documented and thoroughly negotiated. The details of the provision can make the difference between the seller receiving the deferred payment or not.

Key issues to consider when negotiating an earnout include:

- *Amount and timing.* The larger the amount that is subject to the earnout, the greater the risk to the seller. The shorter the measurement period, the less likely it is that subsequent events might intervene to make the attainment of the goals more difficult.
- *Number of goals.* Is there more than one goal? Is the payout all or none or are there subgoals that would earn partial payment of the earnout?
- *Measurability.* Readily measurable goals are important. If the goal cannot be easily measured by agreed-upon methods, the more likely it is that there will be a later dispute over whether the goal was attained.
- *Resource commitment.* Has the payor agreed to allocate sufficient manpower, funding, and physical resources to make the goal attainable?
- *Alignment of interests.* Is it in the payor's best interest for the company to meet the goal and make the earnout payment? If not, no amount of resource allocation can be expected to achieve the goal.
- *Retention of recipient in management.* Will the recipient of the earnout remain in a position with the company that will enable him to effect the accomplishment of the goal? If not, the recipient is relying on the payor's good faith, contractual commitments and, hopefully, alignment of payor's interest with the recipient's improve the odds the earnout will be paid.

*See: Earnups, LBO (Leveraged Buyout), MBO (Management Buyout).*

**Earnups** refer to arrangements structured into leveraged or management buyouts that enable management to earn more equity in the company if the company succeeds in meeting agreed-upon goals. In management led buyouts, earnups have less to do with financing than they do with rewarding management for later performance. In investor led buyouts they are a technique for attracting good people to manage the acquired company.

Earnups are sometimes used by new owners after acquiring a company to entice the existing company executive team to remain with the company. If the executives stay and achieve the owner's goals, they can earn an ownership share in the company. The mechanism used to accomplish this might be a qualified stock option grant that vests only after the goals are met or a restricted stock grant that remains unvested until the goals are met. The goals can be whatever the parties negotiate – sales, profits, or even remaining with the company for a period of time. *See: Earnouts, Golden Handcuffs, LBO (Leveraged Buyout), MBO (Management Buyout), Management Agreements, Vesting Schedules.*

**83(b) Election** is an option employee shareholders have under Section 83(b) of the Internal Revenue Code. It entitles them to choose when they will be taxed on shares they purchase from their employer when their shares are not fully vested and remain subject to restrictions which may or may not lapse.

Anyone who receives stock in connection with the performance of services for a company should know about Section 83 of the Internal Revenue Code. Unless an 83(b) election is made, Section 83 can require the shareholder to pay taxes at ordinary income tax rates when the restrictions on his stock lapse. The tax is computed on the difference between the value of the stock when the restrictions lapse and the price paid for the shares. This tax must be paid even if the shareholder cannot, as is typically the case with private company shares, sell his stock to generate cash.

Section 83(b) entitles the shareholder to make an election within thirty days after he purchases the shares to prevent this unwanted attribution of income. The election (basically, filing the proper form) causes the shareholder to be taxed at the time of the purchase, instead of the date of vesting. This earlier tax is based on the difference between the purchase price of their shares and the value those shares would have had when they were purchased if they had been fully vested.

Why would someone choose to be taxed earlier instead of later? Because, as is often the case in early stage growth companies, the initial low purchase price for the shares may equal the actual market value of those shares at that time. When this is the case, making an 83(b) election creates no tax liability at the time of purchase and prevents tax liability arising when the restrictions lapse on the stock. This effectively defers the employee's tax obligation until he sells the stock.

Even an employee who purchases stock for less than its value, may choose to make the election. If the employee believes the stock will increase dramatically in value, he may prefer to be taxed now on a relatively small amount rather than risk being taxed on a larger amount when the stock fully vests.

The chart below, which assumes that the shares were sold at a discount to the employee, illustrates the workings of Section 83(b).

## 83(b) Election Comparison

|  | No Election | Election |
|---|---|---|
| Price of shares | $10,000 | $10,000 |
| Share value at purchase | $12,000 | $12,000 |
| Value taxed on sale | none | $2,000 |
| Share value when restrictions lapse | $90,000 | $90,000 |
| Value taxed when restrictions lapse | $80,000 | none |
| Value taxed when shares sold for $100,000 | $10,000 | $88,000 |

As the chart illustrates, failure to make an 83(b) election can have damaging effects. If, as everyone involved hopes, the company increases in value during the vesting period, the shareholder who failed to make the election will have to pay taxes on the difference between the increased value of the shares on the date they vest and the amount he paid for them. At the same time, the shares are likely to be illiquid because of restrictions that apply to resales of unregistered securities.

As a result, the shareholder may owe the federal government a substantial tax payment (resulting from his choice not to make an 83(b) election) without having the means to pay it. In the example, failure to elect to pay taxes on a $2,000 gain results in the employee owing taxes on $80,000 of "paper income" when the restrictions lapse.

The provisions of Section 83 are complex and cannot be completely explored here. They apply in situations when a casual observer would not think they should. As a result, any person who receives or purchases securities that are subject to vesting or other similar restrictive provisions should consult with a qualified attorney or accountant to determine whether the filing of an 83(b) election is appropriate. *See: Restricted Securities, Vesting Schedules, Vesting Stock Grants.*

**Emerging Growth Companies** is a phrase used by private equity investors and entrepreneurs to describe young companies that have good prospects for rapid and sustained growth. They are the kinds of companies that venture capitalists are eager to support because their rapid growth promises to create healthy returns for investors.

The phrase reflects the fact that the company's past progress and clearly articulated business plan give investors confidence that the company is "emerging" as an attractive investment. Emerging growth companies can be in any industry.

Emerging growth companies in industries whose public company stocks tend to sell at high multiples of company earnings frequently attract more attention from investors than those in industries whose public companies sell at lower multiples. This is because it takes fewer dollars of earnings to support high stock prices for investor shares in these industries. Technology oriented companies have attracted a lot of venture capital investment not because of their technology orientation, but because they tend to be in industries that support high ratios of share price to company earnings.

Emerging growth companies include any company that presents good potential for rapid and sustained growth in excess of industry averages. Low- or no-technology companies with the potential for rapid and sustained growth are being funded. The investor's primary concern is their return on investment when the company stock attains liquidity, not the glamour of technology. *See: High Tech, Life Style Companies, Price-Earnings Ratio, ROI (Return on Investment).*

**Employment Contracts** are agreements used to set out the terms of an employee's employment. Not all employees have employment agreements. Those who do not are frequently referred to as employees-at-will. In many states, employees-at-will may have their employment terminated without advance notice or cause, unless their right to remain employed is protected by an anti-discrimination law such as those that protect senior age and minority workers.

Employment contracts are used for a variety of purposes, including attracting key people to join a company by setting out their salary, benefits, and severance rights. They can also define job duties or create secrecy and noncompetition agreements to protect a company. Employment contracts can provide protections against arbitrary firings in the form of severance payment obligations the company must provide unless employment termination is for a cause specified in the contract. When properly written, employment contracts can help companies avoid expensive fights over trade secret infringement claims made by former employers of newly hired company personnel.

Employment contracts with key employees are important to many investors. Young companies usually depend more on the talents of a small group of people than do their larger, more established competitors. Because of this, most investors require assurances that a company's key people will remain after funding. They want to know that the people they evaluated will stay around to run the company after their money is invested. At the same time, entrepreneurs often want protection against being fired when new investors are brought in. Not surprisingly, negotiations over who will receive employment contracts and what the terms of those contracts will be are often important parts of a financing discussion.

Employment contracts do not always make sense for a company, however. As a general rule, employment contracts should be avoided unless they serve a specific company purpose. Giving an employee a contract that guarantees his employment for a period of time does not further company interests unless it is necessary to secure an important benefit for the company, such as convincing the employee to take the job. Because of the personal-service nature of employment, employment contracts are usually ineffective at forcing an employee to stay with a company. They are even less effective at keeping an employee interested in doing a good job. At the same time, however, employment contracts can cause management to retain an employee longer than it wants or to pay a departing employee a premium to leave.

Investors, in general, do not like management contracts that are cash rich . They expect entrepreneurs to sacrifice present earnings for the prospects of long-term capital appreciation. Managements that crave large salaries and elaborate executive benefits can scare away venture capitalists. Contracts that insure management employment for too long or in circumstances that could jeopardize a shareholder's investment also cool investor enthusiasm.

Venture investors want the freedom to remove management if it proves to be ineffective. Their ability to do this, of course, depends on whether the securities they buy or the contracts they enter into entitle them to take such actions. So long as management controls a majority of the company's board of directors and has not conceded contract rights to investors that convey this right, outside investors are left with the task of persuading other board members before they can effect a change. At the same time, managements want some security against arbitrary firings. This is particularly true when management finds it has lost control of the board after a financing. *See: Compensation and Bonus Plans, Confidentiality Agreements, Golden Handcuffs, Noncompete Agreements, Vesting Schedules.*

**Entrepreneur** is someone who starts and operates a business. The term includes those who accept the many risks inherent in operating a fledgling enterprise in pursuit of profit. Entrepreneurs forsake the relative security of a job to take on the challenge of building a successful company.

Most entrepreneurs invest great amounts of time and effort, at considerable sacrifice to themselves and their families, for the privilege of starting their own business and being their own boss. Entrepreneurs come from all walks of life and have different degrees of experience and ability.

What do venture capitalists and other sophisticated investors look for in an entrepreneur? In what type of people do they like to invest? Here are a few characteristics commonly found in successful entrepreneurs:

- *Achievement.* Relevant past experiences are considered a prime indicator of an entrepreneur's prospects for success. Someone who has been successful in the past is more likely to be successful in the future. Obviously, the most relevant achievement an entrepreneur can have is to have started a business in the same industry. Next to that, success in managing a business or division of a business is preferred. In some business models, product development success or inventive achievement are crucial.

- *Knowledge.* Knowledge of the industry and where the new product or service will fit is essential. An accurate study of the industry may give an entrepreneur this knowledge, but actual experience in it is a real plus, particularly if that experience is coupled with a history of successful innovation in the industry. Knowledge about managing people and growth is also important.

- *Drive.* A key factor in entrepreneurial success is drive. Experienced investors look for capable entrepreneurs who are driven to succeed and who understand that hard work and long hours are required to make the company a success. A tenacious entrepreneur with enthusiasm for his company is a must. Surveys show that entrepreneurs work long hours. Practical experience shows that an intense desire coupled with a sharp focus on business building priorities makes for a promising entrepreneur.

- *Intelligence.* Raw intelligence, rationality, insight, and creativity are important. Advanced degrees from universities are nice and may evidence intelligence, but what an investor really wants is an entrepreneur who can analyze a complex problem, understand it, and arrive at an appropriate solution quickly.
- *Flexibility.* Blockheads do not make good business builders. A flexible entrepreneur is one who can adjust his approach to meet unexpected problems. He is one who can accept criticism and advice from others, including his investors. Most important of all is the entrepreneur's ability to learn from his mistakes and grow with the increasing demands of his expanding company.
- *Management.* A successful company's management will be faced with personnel and management problems that would stretch the patience and creativity of the best of managers. A good manager must be able to work with and motivate people. He must also keep a tight rein on cash flow, cash control, manufacturing, and sales.
- *Integrity.* Investors want an entrepreneur who is honest and open with them. They want someone who has a realistic understanding of his own strengths and weaknesses. People like this are more likely to face up to challenges quickly and constructively and to make realistic appraisals of their products and their marketplaces.

All entrepreneurs have faults. Few have all the qualities identified above. This is one reason most investors prefer to invest in management teams. Not only are investments safer for not being reliant on the good will or health of one individual but investments in teams often benefit from better decision-making that includes more perspectives. The more of these ideal characteristics an entrepreneur or his team have, the more likely it is that the company will get funded. *See: Commitment, Due Diligence, Ethics, Five Factors, Management Team.*

## *The Seven Deadly Sins of Fundraising*

1. *Don't insist on a nondisclosure agreement from investors up front. Venture capitalists typically read a hundred business plans for each company that they fund. It would be impossible for them to process this kind of deal flow if every one expected a nondisclosure agreement. You don't have to reveal all of your technology in the first document you send the venture capitalist. Describe enough to get them interested and consider a nondisclosure agreement later if funding conversations progress.*

2. *Don't focus on the technology and ignore the market, competition and customers. Remember your business plan is selling your company, not your product. A meeting with an investor is not the same as a sales call to your customer. An investor wants to know how you're going to build, sustain, and run a profitable company. A venture capitalist will generally assume you have good technology. They want to know why lots of people are going to pay you a profitable price and that you can deliver product to them.*

3. *Don't practice top down sales forecasting. "Two percent of a billion dollar market will make us a $20 million company." Wrong! Markets typically shake out to a company with 50% market share, another with 30%, and a whole flock splitting the remaining 20%, none of which are making any money. You need to define a market where you're #1 or #2 in market share.*
*Build your sales forecast from the bottom up using this formula:*
*(# of sales people you can hire) times*
*(# calls they can make) times*

*(conversion rate) times*
*(revenue per sale) = Projected Revenues*
*Projected Revenues/Target Market = Market Share*
*You need to define your market and sales channels so this bubbles up to more than a 30% market share.*

*4. Don't use four significant digits everywhere. Projecting market growth, product roll out schedules and sales costs are, at best, educated guesses. Don't crunch the numbers forever. They're estimates. Everyone understands that.*

*5. Don't position investors as necessary-but-unpleasant "mushrooms". You need to face it, accepting venture capital funding is like getting married. At the very least, you're going to be sitting across the table from each other once a month for 3-5 years. You need to accept your investors as part of your management team.*

*6. Don't fill your business plan with typos, errors, chart junk, repetition, or inconsistencies. Your plan makes your first impression and often your only impression with an investor. Spelling counts as does accuracy, conciseness, and clarity.*

*7. Don't expect to acquired by Microsoft. They're only one company. They can't buy everybody. Likewise not every company in a portfolio will do an IPO. For every company that does an IPO, five are acquired. Keep your options open and be realistic with your exit strategy. Keep in mind that companies need to generate 50% year after year return on assets to be attractive to venture capitalists.*

> *Stephen Fleming, Chief Commercialization Officer, Georgia Institute of Technology*

**Equity** is the ownership companies sell to investors to raise money and that entrepreneurs retain to realize value from the businesses they create. In corporations, equity is represented by the company's stock. In partnerships and limited liability companies, it is represented by partnership or membership interests. The instruments that confer equity ownership can be designed to create specific rights to vote on or approve specified company matters, preferences for dividends or distributions, conversion rights, or liquidation rights.

Equity is the most permanent form of investment in a company. Equity does not require repayment and so does not deplete company cash, as debt repayments do.

Corporate equity, in the form of stock ownership, is different from rights a person may have under a note, debenture, or other debt instrument. Convertible debentures have characteristics of both debt and equity. They are treated as debt until the holder elects to convert them. Then they lose their debt characteristics and become equity.

Equity has an element of magic. Some of the most outrageous, unlikely, seemingly ridiculous business ventures have been undertaken with the object of creating equity. The pursuit of equity and the wealth it can create helps to secure the funding necessary to create new businesses and industries. *See: Cash Flow, Common Stock, Convertible Securities, Debentures, Equity Penalties, Preferred Stock, Preferred Stock Umbrellas.*

**Equity Kickers** refer to stock options or warrants to purchase stock that are given by a company to a lender or other party as an inducement to lend money to a company or provide some other value. *See: Earn-ups, Options, Warrants.*

**Equity Penalties** are agreements, usually contained in written contracts, that increase an investor's ownership percentage upon the occurrence of a specified event, such as the failure of the firm to reach a sales level on a given date. By increasing the investor's share of the company, equity penalties decrease the share of other investors, including management.

Equity penalties include any arrangement that causes management's stock ownership percentage to decrease when the company fails to achieve a goal. Equity penalties can take the form of investor options, specialized antidilution protections, or restrictions that prevent management shares from vesting.

Equity penalties are often legitimately included in private company financings.. They are used to allocate risk among the parties. Sometimes, however, equity penalties sneak into a deal late in negotiations as a sweetener for the investor. The first hint that an investor wants this type of sweetener often comes when the investor suggests to management that if the company does not meet the projections in its business plan, then his investment will not be a good one.

To get the funding, management probably reassured the investor several times that the company's projections were reasonable and attainable. Now the investor suggests that if the company does not meet its projections, his return on investment will not be high enough to justify his investment. The fair thing to do, he says, would be to increase his equity percentage if the company fails to meets its projections.

At this point, many inexperienced entrepreneurs get heartburn. They have spent a lot of time with the investor and have become accustomed to thinking of the deal as done. If they refuse this request, they might lose their funding. The temptation to concede is great. But is the request reasonable? Should management concede the investor's request? Usually not.

Most investors know how difficult it is to accurately project results and do not really expect management to concede this issue. After all, the value of management's investment also diminishes if company projections are not met. And one reason the investor is getting so much equity for his money in the first place is because of the risk inherent in the investment.

When an investor insists on equity penalties and management has neither the time nor inclination to look for other investors, it should nonetheless try to get the investor to require "extra" equity only if the company does not attain

70% or 80% of projected results. Management should also try to work in a time cushion. If the projections show the company reaching a certain result on January 1, for example, management should try to get until April 1 to reach 80% of the projections.

Finally, management can suggest that if it makes sense for the investor's percentage to increase if the company fails to make its projections, that it also makes sense for his percentage to decrease if the company exceeds them. Investors will often concede the fairness of this proposal and, to avoid conceding some of their upside potential from better than anticipated results, will console themselves with their original offer for a fixed percentage of the company. *See: Benchmarks, Business Plan, Earnouts, Earnups, Negotiation, Projections, Take Away Provisions, Vesting Schedules.*

**ESOP Buyouts** are a specialized form of company buyout that creates an exit for all or some of the company's shareholders. ESOP buyouts involve purchases of company stock by qualified employee stock ownership plans established as retirement plans for company employees. These benefit plans are designed to invest primarily in the securities of sponsoring company. They receive annual contributions determined by the plan sponsor. Because these buyouts involve the use of these specialized tax qualified plans, they must be carefully structured to comply with applicable tax laws. In general, these buyouts involve the establishment of a qualified employee stock ownership plan by the company, the use of the plan to borrow money from a third party lender, the guarantee of the plan's loan by the company, and pay out of the purchase price to the selling shareholders. The plan later repays the loan using the company's annual contributions and allocates the purchased shares to the plan participants as the debt is paid off. *See: Exits.*

**Ethics** are critically important in venture capital transactions. The relationship of entrepreneur and venture investor is so intertwined that when one acts unfairly, the other almost always suffers. Even when the parties carefully document their agreements, either party can be injured by the unethical behavior of the other.

Unethical behavior should not be confused with actions taken by a party that are consistent with their contractual obligations but contrary to the best interests of another party. Investors can be expected to act in their own self-interest, even when those actions are at the expense of company management. Despite protestations to the contrary - that investor and company management have the same best interests of the company at heart - investor interests and company management interests are inherently different. That's why financing agreements are carefully negotiated and documented, to balance and articulate the interests of the two parties in a fashion that, after all the give and take, is acceptable to all.

Investors recognize the need, in addition to careful documentation of deal terms, to invest only with people they trust. Consequently, sophisticated investors direct a lot of energy and resources into investigating the company and the entrepreneur they are investing in. Entrepreneurs should be just as careful to examine the backgrounds and resources of potential investors before taking their money. Much of this investigation is directed to determining the quality of the management team's judgment and their reputation for honesty.

An unfair or reluctant investor can cause real problems for a company. An investor who delays or fails to provide funding he has agreed to provide, can steal a company of its promise and starve it for cash. This cash shortage can delay expansions and product developments. It can cause the collapse of companies that are not yet profitable. At the very least, it distracts management from the day-to-day management of the company and forces it to deal, instead, with the cash crisis created by the investor.

What is more, this same cash crisis can prevent a company from enforcing its contracts against its investor. Even if the company's contracts require the investor to fund, the company may be unable to force the investor to live up to his bargain. This is because the investor's unwillingness to fund takes away the two assets management needs most to force him to do so - money and time. In many cases, the company simply cannot afford to spend its money or time trying to force an unwilling investor to fund. Even if it could, the actions required to force investment would be a serious drain on the company and might frighten other investors away. After all, how many investors want to put money into a company that is suing its prior investor?

At the same time, the investor may frustrate management further with new demands that make it difficult for the company to obtain money from other sources. As a result, just when management needs to concentrate its efforts on building its company, it is forced, instead, to find cash and deal with an uncooperative investor who has acquired significant rights in the company.

The best way to avoid these problems is to be careful when selecting investors, to investigate their reputations, and to try, when possible, to deal only with people who are trustworthy. Reputable investors will even help entrepreneurs investigate their reputations by giving them the names of managers of companies in which they have invested. Company counsel and accountants will often have resources for checking into investor reputations as well. *See: Adventure Capitalists, Cash Flow, Due Diligence, Stage Financing, Unlocking Provisions.*

# Real World Conflicts in Fundraising

*If you think ethics are an abstract concept for venture financings, consider this real world example of a start-up biotech company's experience with a prominent venture capital firm. In the world of early stage financings, roles and expectations can take surprising turns. In this case, everyone lost and a promising inventor saw his hopes of building a business dashed by an investor unwilling to meet its contractual obligations.*

*After considerable effort, an aspiring inventor sold his plan to expand his fledgling research business to a leading venture capital firm. The proposal was for $4 million in equity financing to be paid at closing contingent only on the inventor finding a business manager acceptable to the investor. The inventor had already plowed years of effort and invested substantial amounts of money to get his company operating and to acquire key patent rights from a university.*

*Within weeks the investor and the inventor settled on an individual identified by the investor to fill the role of business manager. As part of the deal, the business manager was to receive options to purchase up to 10% of the company that vested over a four-year period. Because this was a 'friendly' deal and because the lawyer the company had used also happened to be the lawyer for the venture capitalist, the inventor and his new found business manager partner chose to forgo engaging separate counsel to help them review the paperwork. For the $4 million investment, the investor was to receive 51% of the company's stock and the right to elect two of the company's three directors. The inventor was to fill the other spot on the board.*

*Troubles started when the inventor arrived at the closing. The investor, who was purchasing a Series A convertible preferred stock, had decided at the last minute not to invest the total $4 million at closing. Instead, he agreed to fund $2* *million at closing and an additional $2 million in one year. Without viable alternatives, the inventor acquiesced. Twelve months later when the second $2 million came due, the investor had cooled to the company and refused to provide the additional funding. Without the funds the company would collapse.*

*Notwithstanding the investor's clear obligation to provide funding, the company's options were limited. Cash was tight and the company had no alternative investors. With the existing investor unwilling to provide the funding he was contractually obligated to provide, the company had little prospect of attracting a new investor.*

*Suing the investor to force funding was problematic. A lawsuit would be expensive and time consuming. Even a favorable result would come too late to save the company from financial ruin. Not only that, the investor promised to use its majority position on the board and as a shareholder to liquidate the company if it the investor forced it to put in the second $2 million, pointing out that it's preferred security would entitle it to take the $2 million back in a liquidation before the inventor saw a penny.*

*Was this a violation by the investor of its contractual obligations? Absolutely. But the investor had more on his mind than just questions about his duties to his portfolio company. He was also concerned about his duties to his investors to minimize losses when he could and he was convinced that further investment in the company would result in increased losses. The investment, he now believed, was a mistake and he was willing to take some risk to avoid throwing new money into a bad situation.*

*The inventor contributed to his own woes as well. His naivety allowed him to close the investment without advice of counsel and he had engaged investor counsel to be his lawyer after the closing. As a result, he missed fundamental issues in his financing agreements that exacerbated his situation. For example, when he accepted half of the money originally promised, he should have insisted that the investor take half of the stock originally promised and reduce his board representation until the rest of the money was received. He could have also negotiated for a penalty in the event the investor later reneged.*

*Also, using the investor's counsel for his lawyer may have contributed to his demise. Owing duties to both parties may have prevented counsel from proactively advising the inventor about the risks inherent in his deal structure. When the issue surfaced, counsel resigned the company account but continued to represent the investor, further complicating matters for the company and the investor.*

*What was the biggest mistake? Clearly the most costly mistake was the inventor's failure, in the excitement of finding a investor, to investigate the investor's reputation with other entrepreneurs. Had he done so, he might have avoided the situation entirely.*

*And, how did it end? Not as badly as it could have for the inventor. He learned from his mistake and engaged qualified counsel to advise him. After much discussion, the investor, probably on advice of counsel and in order to avoid publicity and exposure to liability, agreed to sell the inventor all of the investor's stock in the company for $1 plus a waiver of the inventor's rights as a significant shareholder to sue the investor for failing to provide the funding.*

## Executive Summary. *See: Summary.*

**Exits** refer to the methods investors use to change their private company investments into cash. Because of the largely illiquid nature of private company stock, caused by the absence of public markets for the stock and legal restrictions on trading privately issued stock, entrepreneurs need to be sensitive to the liquidity needs of their investors. Until an investor actually converts its investment into cash, any profits it may attribute to its investment are only "paper profits."

It is important for a fundraising plan to display an awareness of the investors' eventual need to exit. Entrepreneurs need to be prepared to discuss, at least in general terms, the likely ways the investors will later turn their investment and profits into cash. The most common ways investors exit private company investments are through the sale of the business, public securities offerings, recapitalizations, direct investor sales, and contractual liquidity agreements. In order of attractiveness to investors, these common exits are summarized below.

- *Business Sales.* Selling the business converts the stock of company stockholders into new value. To the extent the consideration received is cash, the company's investors are made totally liquid. When notes or stock are exchanged for some or all of the consideration, the investor's liquidity event is delayed until the note is paid or the stock consideration is sold. Investment bankers frequently discuss four distinct types of company sales as possibilities for companies seeking a buyer.
  - o *Strategic Buyer Sales.* These are sales to other operating businesses where the company being acquired supports an operational need of the acquiring business. For a number of reasons, including potential savings and value enhancement from synergies inherent in combining the two businesses, strategic buyers often pay higher prices than financial buyers.
  - o *Financial Buyer Sales.* When the purchaser is an individual or an equity fund that buys businesses for its own account, the sale is considered a financial buyer sale. Financial buyers frequently use borrowed funds to leverage their investment and reduce the number of equity dollars they

invest. The assets of the purchased company are often pledged to secure the buyers debt after the sale is completed.

- o *Leveraged Buyouts*. These are sales, often lead by company management, where the buyer acquires control of the company using equity and debt, usually with the debt being secured by the assets of the company. When the company's existing management team is included in the buying group, the management team's duty to the company's shareholders is likely to conflict with its self interest in cutting a good deal for the buyer. In this circumstance, company shareholders need to be sensitive to whether the pricing is fair and whether other sale opportunities have been actively pursued, particularly if the shareholders are taking promissory notes for any portion of the purchase price.

- o *ESOP Buyouts*. These are purchases of company stock by qualified retirement plans that have been designed to invest primarily in the securities of sponsoring company. ESOPs are defined benefit plans that receive annual contributions determined by the plan sponsor. Because these buyouts involve the use of specialized tax qualified plans, they must be carefully structured to comply with applicable tax laws.

- • *Public Securities Offerings*. Principally designed to generate investment cash to the company, initial public offerings also create a public market for company securities and frequently include the registration of a limited number of shares of investor stock. In practice, investment bankers limit the number of investor shares that may be included in the company's first offering and often require management and key investors to agree not to sell shares into the public market for a period of time, often six to twelve months. As a consequence, the act of going public is frequently not an efficient means for quickly liquidating shareholder investments.

- *Recapitalizations.* These are selective buyouts of investor stock undertaken to provide a liquidity event for one or more investors or to realign company ownership. In a "recap," the company uses accumulated cash, borrowed money or debt instruments to purchase some or all of the stock investment of identified investors. This creates an exit event only for the investors who sell their stock. When the company borrows to obtain the purchase price, the recapitalization is frequently referred to as a leveraged recap.

- *Direct Investor Sales.* After the restrictions on resale imposed by state and federal securities laws expire, investors are free to sell their shares directly to a willing buyer provided they have not entered into any contracts further restricting their freedom to sell.

- *Liquidity Agreements.* Sophisticated investors frequently require agreements that give them contractual opportunities to cash out in the future. These liquidity agreements include registration rights agreements that entitle investors to include shares in a company public offering or to require the company to register their shares for resale. Cosale agreements require management to include investor shares in sales they negotiate for themselves. Puts require the company, at the investors' direction, to repurchase shares at an agreed upon price. The use of convertible debt, such as convertible debentures, enables investors to choose to be repaid as debt on a fixed schedule instead of converting into equity. Buy-sell agreements enable investors to force the purchase of their shares at the risk of having to buy the shares of another party.

An understanding of these common exit strategies can help management prepare for the inevitable questions from investors. It can also help them understand and structure better terms for their financings. *See: Business Plan Format, Buy-Sell Agreements, Cashing Out (or In), Convertible Debentures, Co-Sale Agreements, Downside, ESOP Buyouts, Going Public, IPOs (Initial Public Offerings), Liquidity Agreements, Puts, Recaps, Restricted Securities.*

# F

**Factoring** is a form of receivables financing. The factor (or lender) pays the company a discounted portion of the company's receivables and then collects those receivables directly from customers as they become due.

Factoring differs in popularity by industry. It is perhaps most widely used in the garment industry, where orders are shipped well before the season when they are to be sold, but vendors do not pay for the merchandise until it is sold. A factor will buy the invoices from the manufacturer at a discount. The manufacturer receives the factor's money and shows the invoice as paid. The factor collects the full face value of the invoice and accepts some of the risk of doubtful accounts. *See: Collateral, Credit Lines, Inventory Financing, Receivables Financing, Secured Loans, Security Agreements, Term Loans.*

**Financing Agreements** are the final contracts that document the outcome of the negotiations between the entrepreneur and the investor and result in company funding. In a typical financing of debt and equity, the financing agreements might consist of a stock purchase agreement, a registration rights agreement, an investors rights agreement, a shareholders agreement, a loan agreement, a note or debenture, a charter amendment to create the security being sold and the stock certificates issued to the investor. Security interests in company assets are common in debt financings.

The financing agreements for an equity funding establish a snapshot of the company's business activities and establish ground rules for the parties' relationship going forward. The snapshot includes detailed disclosure of the company's historical financials, major contractual commitments, the status of the company's intellectual property portfolio, the capital structure of the company, and outstanding claims and litigation against the company. The ground rules take the form of agreements regarding representation on the board of directors, investor involvement in company planning, and investor rights to approve and veto certain major decisions. These agreements can also govern how proceeds from the financing are applied, who participates in future public offerings, what rights investors have to participate in future financings, and what restrictions are placed on management's future freedom to engage in competitive activity.

Preparation of the financing agreements for an equity investment typically begin during and parallel the investor's due diligence investigation into the company. In fact, the preparation and review of the extensive schedules most financing agreements contain forms an integral part of the due diligence process and serves to record the factual basis on which the investor relies in making it's investment decision. As a consequence, the stock purchase agreement alone might be thirty forty pages with many pages of exhibits detailing many pertinent facts about the company and its business.

The provisions of a stock purchase agreement also typically identify the amount of the investment and the conditions under which funds are released. They spell out the types of securities the investor receives and special shareholder rights granted to the investor. Financing agreements also contain provisions that govern the ongoing relationship of the investor and management. Many contain penalties if the company's results do not meet expectations.

Because of their breadth and the far-reaching effects their provisions can have on a company and its continued viability, financing agreements should be reviewed carefully with the assistance of qualified legal counsel. Each provision should be considered for its long-term impact as well as its short-term benefits.

For more information about documents commonly found in a venture capital financing see the *Deal* entry. For a more complete description of the documents used to complete a sale of stock in a venture capital funding see the *Venture Capital Deal Structures* entry. *See also: Affirmative Covenants, Boilerplate, Closing, Convertible Securities, Debentures, Due Diligence, Investment Reps, Investor Rights Agreements, Lawyers, Letters of Intent, Management Agreements, Promissory Notes, Negative Covenants, Negotiation, Operating Covenants, Registration Rights, Reps and Warranties, Shareholders Agreements, Structure, Venture Capital Deal Structures.*

**Finders** are intermediaries who assist entrepreneurs in finding investors but who are not licensed as registered broker-dealers. While federal securities laws do not require all money finders to be registered, finders are generally more limited in the services they may perform for a company and restricted in how they may charge for their services. In fact, the manner in which an agent charges for his services or the extent to which an agent is involved in negotiations may cause an agent to be classified under current rulings as a broker instead of a finder. If a finder is not a registered broker dealer, such a classification can create difficulties in finding an applicable state securities law exemption for a funding.

In practice, many finders ignore the limitations and actively participate in negotiations and charge in the same manner as brokers. All of the considerations applicable to engaging a broker, which are described in the *Brokers* entry, apply equally to engaging a finder. *See: Brokers, Finders Fees, Investment Bankers.*

**Finders Fees** are commissions companies pay to third party finders for locating investors. Fees can consist of retainers, hourly charges, and performance payments that are contingent on obtaining investment. *See: Brokers, Finders, Investment Bankers.*

**First Refusal Rights (Company)** are rights that give an investor the first opportunity but not the obligation to participate in future company financings. Inasmuch as they do not guarantee that the recipient will actually provide the funding, the granting of these rights is generally best avoided when possible. Not only do they fail to guarantee funding, they can make it more difficult to close a funding.

Contractual first refusal rights are usually structured in one of two ways. The first variation allows the company to negotiate with others for needed capital, but only if it gives the first investor a right of first refusal to provide the desired financing on the same terms management negotiates with its other investor. Under this variation, management can discuss but cannot close a funding with another investor until the first investor declines to take the deal.

The other type of first refusal right requires the company to present the first investor with the opportunity to invest on terms suggested by the company. If the first investor does not make the investment, the company is then free to negotiate with others to provide the funding on terms no more favorable to the new investor than those presented to the first investor. This right is sometimes referred to as a right of first negotiation.

Both variations complicate a company's fund raising efforts. The first form can make it very difficult to attract a serious outside investor. This is because savvy investors are reluctant to negotiate with managements when they know the deal they make can be taken away by another investor. In fact, many investors will not even talk with a company's management unless it has the ability to close the deal it is offering.

The second variation complicates a company's efforts to secure financing because it requires the company to construct an investment proposal for the first investor before it has had an opportunity to shop around to see what the best available deal is. It requires the company to begin looking for money earlier because of the time it takes the first investor to evaluate the investment proposal. If the first investor declines to make the requested investment, the company is still restricted in the terms it can offer to secure the money it needs.

Managements prefer to avoid rights of first refusal when possible asking, instead, that investors be comforted with company exhortations of loyalty and the reality that money is hard to find. If the right of first refusal is insisted upon, the second form of right of first refusal is generally preferable. Under that scenario, once the company has presented its investment proposal to the first investor, it is free to go and negotiate with others. Unlike the first variation, the company will be able to tell those other investors that it can close the deal it is negotiating.

It is usually wise for management to consult with existing venture investors before conducting a fundraising effort. As a practical matter, their consent will likely be required to create the security needed to close the funding and company efforts will be enhanced if they enter the fundraising process with a commitment from their existing investors to provide part of the new round of funding, especially if their commitment is to provide funding on the terms negotiated by the new investor. *See: Antidilution Provisions, First Refusal Rights (Shareholder), Options, Preemptive Rights, Warrants.*

**First Refusal Rights (Shareholder)** refers to a common feature in venture capital financings that give the investor the first option to purchase management's stock when management desires to sell. These first refusal rights protect investors by making it more difficult for management to sell its stock and by making it possible for them to prevent an unwanted new investor from purchasing management's shares.

Often used with co-sale provisions, these first refusal rights usually are structured to permit both the investor and the company to buy the shares. If the shares are for sale at an attractive price, the investor and remaining management may direct the company to purchase the shares. Doing so increases the ownership percentage of existing shareholders by reducing the total number of outstanding shares. The shares so purchased go into the company's treasury, making them available to use to attract a qualified person to replace the selling manager.

Infrequently, management can negotiate for first refusal rights from an investor in exchange for the first refusal rights given by management. When these rights are received, they are usually exercisable by both company and management. First refusal rights should terminate with a public offering or sale of the company. *See: Buy-Sell Agreements, Co-Sale Agreements, First Refusal Rights (Company).*

## *Venture Capital Bets On Management*

*Stanley Pratt, noted venture capital authority, once identified the five principal factors venture capitalists look for in a company as management, management, management, market niche, and product or service.*

*Other venture capitalists point out that the potential for large long-term profits is also critical. And having the right product at the right time is an important intangible. A product that is too revolutionary may be too far ahead of the market to succeed while one that is not revolutionary enough faces an uphill battle to distinguish itself.*

*Nonetheless, surveys show that management capabilities are critical. Most experienced investors have seen plenty of good, even spectacular, ideas fail. At the same time, most have watched companies succeed in ways they did not anticipate when funding was solicited. The quality and resourcefulness of management is what makes the difference.*

*It should come as no surprise then that when surveys are conducted to ascertain what qualities venture capital investors value most when evaluating an investment proposal that management related qualities always factor prominently into the list. Consider, for example, the following 'top ten' criteria considered most essential in one survey of 100 venture capital fund managers.*

1. *Management's ability to sustain intense effort.*
2. *Management's extensive knowledge of its market.*
3. *Significant potential for high return, at least ten times return in five to ten years.*
4. *Management's demonstrated leadership.*
5. *Management's ability to assess and react appropriately to risk.*
6. *The ability to liquidate the investment.*
7. *The likelihood of significant market growth.*
8. *Management's past success in growing companies.*
9. *Management's ability to articulate its value proposition well.*
10. *Quality of protection for the company's intellectual property.*

*See: Business Plan, Entrepreneur, Management Team, Value Added, Windows.*

**Flip** refers to the practice of selling a company or an investment made in a company soon after the purchase to make a quick gain. Flips are most often seen in leveraged buyouts or other whole company acquisitions where circumstances permit a bargain purchase. When this is so, the opportunity sometimes arises for the purchaser to resell or "flip" the company in a short period of time to another buyer at a higher price.

**Follow-On Fundings** refer to investments that occur after an investor's initial investment in a company. In contrast to stage financings, which are made over time in agreed-upon amounts as a company meets specified milestones, follow-on fundings do not result from preexisting agreements by an investor to provide funding at a later time. Rather, they refer to an investor voluntarily participating in a later round of funding, the terms and conditions of which are negotiated at the time of investment.

Follow-on fundings often include new investors. Sometimes follow-on fundings are provided entirely by a company's existing investors. An investor's ability to participate in later rounds of funding can be important to a company's success in raising funds.

Often, new venture capital investors expect existing venture capital investors to participate as evidence of the existing (insider) investor's confidence in the company. A venture investor's unwillingness to participate in a later round of financing can dampen the enthusiasm of outside investors which, in turn, can result in lower valuations or the inability to raise funds on reasonable terms. Consequently, an investor's financial ability to participate in later rounds of funding should be considered an important factor when investigating possible investors for a company. This is particularly true with institutional investors, such as venture capital funds, who invest in companies after the seed capital stage. See: *Due Diligence, Negotiation, Preemptive Rights, Stage Financings*.

**Forbearance Agreements** refer to contracts entered into between a lender and a borrower under which the lender agrees to forbear from demanding immediate payment and foreclosing on the borrower's property in exchange for the borrower's promise to take certain specified actions. Those actions typically include amending the terms of the loan to increase its short-term cost, agreeing not to borrow further against the loan, and agreeing to a payoff schedule. See: *Benchmarks, Cure Periods, Default.*

**Forecasts.** *See: Projections.*

**Franchising** refers to a form of licensing that businesses use to expand and generate revenue. It is generally characterized by the license from a franchisor to a franchisee of a trademark and system of doing business. In return for the license, the franchisee pays the franchisor an up-front fee, which is often substantial, and agrees to pay the franchisor a percentage of sales or some other royalty in the future.

For the right kind of business, franchising can reduce the need for outside capital by enabling the franchisor to obtain capital from its franchisees. In most franchising arrangements, the cost of expanding to a new unit is borne by the franchisee. The franchisor advises the franchisee in the best methods of establishing his unit of the business and charges him a fee to cover the cost of providing that advice and to make a profit. After the business begins operating, the franchisee pays the franchisor a percentage of sales or other agreed-upon royalty.

Franchising does not usually replace the need for outside equity. Capital is almost always needed to develop the franchise system and protect the trademark. Typically, franchising is pursued only after the company has owned and operated successful units of its business itself. This operation takes time and usually requires considerable capital to fund. Traditional venture capital and other equity sources are receptive to funding businesses that plan to grow through franchising.

Establishing a franchise program requires the preparation of an extensive franchise disclosure document, which provides information about the franchisor and the franchise program. Careful compliance with both federal and state franchise and business opportunity laws is a must. Failure to comply with all of the requirements can result in significant liability to a company and its managers. *See: Licensing, Trademarks.*

**Fully Diluted** is a phrase with multiple meanings that is frequently used by private company investors to express the method thay are using to compute company valuation. The term often first appears in an investor's term sheet in defining the value the investor places on the company for investment purposes. For example, and investor might provide that it will purchase $5 million worth of company stock at a post-money valuation of $25 million on a "fully diluted" basis. Often, the term is not more fully defined until the actual financing agreements are drafted.

Fully diluted refers to the number of shares a company will be considered as having issued for the limited purpose of determining how many shares of stock an investor will acquire. In the preceding example, if the company has 4 million shares on a fully diluted basis, the investor's $5 million dollars would purchase enough shares so that after the investment the investor owned 5/25ths of the company's stock. In this case, the investor would acquire 1 million shares, enough to equal 5/25ths or 20% of the company's 5 million shares of stock outstanding after investment. If, instead, the phrase "fully diluted" is defined to include not just outstanding shares but also another 1.0 million shares subject to options, say 6.25 million shares instead of 5 million shares, the investor would acquire 1.25 million shares so that his 1.25 million shares would represent 1.25 million of 6.25 million shares or 5/25ths of the company's shares after the investment.

As illustrated above, the manner in which "fully diluted" is defined directly effects how many shares a company must sell to raise capital. Elements included in a definition of fully diluted, in order of descending frequency of appearance, are:

- *First,* shares of capital stock that have been issued to and are still held by the company's shareholders;
- *Second,* shares of stock that have not yet been issued but that can be purchased under outstanding options or warrants that have been issued by the company;
- *Third,* shares of stock that have not yet been issued but can be acquired upon conversion of existing rights to convert debt or other rights, as in shares a lender can acquire under a contract that lets it convert some or all of its debt into stock;
- *Fourth,* shares of stock that have not yet been issued but have been reserved (and are therefore available) for issuance to company employees under a company stock plan but that have not been issued or committed to employees by the issuance of options, warrants or other stock plan grants;
- *Fifth,* shares of stock that have not yet been issued but are reserved (and are therefore available) for issuance to identified future business partners upon completion of anticipated business deals;
- *Sixth,* shares of stock that have not yet been issued but are expected to be needed to complete business deals in the future; plus,
- *Seventh,* any other shares that might be issued in the future.

Obviously, the more shares and prospective future shares an investor can throw into a definition of fully diluted, the more shares the investor will receive for an investment he proposed to make that is based of a fixed, fully diluted valuation of the company. Consequently, a company's management is wise to consider the meaning given to this term in an investor's offer before agreeing to the proposal.

Two ways to improve a proposed valuation are to increase the valuation amount given to the company and to reduce the scope of what fully diluted is defined to mean. *See: Fair Market Value, Financing Agreements, Letters of Intent, Offering Memorandums, P/E, Price-Earnings Ratio, Pricing, Term Sheets, Valuation.*

**Geography** refers to the impact location can have on fundraising. Companies that are conveniently located to potential investors are easier for investors to monitor and, therefore, more likely to get funded.

Venture capital funds and other sophisticated investors invest more than money in companies. They invest time and expertise as well. Oftentimes, an investor's experience and business contacts can be invaluable to a company.

As a consequence, investors operate most efficiently when the companies they invest in are located relatively close to their headquarters. For many professionally managed funds, companies located near a major city where the investor can make a visitation in a single day get preference over companies that are more remotely located.Several venture capital investors we know invest only in cities they can travel to and back in one day.

When selecting investors to approach, geography suggests that a company should stay as close to home as possible. When approaching a fund located a long distance away, management should be sensitive to the fact that the investor may want to make a joint investment with a local fund or one that has a portfolio of investments near the company's headquarters. *See: Networking, Syndications, Value Added. See also: Shopping, Specialty Funds.*

**Going Private** refers to a process through which a publicly traded company changes its ownership in such a manner that the company is no longer traded as a public company and no longer subject to the many reporting and governance requirements imposed upon public companies.

Why would a public company consider going private? Here are a few of the reasons most frequently cited:

- *Cost.* Being public is expensive. The extensive reporting requirements and securities filing obligations for public companies require significant management commitment and substantial fees to attorneys, accountants and other professionals. Since the enactment of Sarbanes-Oxley with its increased business governance and accountability standards, estimates of the cost of compliance with securities laws for public companies range from $500,000 to more than $1 million per year. Directors and officers insurance is also more expensive for public companies than for private companies.

- *Focus.* Annual and quarterly reporting requirements imposed on public companies by the SEC create pressure on managements to improve performance each quarter. Removing this pressure can lead to better, longer term decision making that benefits the company.

- *Stability.* Privately held companies are less exposed to hostile takeovers. The absence of a public market for their shares can make it more difficult for a hostile acquiring group to succeed without agreement of company management.

- *Privacy.* Without the public reporting requirements, competitors will know less about the company's business and management will receive less scrutiny of its actions.

- *Litigation.* The accountability standards imposed by Sarbanes-Oxley put the CEO and CFO at risk if erroneous financial statements are disclosed. Being private reduces the likelihood of shareholders suits against management and the board of directors.

Companies go private whenever they can reduce the number of their shareholders to fewer than 300 and relieve themselves of the obligations to file reports with the SEC. The rules of the SEC require public companies to provide shareholders with extensive information about any transaction that causes them to go private. The SEC's disclosure requirements and the potential for conflicts of interests make going private transactions complex and cause most companies to establish special independent committees of their boards of directors to review the fairness of the proposed transaction. These committees routinely engage independent financial advisors to assist them in their review.

Factors that might lead a company to consider going private include an under performing stock price, low trading volume, low market capitalization and lack of coverage by stock analysts. When these attributes are combined with a strong balance sheet, substantial assets, good growth potential and healthy cash flow, a company has the qualities to attract financing and support paybacks that may permit it to reasonably consider going private. When stock prices are low, volume is low and coverage is absent, management may reasonably conclude that their company would be better off and able to compete more effectively in the marketplace if it were relieved of the burdens and costs of being public.

Privatization frequently occurs at the urging of management, a majority owner or a private equity group and typically takes one of three forms – a merger, a tender offer or a reverse stock split. In a merger, the company signs a merger agreement with another company and sends a descriptive proxy statement to its shareholders soliciting votes to approve the merger. If the shareholders approve, the merger is consummated in a manner that converts the public company's shares into rights to receive cash or appraisal rights and leaves the company with fewer shareholders. The transaction is followed with a Form 15 filing with the SEC and delisting from its stock exchange.

Going private through a tender offer involves an acquiring party who buys shares directly from the public company's shareholders. The purchaser sends a written tender offer to the public company's shareholders offering to buy all of the shares of the public company on condition that enough shareholders tender their shares for purchase that the purchaser will own at least 90% of each class of the company's shares after the tender. Upon acquiring 90% of the outstanding stock, the purchaser is able to complete the acquisition of the shares still held by other shareholders by filing a short-form merger converting the outstanding shares into the right to receive the same per share amount of cash offered in the tender offer or, alternatively, appraisal rights. Upon completion, the purchaser files a Form 15 and delists the company from its stock exchange.

In a reverse stock split privatization, the least frequently employed method, the company cashes out shareholders by reducing the number of company shares. By declaring a reverse stock split and cashing out fractional shares, the company effectively reduces the number of shareholders by buying out the smaller holders. For example, in a 10,000-to-1 split, shareholders who own more that 10,000 shares would receive 1 share for each 10,000 shares held and would be cashed out for any group of less than 10,000 shares they held based on a formula based on current market value. Shareholders who held fewer than 10,000 shares would also receive cash. If the split reduces the number of shareholders below 300, the company can take the remaining steps needed to go private.

Whatever the form, going private transactions create potentials for conflict that are not present in arms-length transactions with third parties. These conflicts create risks for directors and managers that lead prudent managers to consult closely with qualified legal counsel throughout the process. The potential for lawsuits from dissatisfied shareholders is real in going private transactions. To mitigate this risk and assure fairness throughout the process, boards routinely appoint special independent committees and engage professional investment bankers to oversee the process. Independent financial advisors are also common in going private transactions. Their role is to provide objective validation of the process and valuation used to price share purchases. *See: Going Public, Sarbanes-Oxley. See also: Revolution in Public Company Governance.*

**Going Public** refers to the process of a company conducting an initial public offering of its securities to the general population of equity investors. The securities typically offered are the company's shares of common stock. Going public is accomplished by registering company securities with the federal Securities and Exchange Commission and state securities commissions through the preparation and filing of a detailed offering circular called a prospectus. After review and approval by the Securities and Exchange Commission, the prospectus is then distributed, typically by one or more underwriters, to potential purchasers and the company's stock is sold to the public.

Going public is a goal of many companies. It enables them to raise money from the public, creates a market for subsequent sales of their stock and raises their public profile. It also creates an easily ascertainable market value for shares.

Many entrepreneurs consider going public a business rite of passage that legitimizes their efforts and confirms their success. Many plan long and hard for the opportunity to run a public company. Most who take their companies public, believe that the offering proceeds generated by their offering and other benefits of being a public company are worth the effort and expense required to complete a public offering.

But going public is not the right decision for every company and does not guarantee future success. It is expensive and adds recurring duties on company management that are costly and time consuming. Seeking funds from private investors or from traditional lending sources may make more sense. At times, going public may be impossible because of market conditions unrelated to a company's strength.

Determining whether going public makes sense requires consideration of a number of factors including timing, company history, future prospects for growth, and management's personality. The advantages and disadvantages of going public should be weighed carefully before a decision is made to seek funds in the public markets. The advantages of going public include:

- Lower cost of capital
- Capital for continued growth
- Increased shareholder liquidity
- Access to public capital markets
- Public tender for acquisitions
- Public markets for employee securities
- Enhanced company image

The disadvantages of going public include:

- Expense
- Increased governance requirements
- Loss of confidentiality
- Periodic reporting
- Reduced control
- Shareholder pressure
- Restrictions on stock sales

**Advantages of Going Public.** The advantages of lower cost, increased capital for growth, shareholder liquidity, access to public capital markets, public tender for acquisitions, public markets for employee securities, and enhanced company image convince many that going public is right for them.

*Lower cost of capital.* The cost of capital in the public market is often cheaper than in the private market. Particularly when stock is involved, a public company's ability to sell securities that are freely tradable in a public market enhances their value. This makes it possible for the company to raise money at lower cost by selling shares at higher prices. When this is true, a public company can raise money with less dilution to existing shareholders, including management.

Going public becomes cost effective for most companies when their business profile becomes attractive to institutional investors and their size is sufficient to accommodate the added expense and administrative burden imposed by the disclosure and corporate governance rules imposed on public companies. While institutional investors are attracted to companies for a variety of reasons, in general, they prefer companies whose profiles include industry leadership, sustained growth and profitability over a significant period of time, a significant company valuation, and prospects for continued growth at a rate greater than the industry average. When a company matures to the point of meeting this profile, its ability to attract institutional investors often boosts the price of its stock high enough to make going public the most economical way to raise capital.

*Capital for continued growth.* Public offerings raise significant amounts of cash for their companies. These funds can be used for working capital, acquiring new divisions or technologies, increasing marketing or sales efforts, paying for research or plant modernization, or repaying debt. Because of the amount of cash raised, most public offerings also dramatically improve the company's net worth and debt-to-equity ratio. This, in turn, makes it easier for the company to borrow money from commercial lenders at competitive interest rates.

*Increased shareholder liquidity.* Going public makes it easier for company shareholders to liquidate their shareholdings by creating a public market for company shares. Shareholders who register their shares in the company's offering hold freely tradable shares once the offering is completed. Even company shares that are not registered in the offering become more liquid. Because of information reporting requirements imposed on public companies, holders of unregistered shares often qualify to sell limited numbers of their shares under Rule 144 after a prescribed period of time. If they want to sell more shares than Rule 144 permits, they can also benefit from easier and less expensive methods available for registering their shares that are available to companies that have already gone public.

*Access to public capital markets.* The existence of a public market for the company's stock makes it easier for the company to sell additional equity. If the company's stock does well (that is, increases in price), the company can use the public markets to raise money by selling stock or debt securities.

*Public tender for acquisitions.* The market for company securities created by going public can make it easier for a company to expand through acquisitions and mergers. Because registered shares are easier to convert into cash, a public company can often use stock instead of cash to acquire another business. With the proper deal structure, the use of shares can ease the immediate tax burden of the owner of the selling business thereby , making the acquisition more attractive to the seller .

*Public markets for employee securities.* Liquid stock also makes a company's stock and option plans more attractive to its employees. This can make it easier to attract and retain the key employees.

*Enhanced company image.* Going public, with all the financial disclosure and investor relations planning it requires, usually attracts the attention of the business and financial press. Free publicity, coupled with the perception that going public is a significant milestone of success, can enhance a company's image.

An improved image can make it easier for management to deal with suppliers and customers. Sometimes, privately held companies that compete with public ones find their customers and suppliers reluctant to deal with them on equal terms because of the confidentiality of their financial data. Going public can erase this distinction and make it possible for the company to compete more effectively.

**Disadvantages of Going Public.** The advantages of going public can be substantial, but they can be outweighed by the disadvantages. Particularly since the enactment of Sarbanes-Oxley and its enhanced governance and disclosure accountability standards, the cost and complexity of operating a public company have dramatically increased.

Operating a public company with these new standards is an expensive and time consuming endeavor, one that not every profitable company can sustain. Whether going public makes sense, depends on management's goals and the circumstances of the company. The disadvantages of going public include expense, increased governance requirements, loss of confidentiality, periodic reporting, reduced control, shareholder pressure, and restrictions on stock sales.

*Expense.* Going public is expensive. The underwriter's discounts alone can amount to as much as 6 to 10 percent of the total proceeds of the offering. Other expenses such as the underwriter's out-of-pocket expenses, filing fees, transfer agent fee, legal fees, printing fees, and accounting fees can add another $500,000 or more to a company's cost of going public. Going public is time consuming too, routinely requiring senior management to invest considerable time and effort to complete the process.

Going public also subjects a company to annual and quarterly financial reporting requirements imposed by the Securities and Exchange Commission. It also requires the company to comply with detailed, time-consuming, and expensive rules regarding corporate governance and accountability. Complying with these requirements increases the company's costs of doing business and exposes company officers and directors to liability for failure to comply.

*Increased governance requirements.* Public companies have significant additional duties imposed upon the way they report operations and manage their companies that do not apply to private companies. These duties, which are imposed by the SEC and the rules of the stock exchanges where company shares are listed, include requirements for company boards to have minimum numbers of directors who meet specified independence and accounting expertise requirements. They also specify certain minimum committees each board must have, how often they meet, who qualifies for each committee, and responsibilities of the committees. These and other governance requirements take time and money to implement and create additional oversight of management activities. They also increase officer and director exposure to potential liability.

*Loss of confidentiality.* Going public forces companies to prepare, register and distribute a complete description of the company, its history, its strengths, its weaknesses, and its future plans. Detailed disclosures of financial information are required. Information about the shareholdings and compensation arrangements of management and holders of large blocks is made public. All of this information must be updated and supplemented periodically and as material events occur in reports required by the Securities and Exchange Commission. Once information is filed, it becomes readily available to competitors, employees, customers, suppliers, union organizers and others.

*Periodic reporting.* Going public subjects a company to a number of periodic reporting requirements with the Securities and Exchange Commission. These requirements include annual and quarterly financial reports (on forms 10-K and 10-Q) as well as prompt reporting of material events that affect the company (on form 8-K). The also require officer certification of financial statements.

For most companies, these and other requirements, which force the company to maintain audited financial statements, increase the company's cost and complexity of doing business by imposing more stringent accounting practices and by making additional demands on management's time. Quarterly financial reporting also tends to focus management on 'management by quarter' and can lead to management decisions that favor short-term results over long term planning.

*Reduced control.* Public offerings reduce management's control. This flows in part from the addition of independent directors to the board. If outsiders obtain enough stock to elect a majority of the company's board of directors, managements control is further reduced. Public companies are also more susceptible to unfriendly takeovers because their shares are easy to accumulate.

The risk of reduced control through sales of stock is not a risk limited to public companies, however. Any sale of voting stock to raise money reduces the percentage ownership of management. In fact, sales of a majority of the company's voting stock to a few private investors may make management's ability to retain control less certain than sales in a public offering, which distributes those same shares to a greater number of investors. The larger number of shareholders in a publicly held company can make concerted action by the outsiders more difficult.

*Shareholder pressures.* Even managements that retain voting control over their companies find that going public subjects them to pressures that can affect the way they run their businesses. Shareholder expectations and the quarterly reporting requirements of the Securities and Exchange Commission combine to create significant pressures on companies to continually improve performance on a quarter-by quarter basis. Failure to meet these shareholder expectations can cause a company's stock price to decline, often dramatically, when it fails to meet expectations. When this happens, it becomes more expensive to raise money or acquire other companies using stock. This pressure to meet short-term goals can tempt management to forgo necessary long-term planning when it includes present-day sacrifices that will be reflected in the company's quarterly reports.

Shareholder lawsuits against directors and management are also real factors in public company life. Specialized law firms across the country purchase small shareholdings in public companies for the sole purpose of qualifying as shareholders eligible to sue the companies if stock share prices fall dramatically. When that happens, these firms frequently advertise for clients willing to sue the company in order to generate a class action lawsuit against the company. These suits generate large fees for the law firms and are costly and time consuming for companies to defend.

*Restrictions on stock sales.* Only those shares registered and sold in the offering become freely tradable. Unregistered shares remain subject to the same trading restrictions as they were before the offering. Moreover, the Securities and Exchange Commission imposes restrictions on the ability of major shareholders and company insiders to sell company stock. These restrictions include limitations on the numbers of shares that may be traded and limitations on the ability to trade at all when there is material information known to the company insiders that has not been publicly disclosed.

All of these factors, good and bad, should be considered when contemplating a first public offering. Anyone contemplating an initial public offering should consult with their accountants, attorneys, investment bankers, and other advisers well in advance of taking their companies public. *See: Control, Investment Bankers, IPOs (Initial Public Offerings), Penny Stock, Private Placements, Public Offering, Restricted Securities, Unit Offerings.*

## *The Going Public Process*

*Here is a brief summary of the events involved in taking a company public:*

*Organizational Preparation. Before jumping into a full scale going public effort, management needs to review the company's organizational structure and make changes that anticipate the requirements imposed on public companies. Internal reporting systems need to be reviewed and possibly enhanced. The board frequently needs to be reconfigured to anticipate independence requirements and committee structures imposed by current securities laws and listing requirements of stock exchanges.*

*Selection of Underwriters. Once a decision to go public has been made, company management interviews several underwriters to evaluate their company and discuss the possibility of representing the company in the offering. Interested underwriters meet with company management and investigate the company's business and prospects for conducting a successful offering. Those who remain interested after their investigations, submit proposals to management and the going public process begins. Most underwriters will provide a preliminary estimation of the potential range of price and size of offering for the company. The size of offering and the price at which shares are offered are usually not finally determined until later in the process, so additional pricing discussions will follow.*

*Offering Document Preparation. Applicable securities laws require a detailed registration statement to be prepared, filed and approved by the Securities Exchange Commission before company securities are offered for sale. The preparation of this document requires an intense and coordinated effort by management, the company's lead underwriters, company and underwriter legal counsel, the company's accountants and a company selected financial printer. The completed registration statement must provide accurate disclosure of material information about the company that will enable potential investors to make informed decisions about whether to purchase company securities. The Securities Exchange Commission's role in the process is to review the submitted registration statement of the company to see whether the company has complied with federal securities laws and provided adequate information about the company. The Securities Exchange Commission does not evaluate the merit of the company's offering.*

*The preparation of the registration statement is typically the most time-consuming step in the going public process. Preparation typically begins with an "all-hands" meeting of company management, underwriter and underwriter counsel representatives, company counsel and accountants. A drafting schedule is agreed and responsibilities assigned to get the process rolling. Typically, company counsel, in cooperation with company management, undertake to prepare a first draft offering statement which other team members will review and revise. Several "all-hands" meetings follow where schedules are refined and the offering document is reviewed in the group and revisions are made.*

*Registration Statement Filing. The completed preliminary registration statement is then filed with the Securities Exchange Commission. This registration statement contains a booklet (called the preliminary prospectus) that describes the company and it's offering. This prospectus is used as a selling document. During the waiting period between the filing and approval of the registration statement by the Securities Exchange Commission, the company and the underwriters may distribute copies of the preliminary prospectus that bear "red herring" legends. This legend* declares that the offering's registration has not yet become effective and that the securities may not be sold, nor may offers to buy be accepted, until the offering becomes effective.

*Sales Efforts.* Most underwriters begin marketing the company's securities once the "red herring" prospectus becomes available. Once the registration statement is filed, the managing underwriters usually distribute the "red herrings" to clients and orally solicit indications of interest in the securities. A tour, or "road show," of company managers coordinates with this effort by making management presentations to underwriters, analysts and investors around the country.

*Registration Approval.* While this marketing effort is taking place, the Securities Exchange Commission reviews the company's registration statement and responds, typically within 30 to 40 days, with comments and requests for additional information.

*Final Negotiations and Filing.* Concurrently with completion of the registration process, the company and the underwriters complete their negotiations and the number of shares and offering price are set. After the registration statement is modified to address the Securities Exchange Commission's concerns and to include the price and number of shares offered, the Commission declares the registration statement to be effective and the final prospectus is printed. The underwriters send this final prospectus to their customers along with the confirmation of sale.

*Closing.* The closing of the offering is held after the registration is effective and the sales are confirmed. The company's securities are delivered to the underwriters for distribution and the proceeds from the sale of stock are paid to the company. The closing usually occurs within five days after the registration statement becomes effective.

**Golden Handcuffs** refers to the combination of rewards and penalties given to key employees that compensate them so generously for remaining with the company and punishe them so severely for leaving that it would be absurd for them to quit the company. Golden handcuff arrangements are usually tailored to the employee's specific situation. Programs can include cash, options, and stock bonuses that increase in value over time and that vest only after the employee has remained with the company over a specified period of time or until a specified objective has been accomplished.

There are two ways to encourage valuable people to remain with a company. One is to reward them if they stay. The other is to penalize them if they leave.

Golden handcuffs combine both approaches by mixing generous economic incentives with non-compete agreements and vesting schedules. If the combination of these incentives and disincentives is effective, they can provide powerful motivation for an employee to stay. They do so by raising employee expectations of wealth so high that cannot be readily be met if he leaves.

Golden handcuff arrangements are best structured with the assistance of qualified lawyers and accountants. Care must be taken to understand the tax consequences of the proposed structure to the company and the employee to avoid unwanted consequences. Especially, when the incentives are tied to an anticipated sale of the company, adverse tax consequences of incentives that are not carefully structured can dramatically diminish their value to the employee and their value as an incentive. *See: Compensation and Bonus Plans, Employment Contracts, Golden Parachuttes, ISOs (Incentive Stock Options), Noncompete Agreements, Phantom Stock Plans, Vesting Agreements.*

**Golden Parachutes** refer to contractual benefits granted to key executives that entitle the executives to receive lucrative benefits in the event their company is sold or merged with another company in a transaction that results in the company managers losing operational control. Company boards grant golden parachutes as parts of poison pill plans to discourage hostile takeovers, to attract qualified senior managers to companies when a sale is likely, and to provide incentives to executives who are affirmatively charged to seek out sale opportunities for the company. When a company sale is possible, golden parachutes are believed to benefit the company by securing the continuing services of its senior executives through the sale process and during the transition to new ownership. By delaying the executive's search for new employment until after the company is sold and transitioned to the new owners, the golden parachute makes it easier to attract buyers and complete a favorable sale.

Golden parachutes are usually contained in an executive's employment agreement or an amendment to that agreement. The benefits can take the form of severance pay, cash bonuses, stock options or share grants, and the continuation of executive privileges such as life or health insurance coverage. To secure the intended benefit to the company, golden parachutes are typically structured to require the executive to stay with the company after the closing of its sale for a period of time, up to one year, before the golden parachute benefits can be received. To protect the executive, these agreements also typically accelerate the ability to receive the benefits if the acquirer declines to employ the executive or adds conditions to the executive's continued employment that significantly change the nature of the executive's position or would otherwise amount to constructive termination.

Internal revenue service rules penalize executives and companies that pay too much in golden parachute payments through the imposition of a sizable excise tax and loss of deductibility of payments. As a consequence, most golden parachute agreements are carefully tailored to provide that the total value of the benefit, in all its forms, may not exceed the amount at which the excise tax would begin to apply. This amount is roughly three times the executive's base pay but the calculations of what constitutes base pay and the determination of what benefits are included in such pay make the calculations sufficiently complicated that golden parachute agreements should never be entered into without the advice of qualified legal and accounting counsel. *See: Employment Contracts, Exits, Golden Handcuffs, Liquidity Agreements, Liquidity Events, Noncompete Agreements.*

**Golden Rule** refers to an axiom of business finance that applies most rigorously to companies whose circumstances or lack of planning put them in the capital marketplace without enough time to shop alternative funding sources. The rule - he who has the gold makes the rules – refers to the funding source's ability to dictate terms unfavorable to the company as a condition to providing financing. *See: Deal, Deal Flow, Leverage, Negotiation, Structure.*

**High Tech** refers to companies and industries that offer products or services that are dependent on the application of technology innovations and that rely on this technology innovation as a market differentiator for their company. Many people equate venture capital with high tech investing. The reality is, however, that venture capital investors are more interested in return on investment than they are in sophisticated technology. Many do invest in high tech companies, but only when those companies are also emerging growth companies that promise rapid growth and a healthy return to the investor. *See: Emerging Growth Companies.*

# I

**Incubators** refer to centers that help entrepreneurs start and grow businesses. They are called incubators because they help entrepreneurs hatch ideas into businesses. Sometimes they are also referred to as accelerators or business development centers.

There are privately run incubators and incubators that are associated with universities, government agencies, and regional development authorities. Many specialize to take advantage of a founder's or university sponsor's expertise and work only with entrepreneurs seeking to build a company in a given industry, such as information technology, biotechnology, nanotechnology, or the logistics. Others are less specialized and accept companies from a broad spectrum of industries. Others are affiliated with networks of angel investors or a venture capital fund.

The services incubators typically provide include inexpensive facilities, short term rental arrangements, free or reduced-cost consulting services from accountants, lawyers, or business consultants, assistance in obtaining government grants and identifying sources of capital, and assistance in marketing and public relations. Some incubators provide access to specialized facilities and equipment that would be prohibitively expensive for a start-up company to acquire. Others offer access to specialized expertise from sponsors or access to investors. Entrepreneurs can identify incubators in their locale by contacting their local chamber of commerce, reading local business publications, or by inquiring of their accountant, banker, or lawyer.

Entrepreneurs should take care to evaluate a center before joining one. The number, quality, and costs of services provided vary from center to center. It is appropriate, when considering an incubator, to meet with and question the center's director about the services available and the qualifications of the persons providing them. It is also helpful to speak with entrepreneurs who are working with the incubator and those who have left it.

Incubators can provide valuable services, but beware of "incubator syndrome." The services incubators provide can sometimes sound so good and complete that they lull unprepared businessmen into making the entrepreneurial jump too soon or into relying too much on the center. Joining an incubator is no substitute for entrepreneurial initiative, training, or self-evaluation. Entrepreneurs must remember when joining a center that their personal efforts and resourcefulness are the key to making their business succeed. An entrepreneur with incubator syndrome permits his initiative and judgment to be replaced by those of the consultants who provide assistance at the center. Even if those consultants are superbly skilled and dedicated, they cannot replace the entrepreneur or make his business succeed. *See: Commitment, Entrepreneur, Technology Development Centers.*

**Industry Funds** refer to venture capital funds that limit or focus the majority of their attention on companies in a given industry. *See: Specialty Funds.*

**Integration** refers to when two or more securities offerings are combined into one offering under the rules of the federal Securities and Exchange Commission. When it occurs, it can cause serious problems for an issuing company and its management.

Federal securities rules treat offerings that are integrated under their rules as if they were one offering and require that all of the securities sold in both offerings be registered or qualified under a single registration exemption. If different exemptions were used to clear the two offerings and the sales of securities in the integrated offerings cannot be fit into one registration exemption, all of the sales lose their registration exemption and both the company and management become subject to liability.I Integrations of previous offerings with a company's present efforts to raise capital can also delay the ability to raise money without a public offering. Because of this, it is important to determine what constitutes an offering whenever securities are sold.

Factors the federal Securities and Exchange Commission considers when determining whether two or more offerings will be integrated into one include:

- Whether they are part of a single plan of financing.
- Whether they involve the issuance of the same class of security.
- Whether they are made at or about the same time.
- Whether the same type of consideration is received for the security.
- Whether the offerings are made for the same general purpose.

There are a number safe harbors registration exemptions that can be relied upon to avoid integration. When their requirements are met, they can prevent the liabilities and inconveniences caused  by an integration of offerings. Experienced legal counsel  can guide management safely through the complexities of the federal and state securities laws to avoid integration. *See: Private Placements, Reg D, Restricted Securities, Safe Harbors, SEC (Securities and Exchange Commission), 33 Act.*

**Inventory Financing** refers to loans that are collateralized by a company's product inventory. It is often contrasted with receivables financing or factoring, when the company's accounts receivables are used to collateralize its borrowing. *See: Commitment Letters, Credit Lines, Factoring, Loan Covenants, Receivables Financing, Security Agreements, Term Loans.*

**Investment Bankers** are financial institutions and individuals who assist companies and their managements with their capital needs. They are frequently involved in company efforts to raise capital, through private placements or public offerings. They are also commonly engaged to , sell business units, or purchase other businesses.

Investment bankers can help growing companies develop fundraising strategies, identify financing options, and obtain introductions to funding sources. Some companies look to investment bankers for assistance in building strategic plans or in revising their existing plans to make them more attractive to potential buyers. Others look to them for up-to-date advice on fundraising market conditions. Because investment bankers make a business of raising money for companies, they can help a company analyze its funding needs, identify the most likely or appropriate sources for raising money, and execute a fundraising strategy.

This is not to say, however, that any investment banker can always sell any company business plan to investors. The quality of a company's opportunity and the strength of its management team determine the breadth of options open for a given fundraising. Investment bankers also vary in their capabilities, resources, experience, and contacts. Investment bankers who are experienced with the company's industry and the type of financing it needs, can often help a company raise funds.

Some venture capitalists believe investment bankers are unnecessary, even disruptive, to a venture funding. For the most part, however, the venture capital industry recognizes the legitimate role investment bankers play. Most venture capital firms will not decline to review a company business plan because the company has engaged an investment banker. They typically expect, however, to deal directly with the company's management team through the due diligence process.

Many entrepreneurs prefer to raise funds without the assistance of an investment banker and look to investment bankers, instead, only when they prepare to take their companies public. Then, an investment banker's ability to underwrite (or sell) the company's stock can make its services indispensable. Choosing the best investment banker to lead the underwriting of a company's initial public offering is an important part of conducting any successful public offering.

Investment bankers charge for their services in a variety of ways. Most charge a success fee as part of their compensation, one that is typically computed as a percentage of funds raised. Engagement agreements with investment bankers can be complex and should be reviewed carefully before they are signed. Qualified legal counsel can help a company avoid unwanted obligations by reviewing the proposed agreement with company management.

The *Brokers* entry earlier in this book discusses a number of provisions common to investment banking agreements used for raising capital. The *Underwriters* entry focuses on an investment banker's role in taking a company public. *See: Brokers, Finders, Going Public, IPOs (Initial Public Offerings), Stage Financing, Underwriters.*

**Investment Memorandums** or investment memos are writings that commit an investor to acquire company securities and describe the terms of the purchase. People often use the phrases letters of intent, commitment letters, and investment memorandums interchangeably to refer to short written understandings that precede formal financing documentation. *See: Commitment Letters, Letters of Intent, MOUs (Memorandums of Understanding), Term Sheet.*

## Investment Reps refer to representations made by

investors about the conditions under which they are purchasing company securities. Investment reps customarily appear in financing agreements or in separate subscription agreements.

Investment reps help complete a funding quickly and cheaply. They do so by giving management the information it needs to qualify the security sale under an exemption from the time-consuming and expensive registration requirements of the federal and state securities laws. Investment reps should always be required in writing when restricted securities are sold outside a public offering. Used in connection with a proper exemption from registration under applicable securities laws, these representations help protect a company and management from serious securities liabilities. Some common investment reps acknowledge that the investor:

- Purchased the company's shares for investment only and not with a view of reselling them.
- Made such independent investigation of the company as he has deemed necessary or advisable.
- Has been given free access to company information.
- Is sufficiently sophisticated about investments to judge the merits of investing in the company or has hired someone who is so sophisticated.
- Meets certain minimum wealth standards.
- Will not sell the shares purchased without first complying with applicable securities laws in a manner acceptable to company counsel.

*See: Blue Sky Laws, Investors, Legend Stock, Private Placements, Reg D, Restricted Securities, 33 Act.*

**Investor Qualifications** refer to federal and state securities laws that restrict the number and type of investors to whom a company can sell its securities without conducting an expensive and time-consuming registered public offering. Unless the number and nature of the investors qualify the company for an exemption, the company's securities cannot be sold without a registration.

The exemptions most commonly used to qualify stock sold to a venture capital fund or angel investor is one that relies on the investor's status as an accredited investor under the securities acts. These "accredited investors" are persons or entities which are recognized by the statutes as having sufficient wealth, sophistication (or access to sophisticated advice), and access to company information to fend for themselves when examining and investing in a privately held company.

Often, sales to these investors can be made without having to prepare an elaborate private offering circular. By contrast, most of the exemptions that permit private companies to sell their securities to investors who do not qualify as accredited investors require the company to prepare an offering circular and to pay close attention to the number of investors solicited, the investors' states of residence, and various state "blue sky" limitations on the number of investors who may reside in each state.

Whoever the company's investors are, management should be careful to conduct its stock offering in a manner that complies with all the rules of an exemption from the registration requirements of the federal and state securities laws. Overlooking a single detail can create significant liability for the issuing company and its management.

Whenever an exemption requires a company's investors to qualify as accredited, management should investigate the credentials of the investors to determine whether they meet all of the requirements. The financing agreements should also contain representations from the investors that they are

*Investors, Deal Structures, Legal Strategies - 185*

accredited, that they have had adequate access to the company and its management, and that they are capable of bearing the loss should the investment fail.

Elsewhere in this book, we have discussed the value of dealing with good investors, and the negative consequences of dealing with poor ones. Being accredited does not mean an investor is good or ethical. It means simply that he has sufficient wealth and sophistication to fend for himself. Generally, he is someone who has enough other investments that losing his money on one deal will not break him. *See: Accredited Investors, Blue Sky Laws, Ethics, Investment Reps, Private Placements, Reg D, 33 Act.*

## Investor Rights Agreements are contracts that

spell out special rights investors obtain when purchasing stock in a company. They are common in venture capital financings. The typical investor rights agreement required in a venture capital financing will supplement the financing agreement by providing the investor with various additional contractual rights. Practices vary, however. Sometimes agreements such as those dealing with registration rights are placed in separate registration rights agreements and, sometimes, investor board and information rights appear as terms in a financing agreement. When a separate investor rights agreement is used, the following rights are frequently addressed in its provisions:

- Rights of first refusal or first negotiation to purchase shares of stock management desires to sell.
- Rights of co-sale to participate with a manager in a sale of the manager's stock.
- Rights to register purchased stock in future public offerings.
- Rights to receive regular reports about the company's financial condition.
- Rights to elect a representative or observer to the company's board of directors.

*See: Board of Directors, Control, Co-Sale Agreements, Demand Rights, First Refusal Rights (Company), First Refusal Rights (Shareholder), Piggyback Rights, Registration Rights, Registration Rights Agreements, Shareholders' Agreements, Tag-Along Provisions.*

## Founders' Dilemma – Dividing the Pie

*Two difficult decisions all new companies face during their formation are what form of entity to select for their business and how to divide the ownership of the company among the founders. Often, these decisions are made before outside investors are identified or before it is appropriate for all of the founding management members to join the business on a full-time basis. Frequently, the company's business plans are still evolving and the prospects for long-term success are uncertain.*

*The form of entity decision usually gets determined with the advice of legal counsel who can point out the advantages and disadvantages of the available business forms. The decision often narrows to whether the business will be better served by organizing as a tax pass-through entity or as a taxable entity.*

*For businesses that expect to lose money before they make money, the question typically becomes whether the company will improve its likelihood of raising needed early stage funding from investors if it structures itself so that the losses it generates will be passed through to the investors. If individual investors who would value a tax loss are the likely source of early financing, structuring the company as an S corporation or limited liability company may make sense. If the business is such that management believes it might later be able to sell its assets for more than its stock in a sale of the business, a tax flow through entity might also be appropriate. Otherwise, most management teams chose the C corporation form.*

Deciding how to allocate ownership is a more difficult task. Limitations on available funds and a desire to treat other founders fairly often leads to allocations between founders that do not fairly reward all members of the founding team. Many teams are tempted to divide ownership equally among the original founders. This urge often flows from the absence of a clear rationale for differentiating among team members so early in the process. But members of a founder team rarely make equal contributions to the company's eventual success. Consequently, equal division of founder's equity almost always over compensates one founder at the expense of another. And equal divisions of ownership can jeopardize later rounds of fundraising. The realization of this occurs most frequently after the founder ownership positions have been diluted by investments made by outside investors. If the ownership percentage owned by the key managers is too small because of their generosity to other management team members, new investors may hesitate to commit their funds out of fear that the key manager's ownership stake after the new investment will be too small to provide proper motivation.

For example, if prior fundraisings and management option plan grants reduce the collective ownership of the founder managers to 20%, each of five founders will hold 4% of the company's outstanding stock if their shares were divided equally. If one or two of those two founders are key to the success of the organization, a new investor might be reluctant to invest if his investment reduces the ownership of these two key players to 3%. He might feel better investing if the two key members retained 5% each after his investment, with the remaining 2% divided among the three less important management members. He may feel compelled to try to address what he perceives as an unacceptable business risk as a condition to his providing financing or he may just move onto his next opportunity to avoid the conflict and *anguish caused by trying to adjust the relative ownership percentages of the founders.*

*So what's a founder to do? First, avoid the impulse to divide things equally. Make a concerted effort to evaluate the relative market value of the contributions to be made by each founder. Engage an outside advisor or attorney experienced in working with venture-backed companies to help with this. Second, subject every founder's ownership to future vesting. This is something most venture capital investors will require in any event when you complete your first institutional venture capital funding. Use a four or three year vesting schedule so that if a founder leaves the fulltime employment of the company during that time, the company can take back the shares that have not vested. Third, consider requiring all of the founders to sign a shareholders agreement that includes an option that lets the company, or the other founders, buy the vested stock of a founder that quits. Finally, be prepared for surprises. The stresses of starting a growing company may burn out some of your early partners. Others may not have the skills you thought they had or the judgment needed to operate successfully on a shoestring.*

## IPOs (Initial Public Offerings) refer to the first registered offering of company securities to the general population of equity investors. They are registered with the Securities and Exchange Commission and with the securities commissions of the states in which the company's securities will be offered and sold.

An IPO requires the preparation of a detailed offering memorandum in a form prescribed by the SEC. According to the requirements, the offering memorandum must contain an extensive description of the company, its reasons for conducting an offering, the qualities of the securities being sold, an analysis of the risks inherent in investing in the company, and a description of how the company will utilize the proceeds of the offering. Disclosures regarding the stockholding and compensation arrangements of management and persons with significant stockholdings in the company are also required. Detailed audited financial statements must be provided.

In addition to the disclosure requirements, companies conducting an IPO must also update their internal corporate governance procedures to comply with the requirements of the SEC and the stock exchange where they will list their securities for sale. These requirements include the adoption of governance standards for the company, establishment of required committees on the board of directors, and, often, expanding the board to accommodate the addition of directors who will meet SEC and stock exchange rules regarding independence. Procedures for dealing with whistle blowers must be adopted and loans to managers and directors must be paid off. Often, charter amendments and minute book updates are needed to accommodate the company's plans as it goes public. Internal accounting procedures are frequently added to strengthen down-the-line accountability.

Conducting an initial public offering is a painstaking and time-consuming project that requires extensive due diligence by the company's counsel, accountants, and underwriters and a serious time commitment by management before, during, and after the offering. The offering process usually takes at least three to six months to complete. Typically, these months of preparation include an extensive review of company documents, the preparation of audited financial statements, the adoption of changes to the company's internal reporting methodologies, reconfiguration or expansion of the board of directors, numerous due diligence meetings between company personnel and company advisers, and several drafting sessions (often referred to as "all-hands meetings") for the offering memorandum. The preparation also includes filings and discussions with the Securities and Exchange Commission and with state securities commissions to secure proper registration for the offering, and a "road show" during which the underwriter and company officials take their offer "on the road" to sell the company's securities.

Although IPO schedules vary widely from company to company and are sometimes accelerated or expanded to respond to the perceptions of the company's underwriter as to the best time to sell the company's stock, a representative IPO schedule might look something like this:

## *IPO Schedule*

| | |
|---|---|
| Day 1 | Organizational all-hands meeting to set schedule and assign responsibilities. |
| Day 2 | Begin due diligence interviews and documents review. Distribute officers and directors questionnaires. Begin review of company reporting procedures and the configuration of the board of directors. Begin selection of transfer agent, printer and others. Begin preparation of offering circular by company counsel and required financial statements by the company's outside accountants. |
| Day 10 | Distribute first draft of offering circular. |
| Day 20 | First all hands drafting session to review and revise offering circular. Second draft is re-circulated ten days later. |
| Day 40 | Second all hands drafting session. |
| Day 50 | Final all hands drafting session to make any final revisions and sign offering circular. |
| Day 55 | File offering circular with the Securities and Exchange Commission. Issue press release. |
| Day 65 | Begin road show to sell securities. Proceed with state securities registrations. |
| Day 90 | Receive comment letter from Securities and Exchange Commission. Prepare response or amendment to offering circular, as appropriate. |

| Day 100 | Determine offering price. Complete state securities filings. File amendment to offering circular if necessary. |
| Day 115 | Effective date, offering commences. |
| Day 120 | Closing. Company issues securities. Offering proceeds transfer to the company. |

Of course, the schedule only outlines some of the major undertakings involved in an initial public offering. The process also involves directors' meetings, extensive due diligence meetings, elections of new directors, the formation of audit and compensation committees for the board, the adoption of new governance rules, and the negotiation and execution of contracts with underwriters and others. Often, the process includes the preparation and adoption of employee stock incentive plans or substantial corporate cleanup to get the company's books, records, and systems into proper order to become public. *See: Blue Sky Laws, Going Public, Penny Stock, Private Placements, Public Offering, SEC (Securities and Exchange Commission), 33 Act.*

## The Language of Going Public

*The going public process is complex and has its own language developed over time to describe different elements of the process. Here are a few of the terms used by insiders to describe the process.*

- *All hands meeting. Any one of a number of meetings where representatives of all the parties responsible for completing the company's public offering convene to organize or work on aspects of the offering. The typical parties include company senior management, the lead underwriters, counsel for the company and the underwriters, the company's outside accountants, and the printer. The first all hands meeting is also called the organizational meeting.*

- *Aftermarket. The trading activity in the company's securities after completion of its public offering.*
- *Best efforts underwriting. A public offering where the underwriter commits only to use its best efforts to complete the sale of the company's securities and does not commit to purchase any shares for its own account even if such a purchase would be necessary to complete the offering.*
- *Comfort letter. A letter provided to the underwriters by the company's outside accountants that confirms the accuracy of financial disclosures in the prospectus and provides limited 'negative assurances' that material financial changes have not occurred since the company's last audit.*
- *Firm commitment underwriting. A public offering where the underwriter commits to purchase the shares offered by the company, usually entered into after the underwriter has secured sufficient indication of interest in ordering the shares that the underwriter is at little risk of being unable to sell the shares.*
- *Green shoe. An option granted to the company's underwriter that allows the underwriter to purchase additional shares of the company's stock at the original offering price for a period of time after the offering. The name comes from the first company to grant this option to an underwriter. The purpose is to provide the underwriter shares to sell to buyers in the event of an over-allotment.*
- *Issuer. The company selling securities in a public offering.*
- *Lead underwriter. The underwriter in charge of the offering is called the lead or managing underwriter. The lead underwriter coordinates securities sales through its own distribution channels and the*

distribution channels of one or more other underwriters. It's name appears in the lower left had corner of the company's prospectus, with other participating underwriters appearing on the lower right hand corner.

- *Lock-up agreement*. A contract between certain company shareholders and the underwriter in a public offering that requires the shareholders to refrain from selling shares for a period of time, typically 180 days in an initial public offering.
- *Organizational meeting*. The first all hands meeting of company officers, underwriters, lawyers, and accountants to organize the team's efforts toward completing all steps necessary for the anticipated public offering.
- *Over allotment*. Underwriters typically take orders to sell more shares than are made available by the company in a public offering in anticipation that some purchase orders may be withdrawn. This is referred to as an over allotment.
- *Preliminary prospectus*. The company's offering memo used to solicit indications of interests from prospective buyers before the company's registration becomes effective.
- *Prospectus*. The final offering memo delivered to each purchaser of shares. The prospectus contains a detailed description of the company's business, financial disclosures, and a discussion of risks attendant to investing in the company.
- *Quiet Period*. The period beginning when the company and its underwriter reach a preliminary understanding respecting a public offering until 25 days after the effective date of the public offering registration. During the period, the company is subject to various restrictions on its public statements.

- *Red herring*. *The preliminary prospectus, sometimes called a red herring because it bears a legend on its cover page in red ink.*
- *Road show*. *Meetings between company management and prospective investors conducted during the quiet period and arranged by the company's underwriters. The purpose of the meetings is to generate interest in buying its securities.*
- *Underwriting agreement*. *The contract in which the underwriter commits to conduct the company's offering.*

*See: Going Public, IPO (Initial Public Offering), Public Offering, SEC (Securities and Exchange Commission), Underwriters.*

## ISOs (Incentive Stock Options)

**ISOs (Incentive Stock Options)** refer to rights companies grant employees to purchase stock in the future at presently designated prices. ISOs are frequently used to attract new employees and motivate existing employees by giving the employee the right to purchase company shares in the future at present-day prices. If the company is successful, and its stock increases in value, the employee can purchase shares of company stock in the future at a price far below the then fair market value of the shares. By creating this potential windfall, incentive stock options motivate employees to work hard to make the company succeed.

ISOs are issued under guidelines adopted by the company's board of directors. These guidelines are commonly referred to as plans. Federal tax laws recognize two types of ISO plans: qualified stock option plans and nonqualified stock option plans. Preferential tax treatment is given to the holders of options issued under qualified plans. The preference is that the option recipient recognizes no ordinary income tax gain for federal income tax purposes when the option is issued by the company or exercised by the holder.[1]

Employees who hold nonqualified stock options realize income, taxed at ordinary income tax rates, when they exercise their options if the fair market value of the shares purchased exceeds the price they pay for the shares under their option. If the fair value of the shares underlying a nonqualified stock option is significantly greater than the option exercise price, the employee's tax obligation can be substantial when the option is exercised. Since the employee's profits in the stock may not be liquid (i.e., the stock may be restricted or the market for the stock may be limited), he may have to pay those taxes from other resources.

By contrast, qualified stock option holders incur no federal tax obligation until they later sell their stock at a profit.[2] No income is realized when the option is issued or exercised. If the stock is held for at least one year and then sold, the gain realized is taxed at capital gains rates. When capital gains rates are lower than ordinary income rates, as they are at this writing, the difference between paying taxes at ordinary income rates when a nonqualified option is exercised and being able to defer those taxes on a qualified option until the stock is sold and then only pay lower capital gains rates makes qualified options even more attractive.

Securing the benefits of qualification with the IRS requires careful planning and close attention to detail. Qualified options may be issued only under a plan that meets the requirements set out by the Internal Revenue Service.

---

[1] Caution! As explained later in this entry, alternative minimum gains taxes now change this for many option holders when they exercise qualified options to purchase shares. The tax applies to individuals who make more than a specified amount (which is less than $80,000 per year) and taxes the individual on the difference between the exercise price and the fair market value of the shares when he exercises his qualified option.

[2] See footnote 1.

These include having the plan approved by the company's shareholders within twelve months after it is adopted by the company's board of directors. Qualified plans must also identify the types of employees who may receive options and the total number of shares that may be subject to options issued under the plan. Each option may have a term of no more than ten years and must be issued within ten years after the date the plan is adopted. Qualified options may be issued only to employees. Except in certain limited circumstances, employees must exercise their options while they are employed by the company or within three months thereafter.

Qualified options may not be transferred except on death and their exercise price must be at least as great as the fair market value of the underlying stock at the time the option is issued. For any employee who holds 10 percent or more of the company's stock, the exercise price must be at least 110 percent of the fair market value of the company's stock when the option is issued, and the option term cannot exceed five years. The total fair market value of stock subject to qualified options that can vest in one employee in one year cannot exceed $100,000.

Plan administrators (usually management) must be careful when they accept notes in lieu of cash payment when a qualified option is exercised. The notes must be full-recourse and must bear interest at least equal to minimum rates established by the IRS. If they do not, the IRS-imputed interest rules will apply. This will require the employee to pay tax on the imputed interest and may, because imputed interest is not included in the option exercise price, cause the latter to fall below fair market value. If it does, the option may not be treated as qualified.

Stock option plans that do not meet all of the IRS requirements will be treated as nonqualified by the IRS. This means the employee will not receive the tax advantages of holding qualified options. However, they also will not be subject to the $100,000 value limitation or to the requirement that they be employees. Nor must the term of their options be tied to employment. And, below-market interest rate loans used to exercise options will not have a disqualifying effect. If the employee is sufficiently wealthy to pay the taxes, or if the term of the option is long enough to permit him to exercise the option after the company's and his stock becomes tradable in the public market, the nonqualified stock option may still create a viable incentive for the employee.

Nonqualified options issued to employees also entitle the issuing company to expense against its income tax obligations an amount equal to the compensation income attributed to the employee upon the exercise of the option. The amount of this deduction is the same as the amount of income attributed and taxed to the employee because of his exercise of the option - the difference between the option exercise price and the fair market value of the shares purchased. In order to obtain the deduction, however, the company must be sure to withhold the proper amount from the employee's income.

The use of options should be considered carefully so they can be tailored to fit the employee's and the company's needs. Qualified stock options can be used to advantage in most situations and can benefit the employee by giving him the opportunity to share in the future appreciation of the company's stock. To qualify the options the employee receives, however, the company and its management must be careful to structure the option plan to meet all of the IRS's requirements. This usually means engaging a qualified professional to establish and administer the plan.

Also, certain individuals, particularly those who are attempting to shelter income from federal taxation, must be careful to consider the alternative minimum tax (AMT) consequences of obtaining rights under a qualified plan. The difference between the holder's exercise price for the shares in a qualified plan and the fair market value of those shares when he exercises the option is a potential tax preference item that may become subject to the alternative minimum tax. The application of the AMT rules can make qualified options less attractive to these individuals. Those persons with AMT concerns should consult their tax adviser before accepting qualified stock options. *See: Board Committees, Compensation and Bonus Plans, Golden Handcuffs, Junior Common Stock, Options, Phantom Stock Plans, Qualified Stock Option Plans, Restricted Share Grants, Warrants.*

# J

**Joint Ventures** refer to business projects undertaken cooperatively by two or more parties where each contributes different skills and resources and shares in the results of the endeavor. Unlike straight financings where one party's contribution is limited to money, joint ventures usually include active participation by all parties. For example, one party might contribute technology and product development expertise while the other manages product manufacturing and marketing and provides the financing to get the product to market.

Joint ventures can be structured as contractual arrangements between two or more parties or as specialized partnerships. Corporations and limited liability companies can also be used to implement joint ventures, with special contractual arrangements among the owners. Extensive negotiation to determine the precise roles of each party is commonplace.

The most promising joint ventures are those where the contributions of the parties compliment one another and the parties duties and expectations have been thoughtfully and thoroughly documented. An example of complimentary parties who might make good joint venture partners might be an early stage company with a promising medical device in development that needs regulatory clearance and an established device distributor who has funds to back the venture through the regulatory approval process and sales people to distribute the product once it is marketable.

The issues commonly addressed in joint venture negotiations include the nature, scope and timing of each party's contributions, form and tax consequences of the venture, technology and intellectual property rights, limits on the scope of the joint venture's activities, management and decision making authority, reporting obligations, ownership and allocation of profits and losses. Some of the matters typically considered in each of those items are discussed below:

- *Nature, scope, and timing of contributions.* What resources will the joint venture need to succeed and how and when will they be made available? Contributions routinely include cash but other resources are also possible contributions. If one party has a facility or other asset available, such as computer capacity, the asset or use of the asset might be a contribution. Specialized capabilities or personnel might also be contributed. For example, a manufacturer might join up with a distributor to create a joint venture to develop products the first party will manufacture and the other party will distribute.

- *Form and tax consequences of the venture.* Will venture be operated as a series of contractual obligations between separate parties or will their be a company established to conduct the venture's business? If a company is established what form will it take? Will it be a corporation, partnership, a limited liability company or something else? Whatever the choices, both parties will want the structure to be tax efficient.

- *Technology and intellectual property rights.* Knowledge, know-how and even patent rights are frequently contributed to joint ventures. Intellectual property is almost always developed by the joint venture as a consequence of its activities. In each case, the rights of the joint venture company and the joint venture partners in this intellectual property must be clearly delineated.

- *Limits on the joint venture's activities.* Joint ventures are typically focused on a specific task and limited in the scope of the activities in which they may engage. This gives the venture direction and protects each of the venture partners from having the joint venture cannibalize other business operations. For example, a video game developer may be willing to joint venture with a European distributor to develop and market a new game conceptualized by the distributor but only if the joint venture is limited to developing games of a certain limited description. The distributor may be willing to provide its distribution capability only if it gets a royalty on sales of the product outside of Europe.

- *Management and decision making authority.* How will the joint venture be managed and who will make major decisions in the future? Will company be essentially independent when it comes to operational decisions or will the joint venture partners be consulted? Often, the party who contributes the critical expertise or capability to a given venture function will negotiate for control or input into decisions that fall within their domain. Balancing the parties' interests with those of the joint venture in a way that promotes an efficient operation is critical.

- *Reporting obligations.* What kind of financial and progress reports will each of the parties receive? How often will they be delivered and what kind of information will they contain? Will the joint venture's financial results be audited? How will access to proprietary information that has competitive ramifications be restricted?

- *Ownership and allocation of profits and losses.* How will the profits and losses of the venture be allocated among the joint venture parties? Will one party receive a royalty from sales of the venture's product? Are there other payments, preferences or rights distributions that need to be documented?

In addition to all of these matters, joint venture agreements also frequently spell out in detail what happens to the assets, inventions, inventory and personnel of the joint venture if operations cease. These termination agreements also typically spell out what the parties' responsibilities are to one another after the termination. For example, if the intellectual property and license rights to continue to pursue one or more activity of the joint venture after termination, the other party may be entitled to receive royalties or other payments if the continuing party succeeds. The party receiving the payments may be prohibited from competing in the market for a period of time or both parties may be free from constraints and permitted to use the intellectual property generated by the joint venture. The agreements between the joint venture partners will determine their relationship during and after the life of the joint venture. *See: Licensing, Off Balance Sheet Financing.*

## *Joint Venture Checklist*

*Creating a successful joint venture requires careful planning and a measured approach to your joint venture partner. Sometimes a good partner for a joint venture is also a potential competitor for the product or service to be provided by the venture. Here are some suggestions on how to take your idea for a joint venture and bring it to a successful conclusion.*

- *Explore the opportunity. Do this on your own before you contact potential partners. Review the potential market rigorously. Determine that the venture's business is worth your effort. Do the same internal review you would of any new initiative for your company. Determine whether there are any factors, such as proprietary technology or patents, that will protect your company's position from the potential venture.*
- *Establish your short-term and long-term goals for the venture. There is an old saying, when you don't know where you are going any path will get you there.*
- *Determine what contributions you need from a partner. Break down the essential elements to make the business a success and consider which of the elements can be best provided by you and which can be better provided by the right partner.*
- *Investigate potential partners. Using your list of contributions needed from partners, identify partners who have the capabilities and resources to make the venture a success. Make initial contacts with potential partners.*
- *Confidentiality agreements. Consult with your legal counsel before you disclose too much about your potential venture. Counsel can help you determine what contractual protections are appropriate and when they should be completed as part of the process. Consider no-hire agreements along with secrecy agreements to protect against having your people hired away from you.*
- *Negotiate terms. Determine what each party needs to contribute to make the venture a success and how each party benefits from the activity. Focus separately on each of the following areas to create a successful structure for your venture.*

- *Quantify contributions and allocate duties.* Contributions can include technology licenses or grants, use of physical facilities, loan or transfer of key employees, money, and commitments to fund or complete required milestones. Market expertise or commitment of sales capability can also be contributed. Be as specific as you can about who is responsible for each how that success is measured.

- *Establish funds flow.* Determine what resources will be needed and who will provide each. Pay close attention to the need for capital resources to support the venture. Agree on reasonable cash flow projections for future operations and provide for how additional resources are accessed and at what cost.

- *Determine ownership and allocate profits.* Ownership and profits allocation can take many forms to suit the parties. The actual venture can be owned in varying percentages. Securities can be created to provide preferences in different situations. Technology licensed to the venture can generate royalties or other income. Margins on the venture's products can be specifically allocated between the parties depending on their functions.

- *Resolve intellectual property questions.* If technology or other intellectual property is being contributed or developed specify carefully the rights of each party and the joint venture to such intellectual property. Allocate duties respecting the intellectual property – such as patent prosecution and maintenance – appropriately.

- *Agree on how the venture will be managed.* This discussion often revolves around which party will have more control if things do not go as anticipated. But other considerations, such as how each party participates in and is informed about the venture's activities, are just as important.

- *Include break up provisions. Specifically provide for the dissolution of the venture if it does not succeed. Also, provide for resolution of differences between the partners.*
- *Review the legal structure and tax and regulatory consequences of the venture. As you would with any serious new business venture, engage attorneys, accountants, and regulatory experts as needed to make sure the structure you are implementing will have the desire effects.*
- *Put it in writing. With the allocation of various rights and duties between parties, joint ventures need to be thoughtfully documented. Get your legal counsel involved early to avoid costly mistakes.*
- *Get to work. Start your operational level discussions early. To the extent you are comfortable relying on existing confidentiality agreements, get your people together even before the joint venture agreements are closed to get your new business off to a fast start.*

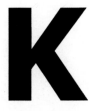

# K

**Key Man Insurance** is life insurance purchased by a company or investor on the life of an important member of a company's management team. Key man policies insure the lives of executives who are "key" to making the company a success. Many investors insist on key man insurance as a condition of financing. Sometimes lenders require key man insurance as well. Key man policies are typically payable to the company. The purpose is to provide the company with additional financial resources in the event of the death of its key executive. The resources can be used for any appropriate company purpose, including to use in attracting a suitable replacement for the lost executive.

# L

**Lawyers** are important service providers for growing business and the investors who fund their growth. They advise and help implement organizational and growth strategies and are routinely participate in the negotiation and documentation of company contracts. Lawyers have different specialities and different levels of experience. Those who understand  corporate finance and business structure can provide valuable assistance to growing companies  in their formation, financing and other business efforts.

Venture capitalists routinely use lawyers to prepare and even negotiate their financing agreements. Entrepreneurs should do the same and they should do so early in the process, before a term sheet or letter of intent is agreed to. Waiting until after the terms of the deal are fixed reduces the ability of the entrepreneur's counsel to help the entrepreneur get an appropriate deal.

Once in a while, management teams come across investors who encourage them to keep things simple and hire a lawyer only after the economic terms of the deal have been finalized. What management will miss out on if they take this advice is the benefit of counsel's experience with similar venture financings that can help shape a deal that is easier to live with and more in line with commercial norms.

The investor who advises an entrepreneur not to seek professional advice frequently does so from a desire to move things along or for other personal motives. Certainly, the deal will go easier and better for the investor if the entrepreneur forgoes the advice of counsel and negotiates from a position of inexperience.

The negotiation and documentation of venture capital financing involves many issues of critical importance to the entrepreneur. Many of these issues are ones that are apparent only to a person experienced in venture capital finance who understands the legal and practical implications of the way these issues are resolved. Hiring experienced counsel early in the process will improve management's negotiating leverage and, usually, result in a better deal. *See: Letters of Intent, Negotiation, Structure.*

## LBO (Leveraged Buyout) refers to the purchase of a company that uses borrowed money for a substantial portion of the purchase price.

The phrase usually refers to a purchase of a company by its management or outsiders using money borrowed from the seller or a third party lender for part of the purchase price. The remainder of the purchase price usually comes directly from the buyer's management and outside investors, often venture capitalists. If the purchasers are management, the acquisition is also called a management buyout or a management leveraged buyout.

Three factors generally are considered essential to conducting a successful leveraged buyout: the ability to borrow significant sums (leverage) against the company's assets; the ability to retain or attract a strong management team; and the potential for each participant's (including management's) investment to increase substantially in value. The ability of a company to support significant leverage depends upon whether it can service the principal and interest payment obligations that accompany that leverage. This, in turn, requires a company that is capable of generating large sums of cash on a regular basis or that has substantial assets that can be sold to pay off the debt. This usually means a company with an operational history that is strong enough to support the borrowing required to fund the deal.

Attracting a strong management team often translates into finding a business to purchase that already has a strong management team in place that requires few or no changes to make it complete. It is, after all, investor and lender confidence in management's ability to run the company profitably and to expand its operations that make the buyout possible. Attracting and keeping good management usually means allocating a significant portion of company ownership to the key managers in order to motivate them to stay with the company and make it grow.

The potential for increasing the value of the company's stock comes not only from the ability of management to build on an existing base of business but also on the very fact of leverage. The heavy borrowing undertaken to complete a buyout is customarily made directly from the lender to the company. This borrowing, because it is large in comparison to the value of the assets of the company, decreases the value of the company's stock, enabling management and the outside investors to acquire it at lower prices that reflect the company's value as reduced by the leverage. The leverage reduces the stock value to an amount that is low in comparison to the underlying market value of the company's assets and its historical level of earnings. As the company's debt is paid off, the value of its stock increases, in part because of the decrease in the company's debt. This creates wealth for the investors.

As might be expected, sophisticated cash flow analysis is essential to structuring a successful leveraged buyout. Failure to properly project the company's ability to service the debt placed on the company can doom a buyout to failure. This, coupled with the number of parties typically involved in a buyout and the variety and complexity of the financial structures needed to accommodate the divergent interests of those parties, almost always requires the involvement of experienced professionals. These include leveraged buyout specialists, investment bankers, accountants, and lawyers.

Leveraged buyouts often involve sensitive negotiations between company management and the owners of the target company. These negotiations can be difficult because company management must weigh the risk to its job security created by suggesting a leverage buyout against the necessity of conducting those conversations to determine whether the buyout is possible. Price negotiations can be particularly sensitive because the management team seeking to buy the company is often in a better position to guage the company's true value than the owners of the target company. Management also has an incentive to keep the price low. These conflicts can make negotiations intricate and difficult. Some find using an intermediary or a third party valuation expert can help during these discussions. *See: Debt Service, Earnouts, Earnups, Flip, Leverage, MBO (Management Buyout), Spin Outs.*

**Lead Investor** refers to the company's primary provider of capital. When more than one investor participates in a company's financing, the one who invests the most or pulls together the syndicate of investors who provide the funding is referred to as the lead investor. Typically, the lead investor serves as the syndicate's representative on the company's board of directors.

Sometimes, however, all or most of the investors in a syndicate will want to be represented on a company's board of directors. When this is the case, it is often because the syndicate members have different motivations for investing and do not feel comfortable having their interests represented by the lead investor. Sometimes the desire for more than one seat on the board springs from a lack of confidence in the lead member.

Whatever the reason, management should resist attempts to place too many members of a single syndicate on its board of directors. With divergent motivations, too many venture board members can create a serious distraction to the business of running a company. More people add more experience to a board, but too many people in any group make decision making more difficult. *See: Board of Directors, Clubbing, Control, Syndications.*

**Legend Stock** refers to a certificate of equity ownership that carries a description, usually on its face or back, of the restrictions imposed upon the ability of the holder to sell or otherwise transfer its ownership. Most legend stock carries one section identifying the restrictions imposed by state law and another identifying those imposed by federal law. If the holder of the stock has entered into a shareholders agreement or agreed to some other restriction on his ability to own or resell his securities, these will also typically appear on his stock certificate.

The purpose of putting legends on stock certificates is to alert potential purchasers to the restrictions imposed upon the stock. The absence of restrictive language on a share certificate, however, does not necessarily mean that the stock is freely tradable and unrestricted. The legends may have been left off by accident. If they were, the purchaser may acquire fewer share rights than he anticipated unless he investigates to determine what restrictions apply.

A typical stock legend might read as follows:

The shares of stock represented by this certificate have not been registered under the Securities Act of 1933, as amended, the Georgia Securities Act of 1973, as amended, or any other state securities law, and may not be transferred, sold or otherwise disposed of in the absence of an effective registration statement with respect to the shares evidenced by this certificate, filed and made effective under the Securities Act of 1933, as amended, the Georgia Securities Act of 1973, as amended, or any other state securities law, or an opinion of counsel satisfactory to the Company to the effect that registration under such Acts is not required.

The shares represented by this Certificate are also subject to the restrictions as to their transferability as set forth in that certain Agreement dated as of July 1, 2007 between the holder and the Company, a copy of which is on file in the offices of the Company.

*See: Restricted Securities, Shareholders' Agreements, Vesting Schedules, Voting Agreements.*

**Letter Agreements** are binding contracts that appear in correspondence form. They can be used for any purpose that a contract can be used for. Letter agreements are often used when employing executives or for agreements that set the stage for later more involved agreements.

On occasion, letter agreements are used to facilitate the immediate transfer to a company of some portion of a larger financing. In this case they are often used like letters of intent but are made binding on specified deal points that advance the parties' interests. Like letters of intent, which are generally non-binding except in a few procedural particulars, letter agreements often contemplate additional documentation before additional funding is provided. For example, an investor may agree to lend a company $1 million of which $100,000 is needed immediately. This amount can be advanced when the letter agreement is signed while the remaining $900,000 is held pending completion of the final documentation. *See: Bridge Loans, Investment Memorandums, Letters of Intent, Financing Agreements.*

**Letters of Intent** are writings in correspondence form that set out the basic business terms of a business deal. Letters of intent almost always anticipate additional formal documentation before the deal is completed. Major transactions such as company equity financings, joint ventures and business sales are frequently preceded by letters of intent.

Letters of intent can be completed quickly, and serve several purposes. First, by putting the business deal into writing they assure both parties that the other party agrees to the major terms of the deal. Also, they usually establish a time frame for finalizing the details and getting the necessary documentation completed. Letters of intent highlight the agreements of the parties. In so doing, they tend to solidify each party's commitment to the deal and make it easier for the parties to agree on the peripheral issues that have to be dealt with in the definitive agreements.

Although many think of intent letters as unenforceable, most contain some agreements that are binding. Some contain agreements regarding how the company will be operated pending the transaction. When they precede a venture capital financing, they sometimes contain binding agreements for bridge loans or other immediate funding to hold the company over until the formal financing agreements can be completed.

Most financing letters of intent have three things in common. They contain binding agreements by management and the company not to negotiate financing with others for thirty days or more; they provide the investor with access to company records and facilities for due diligence purposes; and they require the company to continue operating its business in the ordinary course. Some also require management and the company to make representations about the company's business plan, financial statements, and management's stock ownership.

When preparing a letter of intent, management should be careful to understand which provisions of the letter are binding and which are not. The alteration of only a few words can mean the difference between a binding obligation and a simple statement of intent.

Management also should be careful to understand the full implications of the proposed deal. Intent letters set the tone for the negotiations of the final financing agreements. Because of this, it can be very difficult to change a poorly considered term of an intent letter even though that term may appear only as an expression of intent. The best practice when working with an important letter of intent is to consult early with legal counsel.

*See: Bridge Loans, Commitment Letters, Financing Agreements, Investment Memorandums, Letter Agreements, Negotiation, Structure.*

## *Sample Venture Capital Letter of Intent*

*Virden NewCo, Inc.*
*New Business Street*
*Atlanta, Georgia 33333*
*Attention: Harold Peters and Paul Carrot*

*Gentlemen:*
*This letter is to set forth our understanding regarding the investment by Nokomis-Atlanta Ventures Ltd., a Georgia limited partnership (the "Investor") of $1,500,000 in Virden NewCo, Inc., a Delaware corporation (the "Company"), whose sole shareholders are Harold Peters and Paul Carrot (collectively, the "Shareholders"). Except with respect to paragraphs, 8, 9, and 10, the provisions of this letter are not intended to be legally binding.*

*Upon execution and delivery of the Agreement described in paragraph 7 by the Company and the Shareholders, the Investors will immediately (i) pay to the Company the sum of $850,000 and (ii) execute and deliver to the Company subscription agreements in Company's standard form subscribing for a total of 16.7% of the total issued and outstanding common stock of the Company after such issuance. The Company shall thereupon issue to the Investor 1,500 shares of its common stock, $.01 par value, equal in number to 16.7% of the issued and outstanding shares of common stock of the Company immediately after the issuance thereof.*

*In addition to the investments set forth in Paragraph 1, the Investor will invest an additional $650,000 in the Company in return for common stock which increases the Investor's percentage of the issued and outstanding capital stock of the Company immediately after such issuance by 8.3% (so that the Investor's total percentage ownership at that time will be 25% of the issued and outstanding capital stock of the Company). This subsequent $650,000 investment will be made only after the Company has achieved certain agreed upon benchmarks, including benchmarks relating to the receipt by the Company of its first order, the first shipment of Company product and the first collection on account by the Company.*

*The Investor and each of the Shareholders will agree to vote their shares of common stock in the Company to elect a slate of directors nominated by the Shareholders, which slate of directors shall always include at least one nominee of the Investor. This agreement will be evidenced by a written voting agreement and expire upon the earlier of February 2, 2010, the sale of the Company to any third party, or the sale by the Company of shares of its common stock in a public offering. All shares of common stock of the Company issued to the Investor and the Shareholders will be marked to bear appropriate restrictive legends, including reference to the voting agreement.*

*The Company will use the $850,000 provided pursuant to paragraph 1 only to fund product development, marketing and inventory expansion associated with the Company's ecommerce security program (the "Failsafe System"). Each of the Shareholders also agrees to submit to a physical examination at the Investor's request for the purpose of enabling the Company to acquire key man insurance. The Company further agrees to purchase key man insurance on each of the Shareholders in amounts reasonably required by the Investor.*

*The Investor will be entitled to one demand registration, at the cost and expense of Investor, and to participate as a selling shareholder in any public offerings of the common stock of the Company initiated by the Company upon reasonable terms and conditions to be agreed upon and set forth in the Agreement described in Paragraph 7 below.*

*As an inducement to the Investor to enter into this letter and the subsequent Agreement contemplated herein, the Company and the Shareholders, jointly and severally, represent and warrant that (i) the total issued and outstanding capital stock of the Company consists of 7,500 shares of the Company's common stock, $.01 par value, all of which are held by the Shareholders, (ii) to their knowledge, the business plan of the Company heretofore delivered to the Investor (the "Business Plan") and all other written information provided to the Investor by the Company do not contain any untrue statement of material fact or omit to state any material fact which is necessary in order to make the statements contained therein not misleading in light of the circumstances under which they are made, (iii) to their knowledge, the financial projections contained in the Business Plan have been prepared accurately based on the assumptions described therein, (iv) the Shareholders have no rights (and know of no other party having any right) in or to* the Failsafe System other than by virtue of their stock ownership in the Company and (v) that within 14 days after the date of this letter the Shareholders will each have entered into written agreements in form reasonably acceptable to Investor (A) not to use or disclose any of the confidential information or trade secrets of the Company, including information relating to the Failsafe System, except for the benefit of the Company and in the ordinary course of Company business, and (B) not to compete with the Company for a period of two years after their employment with the Company terminates for any reason.

The terms and conditions governing the transactions described in Paragraphs 2 through 9 hereof are to be set forth in a definitive agreement (the "Agreement"), which shall be subject to the approval of all of the parties and their counsel. Such terms and conditions shall include among others:

- warranties, representations and indemnities including those usually given in transactions of the nature herein contemplated, satisfactory to the Investor relating to the Company's structure, organization, business, operations and financial condition;

- the usual conditions which must be satisfied before parties to transactions of the type contemplated are obligated to close, including, but not limited to, obtaining of any required consents relating to material contracts, the absence of any litigation or other legal proceeding relating to this transaction or the Company; and

- provisions relating to compliance with all applicable securities laws.

All the parties agree to use their reasonable best efforts to complete the aforesaid Agreement within 30 days. Neither the Shareholders, the Company nor the Company's management will enter into any negotiations with any third parties for the *provision of the moneys described herein during the aforesaid 30 day period.*

*Following execution of the letter, the Company will provide the Investor and its agents with full and complete access to its property, books and records and will allow the Investor and its agents to talk to personnel, customers and independent providers of professional services to the Company. The Investor agrees to hold all information obtained by virtue of such access in confidence and not to release it to third parties without the prior written consent of the Company.*

*From the date of execution of this letter, the Company will operate its business in the manner described in the Business Plan and will use its best efforts to (i) secure at least $1 million in borrowed funds for the Company (even if such borrowing requires the personal guarantees of the Shareholders), (ii) maintain its business as a going concern and (iii) maintain its business relationships.*

*If the foregoing accurately describes our understandings and agreements, please sign, date and return the enclosed copy of this letter to me.*

*Sincerely,*
**Nokomis Atlanta Ventures, Ltd.** *(the "Investor")*
*Floyd Williams, General Partner*
*Read and Agreed to:*
**Virden-Newco, Inc.** *(the "Company")*
*Harold Peters and Paul Carrot*

**Leverage** refers to use of debt instead of equity to increase company funds. Usually, leverage is used to avoid "giving up" equity. The cost of preserving equity is the debt service payments required to service the company's loans. These payments reduce earnings and, when cash flow is inadequate, can require funding themselves. A company that has lots of debt in relation to its equity is said to be highly leveraged.

Leverage is also used to refer to a strong negotiating position caused by a compelling need of the other party. If a company cannot meet a large loan payment without an investor's funding, that investor may use his leverage to obtain concessions from the company he might not otherwise obtain. *See: Bridge Loans, Cash Flow, Cram Down, Debt Service, LBO (Leveraged Buyout), Negotiation.*

**Licensing** is an arrangement whereby an inventor grants another person or company the right to make, use or sell his invention. In many cases, licensing is a viable alternative to starting a company and raising capital. Licensing an invention can be very profitable to the inventor if the invention succeeds in the marketplace and the license agreement is properly structured.

In general, an inventor who licenses his technology to another stands to earn less from his invention than one who builds a new company to exploit it. This is because the inventor transfers the risk and cost of developing and marketing his invention to the licensee. On the other hand, because the inventor does not undertake the time-consuming job of starting and financing a new company, his time is available to explore other interests and develop other products, which may provide additional commercial success.

Sometimes an inventor does better to license his product rather than trying to build a new company around it. If the product requires a large capital investment or if the market is dominated by a strong competitor, the inventor may be more successful licensing his invention than trying to raise venture capital to start a new company. If the channels of distribution are particularly hard to penetrate or name recognition is especially important to his type of product, it may make more sense to license. In short, when the entrepreneur conducts his market research, he should consider carefully whether his product is one that can be successfully developed and marketed by a new company or whether there are factors that indicate that licensing would be more advantageous.

Licensing agreements vary from deal to deal but some issues need to be addressed in any effective license. In a technology license, these include the scope of license, the technology rights included, the payment obligations of the licensee, whether there are development obligations and how those are addressed, what rights the parties have to new inventions, who protects the intellectual property underlying the technology, who bears the risk of intellectual property infringement or liability generated from use of the licensed product, when the license terminates and what the consequences of termination are, and what related transactions are involved. The material below discusses these common licensing issues.

- *License scope and field.* Many licenses provide only limited rights to the licensee. Rights to distribute might be limited to a specified territory such as the United States or the European Community. If the technology has application in more than one area, a limited field license might be granted. For example, technology for a biocompatible material might be licensed to a company that specializes in cardiac products for cardiac and vascular applications while another company is licensed for orthopedic uses.
- *Technology rights included.* The actual technology licensed is often a subject of negotiation. Does the technology include know-how as well as patent rights? Are future improvements developed or acquired by the licensee also included? If so, in what way are they included? Does the license get them without additional charge? Or are the rights limited to first negotiation or first refusal rights? And how broadly described is the field of new inventions?

- *Payment obligations.* What royalties will the licensee pay and how will they be calculated? Are there separate license fees paid for meeting milestones in product development? Are there minimum royalties payable in exchange for exclusive license rights?

- *Development expectations and duties.* Technology is often licensed before everything has been done to enable it to be immediately commercialized. When it is, the license may also contain a development agreement that sets forth who is responsible for completing needed work and how that work will be conducted. The reasons why a product may not be ready for market are many. It may be that the product simply needs tweaking to make it into a salable product or there may be testing that needs to be done to confirm that its qualities are as represented. There may also be regulatory hurdles that have to be met. With medical innovations, these regulatory requirements can be costly and time consuming to fulfill.

- *Rights to licensee developed inventions.* Licensee's frequently develop improvements to licensed technology. These licensee-developed improvements to licensed technology are a subject of interest to both parties. Who will own licensee developed inventions? What rights will each party have to those inventions?

- *Intellectual property protection.* Licensees routinely require representations and warranties as to the licensor's ownership of the technology being licensed. When patents are involved, they also want to know what the licensor will do if a third party violates the patent to compete with the licensee. The obligation to maintain and pursue patents protection is also addressed and allocated between the parties.

- *Allocation of risk.* Three principal risks are typically addressed in a licensing agreement, the risk of damage caused by a party's breaching its contractual obligations, damage and loss of value to the license from loss of patent or intellectual property protection, and damages occurring from personal injury caused by the product produced using the licensed technology. License agreements allocate these risks among the parties. The risk of loss of intellectual property rights usually falls to the licensor. Risks from personal injury may be assigned to either party depending on the circumstances.

- *License termination.* What conditions permit the licensor or the licensee to terminate the license? Are there circumstances that permit the licensor to change an exclusive license into a nonexclusive license? What happens once the license terminates? Are their rights the licensor needs from the license to effectively commercialize the licensed product? Transition agreements that allow the licensee to sell off existing inventory are sometimes included. If the licensee also manufactures the product there may also be provisions that provide licensee with product until it can find alternative supplies.

- *Related transactions.* Many licenses are parts of larger transactions between the licensor and the licensee such as a fundraising or company recapitalization. When they are, the agreements are usually integrated with or made contingent upon the other inter-company transactions. In the life science field, development companies frequently license limited field rights to their technologies to raise capital by relinquishing rights to the technology they are unable to commercialize on their own. In these cases, the technology frequently needs further development or costly and time-consuming regulatory approval. If the technology is important, it may command a sizable up front license fee and significant additional payments when agreed-upon milestones are reached that fund the companies efforts in other areas.

Licensing any technology or right effectively involves attention to detail and an understanding of both technology and markets. Legal issues and their resolution can play important parts in allocating risk and reward appropriately between the parties. Effective legal counsel should be engaged in any serious licensing endeavor. Complex licenses are frequently preceded by letters of intent or term sheets. Engaging counsel at this stage is important. *See: Business Plan Format, Franchising, Letters of Intent, Market Research, Patents, Software Protection, Term Sheet, Trade Secrets.*

## Life Style Companies

**Life Style Companies** are companies that operate without sustainable strategies to achieve the rapid growth or provide the short-term exit strategy necessary to attract venture capital investors. Life style companies are often profitable and valuable but, because they are not geared toward rapid growth, they are not attractive investments for venture capital investors. They are often contrasted with emerging growth companies. Instead of operating from the premise of generating rapid and sustained growth, life style companies look to remain competitive while generating steady streams of income for their operators. Businesses often operate as life style companies because they are not in industries that will support the type of growth needed to become an emerging growth company. *See: Emerging Growth Companies.*

## Limited Partnerships

**Limited Partnerships** are a form of business organization that combine attributes of corporations with those of partnership. Like corporations they can provide investors with the protection of limited liability. Like partnerships they can give management and the investors flexibility in allocating profits and losses among partners.

The limited partnership, together with the limited liability company, is the structure most frequently used by venture capital firms to raise money. They enable investors to receive the profits and losses generated by the fund's investment without the intervention of corporate income tax. At the same time, they give investors the flexibility needed to attract competent fund managers by funding their expenses and salaries and providing them with a percentage of profits for incentive. Limited partnerships are also used by young companies to raise money before they become profitable. Such companies sometimes select the limited partnership or limited liability company structure during formation to enable them to transfer the tax benefits of company losses to investors as a method of making equity investment more attractive to investors.

Limited partnerships have two types of partners, general and limited. Limited partners traditionally provide funding to the entity and, by virtue of their limited partnership status, receive limited liability much like that of a corporate shareholder. The general partners do not receive limited liability and customarily manage the business. Limited partners, unlike corporate shareholders, are generally prohibited from becoming involved with the active management of the partnership. If they do become involved, they risk being treated like general partners and becoming personally liable for the actions of the entity.

Limited partnerships must be structured carefully. Obtaining the tax benefits of a limited partnership depends upon close compliance with Internal Revenue Service rules that govern, for tax purposes, the differences between corporations and partnerships. A limited partnership must qualify as a partnership to obtain the special tax treatment.

There are generally four factors the Internal Revenue Service looks at when determining how to tax a limited partnership: 1) unlimited personal liability for the debts of the entity; 2) lack of centralized management; 3) limited duration; and 4) restricted transferability of ownership interest. If a limited partnership meets fewer than two of these standards, it may be characterized and taxed as a corporation. To avoid this result, limited partnership agreements usually try to qualify under criteria (3) and (4) by making the partnership terminate after a specified period of time and restricting the rights of limited partners to transfer their partnership interests. Whenever a limited partnership is used, management should consult with its attorneys and accountants. Only they can insure management of obtaining the desired tax results. *See: LLCs (Limited Liability Companies), R & D Partnerships, S Corporations.*

## Lines of Credit. *See: Credit Lines.*

## Liquidation Preferences refer to rights built into
the terms of a financial instrument that guarantee the holder the right to get back the money it has invested or some fraction or multiple of the money before other investors are paid. The most common liquidation preference in venture capital financings appears as a term in a convertible preferred stock description that gives to the investor the right to receive back its investment (or its investment and a designated return) when the company is liquidated before proceeds from the liquidation are paid to holders of common shares.

Typically, liquidation events include sales of the business or mergers. In the most common convertible preferred stock liquidation preference, the holder of the convertible preferred stock must choose to receive its liquidation preference or convert into common stock and receive the pro rata share of the liquidation proceeds. If the company's sale generates a value per share that exceeds the liquidation preference to the preferred shareholder, conversion can be expected. A more investor-friendly preference, referred to as a participating preference, provides the holder even more rights. When included in a convertible preferred stock, this preference gives the investor his money back on a liquidation event and then lets him share pro rata with other shareholders in dividing up the remaining proceeds from the liquidation event.

Liquidation preferences are a favored tool of lead investors in down rounds. Frequently, they have been used with extreme preferences, such as three or six times investment, to compensate the investor of a troubled company for taking the risk of investing. Such structures can drastically diminish the value of the securities held by other investors and make it more difficult to attract additional capital. *See: Down Rounds, Pay-to-Play, Participating Preferred Stock.*

**Liquidity Agreements** refer to contracts that provide mechanisms for investors to convert their investments in stock or debentures into cash. They usually appear as provisions in written contracts between investors, management shareholders and the company. Sometimes they appear in the description of the security itself. Liquidity agreements are common in private company investments because of the limited opportunities these companies provide for cashing out. Unlike public companies with an active trading market in their securities, private companies have no readily accessible market for selling their securities. Because many private company investments end up being less successful than expected, the liquidity options afforded by these agreements can be very important to investors.

Common liquidity agreements include puts, which enable an investor to force a company to repurchase his shares for an agreed-upon price, and buy-sell agreements, which enable an investor to force management to either purchase his shares or sell its shares to him. These buy-sell arrangements can make it easier for an investor to liquidate his investment even when management chooses to sell its shares. This is because it is often easier to sell a controlling interest in a company than it is to sell a minority interest (which is what most outside investors hold).

Registration rights also improve investor liquidity by giving the shareholder rights to require the company to register their shares for resale or to include their shares in a company sponsored public offering. Registering the shares makes them freely tradable without the restrictions on resale imposed on unregistered stock. A public offering also typically generates a market for the stock, making it easier to sell company shares.

Convertible debentures increase investor liquidity by giving the investor the option of not converting his debenture into shares of the company's common stock. If the company's stock value does not increase enough to give the investor a higher return from selling the common stock than he can obtain by converting his debenture, the investor can choose to forgo converting to the company's stock and, instead, collect the interest and principal repayment on the debenture. Mixed investment structures that include stock and promissory note purchases also enhance investor liquidity by enabling the investor to withdraw a part of the investment as a nontaxable repayment of debt.

Any agreement that makes it easier for investors to get their money back is a liquidity agreement. All liquidity agreements should be considered carefully. Agreements that create a corresponding company need for funding, such as a put or a promissory note, could be exercised or come due when replacement funds are costly or unavailable. Demand registration rights could force a company to go public at a time when it is advantageous for the selling investor but disadvantageous for the company and management. *See: Buy-Sell Agreements, Cashing Out (or In), Convertible Securities, Co-Sale Agreements, Debentures, Demand Rights, Exits, Financing Agreements, Piggyback Rights, Puts, Registration Rights, Structure.*

**Liquidity Events** refer to events that enable investors to cash out their investments. Repayment of principal and interest are liquidity events for a lender. Sale of stock is a liquidity event for a shareholder. Investors of registered stock can cause a liquidity event by simply selling their shares through a broker.

Private company investors, however, are not so fortunate. They receive unregistered stock that is not freely tradable and that, often, does not have an established market for its shares. This limits their ability to cash out, particularly on short notice. Liquidity agreements are commonly entered into in these situations to help improve the investor's ability to get to a liquidity event. Liquidity events are also referred to as exits, particularly when they involve liquidating all of an investor's investment in a company. A listing of common exits is described in the Exit entry in this book. *See: Exits, Liquidity Agreements.*

## LLCs (Limited Liability Companies) are a form
of business entity that combines the attributes of partnerships with attributes of corporations. They are designed to provide the ownership and tax flexibility of partnerships with the limited liability and streamline management structure of corporations.

The owners of LLCs are referred to as members and hold membership interests to evidence their ownership. Day to day management of the LLC is conducted by managers instead of officers or directors, in the case of corporations, or general partners, in the case of partnerships. The activities of the managers are monitored by the members. The principal organizational charter is the operating agreement, which sets out the company's membership and operational rules. Membership interests are usually transferable only with the approval of other members after all requirements of the operating agreement are met. Profits and losses are shared (and taxed) to members in the manner provided in the operating agreement. LLC members can elect to have the LLC taxed as a C corporation, with its separate taxable identity, or taxed as a pass-through organization, without a separate tax at the entity level.

The flexibility to elect to be taxed as a pass-through organization has made the LLC structure popular with venture capital and other equity funds as well as with new companies. The absence of an entity level income tax makes it possible for venture capital fund managers to deliver the profits (and losses) from their investments directly to their investors without the intervention of an entity tax. New companies that anticipate losses in their early years can use the LLC structure to pass those losses through to their investors, which reduces the after tax cost to those investors. *See: Corporations, Joint Ventures, Limited Partnerships, S Corporations, Strategic Partnerships.*

## Comparison of Business Entities

| | C Corp | S Corp | Limited Partnership | LLC |
|---|---|---|---|---|
| Investors | shareholders | shareholders | partners | Members |
| Management | directors/ officers | directors/ officers | general partner | Managers |
| Liability | limited | Limited | limited (unlimited to general partner) | Limited |
| Earnings Taxed To | corporation | shareholders | partners | Members |
| Profits/Losses Allocated To | corporation | shareholders pro rata to ownership | as provided in partnership agreement | as provided in operating agreement |
| Entity Limits on Ownership Transfer | none | none (but may lose S status) | yes, in partnership agreement | yes, in operating agreement |

*See: Corporations, Limited Partnerships, LLC's (Limited Liability Companies), S Corporations.*

**Loan Covenants** refer to promises a borrower makes to its lender in its loan agreements that serve as the basis for the lender issuing the loan. Loan covenants also serve as performance minimums the borrower must meet during the term of the loan in order to retain the right to continue the loan. When a borrower does not maintain the loan covenants the lender may tender the loan into default and call the loan.

Typical issues addressed in business loan covenants include:

- *Insurance.* This requires the borrower to maintain general liability insurance and insurance to protect such things as plant and equipment or inventory against catastrophic loss. Sometimes the insurance covenant also requires the borrower to maintain key man insurance to insure the life of an important executive.
- *Financial representations.* The borrower warrants the accuracy of financial statements provided to the lender and agrees to provide updated financial statements to the lender on a monthly or quarterly basis throughout the term of the loan.
- *Financial covenants.* The borrower is required to maintain the viability of the business as measured by key financial ratios that can be determined from the borrower's financial statements. Common minimum ratios that borrowers are required to maintain include the quick ratio and current ratio, which measure liquidity. Lenders frequently also require maintenance of minimum return on assets and return on equity. Minimum maintenance requirements may also be

imposed on the borrowers equity, working capital and debt to net worth ratios.

- *Taxes, fees and licenses.* The borrower agrees to make timely payment of all taxes and fees due. This keeps the borrower's assets free from government liens, which would take priority over the lender's liens.
- *Other loans.* Limitations are placed on the borrowers ability to obtain loans from other lenders.
- *Dividends and withdrawals.* Dividend payments and certain other specified withdrawals of cash are forbidden during the term of the loan or limited to specified amounts.
- *Business acquisitions and management changes.* Lender is prohibited from acquiring other businesses or making material changes in its management term without the prior written consent of the lender.

*See: Credit Line, Cure Periods, Guarantees, Key Man Insurance, Personal Guarantees, Secured Loans, Security Agreements, Term Loan.*

# M

**Management Agreements** refer to contracts that govern the manner in which an enterprise is managed or provide for a party to deliver identified management services to a company. When they involve outside investors, they frequently are included in the terms of a shareholder agreement or the terms of their preferred security. Management agreements of this sort can take the form of shareholder agreement provisions that guarantee the election of a management-controlled board of directors or a veto right that prevents certain major decisions from being made without outside investor's consent.

Where outside investors control a company, a management contract can be used to empower the company's managers to operate the company for a specified term. Management agreements also include contracts between companies and outside consulting firms who are hired to perform specific functions. These agreements often contain performance requirements, which, if not met, can cause the agreement to terminate.

Management agreements also include consulting or participation agreements some investors require as a condition to funding. These agreements frequently require the company to pay the investor a regular fee and give him the right to obtain financial reports and participate in management decisions. Most venture capitalists do not require these types of management agreements. Instead, they work their rights to participate in management into their financing agreements and do not charge a separate management fee. Whenever a separate management fee is paid to an investor, management should consider the fee as a part of its cost of capital. *See: Consulting Agreements, Financing Agreements, Pricing, ROI (Return on Investment).*

## Management Team refers to the group of individuals

who are collectively responsible for managing and overseeing a company's operations. In many entrepreneurial companies the management team consists of the founders and one or two key individuals hired after the company was incorporated.

Most venture capitalists prefer to invest in companies led by complete management teams. This reduces their risk in the event the founding entrepreneur becomes sick and enhances the capabilities of the company's management to anticipate and direct the company's growth. Few individuals possess the ability or stamina that is necessary to create and manage a company through all the challenges that come with growth. Investors usually look to the three or four people who are essential to a company's success as its management team.

Because of this, the chances of obtaining venture capital are improved greatly by presenting a complete team in the business plan. Companies with gaps in their management teams should be ready to explain what plans they have to fill the vacant spots. Most investors will want to know about these plans and how the present management team expects to fill the important vacancies. Many investors will help entrepreneurs fill those spots by identifying potential candidates from their network of contacts.

As a rule, however, it is better to present potential investors with a complete management team or with concrete plans to identify and attract additional team members.

Investors know it can be difficult to attract and retain key personnel, particularly in technical areas important to the company where few persons with the requisite skills are available. Thus, presenting a business plan that lacks key players may make an otherwise enthusiastic investor reluctant to invest. *See: Entrepreneurs, Five Factors.*

**Market Price Method** is a common method used to estimate the fair market value of private companies. The methodology estimates the company's value by comparing it to similar publicly traded companies. One common method compares a company's after-tax profits and multiplies it by the average price to earnings (P/E) ratio of its public competitors. Others compare company sales and multiply by an average price to sales ratio. When public company comparisons are used to determine a private company value, discounts are commonly applied to the result. The reason for this is that private company values are thought to be less than their similarly situated public company counterparts because their shares are not freely tradable. This discount is commonly referred to as the liquidity discount.

For example, a private widget company with after-tax earnings of $1.5 million might estimate its fair market value at $15 million if its public company competitors had P/E ratios of ten. If a 20% liquidity discount were applied to the valuation, the company value estimate would be reduced from $15 Million to $12 Million.

If the comparison companies were of comparable size to the company be valued, management might have a high degree of confidence in the valuation. If the companies were significantly larger or involved in noncompetitive businesses, the confidence in the comparison might be lower.

Like all valuation methods, the market price method is imperfect and should be used with other models, such as the discounted cash flow model, when estimating company value. A more detailed description of how a modified form of the market price method using a company's projected financial statements can be used to estimate values of rapidly growing companies is contained in the *Pricing* entry. Another common method for valuing growing companies, the *Discounted Cash Flow* method, is also described in this book. *See: Discounted Cash Flow, Negotiation, P/E, Price Earnings Ratio, Pricing.*

**Market Research** refers to the investigation companies and investors make into a company's market to evaluate whether the company's products will sell and whether the marketplace for the company's products is large enough to support the product sales projected by the company. Every venture capitalist bases his investment decision, at least theoretically, on market research.

Market research requires both an investigation of the market in which the company's product will compete and an analysis of how the company's products will fit into that market. It identifies who the company's competitors are, what their present and future products will look like and sell for, and how price-sensitive its customers are. It also determines who the potential company suppliers will be and whether product components will be difficult to obtain.

Market research should include reviews of available industry data, including industry magazines, web resources, and reports by industry experts. Annual reports of competitors should also be digested. Personal interviews and discussions should not be overlooked. Some of the most insightful information available can be obtained by a telephone conversation with a potential competitor.

Venture capitalists conduct thorough market research and expect extensive and thoughtful research from the entrepreneurs they consider for their portfolios. The thoroughness of management's market research and the conclusions drawn from it should be fully reflected in the company's business plan. If the process of market research is new to management, experienced consultants can be hired to help focus the questions and to conduct the research. *See: Business Plan, Business Plan Format, Due Diligence.*

## MBO (Management Buyout) refers to a leveraged buyout conducted by members of the acquired company's existing management. *See: LBO (Leveraged Buyout), Spin Outs.*

## Mezzanine Financing refers to a hybrid form of investment that falls between pure equity and pure debt. It is frequently used in later stage investments to fund a company's growth opportunity or to enable a company to achieve a critical objective (such as increasing inventories to accomplish greater sales). Mezzanine financings are frequently undertaken when they promise to decrease a company's overall cost of financing by helping the company expand sufficiently to attract a significantly better price for its shares in a later public offering. Sometimes they are undertaken because the market for public offerings is so poor that going public is not a viable alternative. They are also used to fund acquisitions of companies or product lines.

Mezzanine financings are often the last round of investment in a private company before it goes public. When used for this purpose, the mezzanine funds are intended to facilitate the company's efforts to grow its business to a point where its stock will be attractive to the public market or to where it will attract a larger audience and higher price than without the growth supported by the mezzanine financing. By making its stock more appealing (and more expensive) to investors, companies hope to decrease the company's overall cost of financing.

Mezzanine financings appear between senior debt and equity on a company's balance sheet. Typical terms include a convertible subordinated debt instrument or a subordinated debt instrument and warrants. On some occasions, second lien debt instruments or convertible preferred stock is used. Whatever instruments are used, mezzanine financings typically include both a debt and an equity component. In the subordinated debt and warrant structure, the subordinated loan serves as the debt instrument and the warrants give the lender the ability to acquire equity on favorable terms.

In mezzanine financings, the debt portion is structured to be junior in preference to the company's institutional loans and senior in preference to its shareholders. It stands, by virtue of its contractual terms, behind the company's other debt when it comes to preference for payment. Because it is debt, however, it stands before the company's equity holders in preference for payment. The subordination feature is intended to make it possible for the company to obtain other secured or unsecured borrowings from commercial lenders.

Mezzanine investors usually look for returns that are higher than those expected by commercial lenders but lower than those desired by venture capital investors. The return is calculated by combining the value of the interest charged on the debt with the potential return available from the equity interest. When a mezzanine investor seeks an 18 to 20% rate of return, for example, it might issue its subordinated debt at a 12 or 12.5% interest rate and look to obtain the remaining 6 to 8% of its return in the potential value of warrants it acquires with the debt to purchase company stock. *See: Credit Line, Debt Service, Going Public, Investment Bankers,, Loan Covenants,, Secured Loans, Term Loans.*

**Milestones** are performance goals against which a company's success is measured. They are sometimes used to determine whether a company will receive additional financing or whether management will receive additional stock. They are also frequently used in development or joint venture agreements to determine when a payment or contribution is required. Milestones are sometimes referred to as benchmarks, minimums or performance requirements. To be most effective, milestones need to be clearly articulated and measurable. For example, the milestone of profitability is only effective if he parties agree on what profitability means and how it is measured. A milestone like selling a fixed number of products or filing a required regulatory application is easy to measure and confirm. *See: Benchmarks.*

## Minority Shareholder

**Minority Shareholder** refers to an investor who does not own enough stock to elect a majority of a company's board of directors and so cannot control the manner in which the company is run. However, in some cases, a minority shareholder may represent a swing vote in battles for control or may have contractual rights to participate or veto certain actions within a company.

Venture capitalists routinely find themselves in the role of minority shareholders. To compensate for the lack of influence and control normally attendant to being a minority shareholder, venture investors incorporate participation rights and liquidity agreements into their investment agreements. Those rights often include rights to obtain representation on the company's board of directors, receive regular reports on the financial condition of the company, require completion of identified tasks, participate in company budgeting processes, and approve certain types of major actions taken in the future. Venture capitalists also sometimes provide their funding in stages as a method of requiring certain milestones to be accomplished. *See: Affirmative Covenants, Control, Negative Covenants, Shareholders' Agreements, Stage Financing, Venture Capital Deal Structures, Voting Agreements.*

## MOUs (Memorandums of Understanding)

**MOUs (Memorandums of Understanding)** refer written statements describing the main business terms of a deal. They serve the same purpose of term sheets and letters of intent. Usually, most of their terms are intended to be nonbinding statements of intent set forth in anticipation of the parties entering into more detailed and binding deal agreements. *See: Commitment Letters, Letter Agreements, Letters of Intent, Term Sheets.*

**NASBIC** refers to the National Association of Small Business Investment Companies, a non-profit industry association that acts as the voice of the small business investment community (SBICs and SSBICs) before Congress. Their web site can be found at www.nasbic.org. *See: SBICs (Small Business Investment Companies), NVCA (National Venture Capital Association).*

**Negative Covenants** refer to agreements that obligate a party to refrain form taking certain specified actions. In the venture capital context, they are typically used to assure an investor of the right to be consulted before a certain type of agreement is taken. They provide this assurance to the investor by prohibiting the action unless investor consents.

Negative covenants are a staple part of venture capital financings. The negative covenants that are commonly found in venture financing agreements are designed to prohibit actions that could dilute or undermine the value of the investor's stock. Since these covenants also limit management's flexibility, they should be considered and negotiated carefully.

Negative covenants usually appear as part of the financing agreement or in the terms of an investor's convertible preferred stock. They typically prohibit a company from taking one or more of the following types of actions without investor consent:

- *Altering the company's charter or bylaws.* Charter and bylaw changes could reduce preferences granted to the investor's convertible preferred stock or grant greater preferences to others. They could also be used to expand the Board of Directors and reduce investors influence.

- *Changing the character of the business conducted by the company.* The investor wants to prevent management from changing the basic character and focus of the business unless he agrees with it.

- *Paying dividends, issuing new stock, or borrowing funds that are convertible into stock.* Paying dividends reduces available cash for a growing company and may make it necessary to raise additional funds earlier. New stock issuances reduce the percentage ownership of existing shareholders. Venture investors, and usually management, want to minimize the circumstances that require the company to issue new stock.

- *Altering the preferences of the stock acquired by the investor.* This is also covered by the prohibition against altering the company's charter. The issue here is that the investor does not what his preferences reduced or negatively impacted without his consent.

- *Disposing of company assets or acquiring new assets in transactions which fall outside the ordinary course of the company's business.* Investors want to be consulted on extraordinary transactions and events that affect the company. The sale of a division or acquisition of a new line of business that will change the character of the company's business are the types of activities covered here.

- *Selling the business.* This is perhaps the biggest extraordinary transaction, whether it occurs as a sale of substantially all the company's assets, a merger or a sale of stock.
- *Voluntarily dissolving or winding up the company.* This extraordinary transaction will end the company's existence and determine what return, if any, the investor receives.
- Entering into business transactions with management of the company.

The term negative covenants is also used to refer to financial covenants in loan agreements that create defaults when they are not met. Here a negatiave covenant might be something like failing to maintain a specified current ratio or permitting cash to fall below a certain percentage of current liabilities. Failure to meet the covenant creates a default that the lender could tender to terminate the loan. *See: Affirmative Covenants, Management Agreements, Operating Covenants, Reps & Warranties, Structure.*

**Negotiation** refers to the give and take between two or more parties that leads to an agreement. Many negotiations, particularly those that involve something as important and complex as an investment in a growing company, can be lengthy and involve several negotiations and drafts of contracts. Fruitful negotiations involve careful planning and attention to detail.

Negotiations for financing begins when management makes its first contact with an investor. Whether that contact is face to face or made through the mail, the first impression management makes sets the tone for future dialogue with the investor. A solid presentation by management sets the groundwork for a positive exchange with the investor by improving the investor's perception of the company and its management.

Most venture capitalists prefer to make a funding proposal to management rather than react to a proposal prepared by the company. Their proposal is made only after they complete their due diligence, during which management's opinions and expectations about financing are solicited. Usually the proposal is specific as to amount of money, timing of investment, and the number and types of company securities the investor desires.

Once a proposal is made, management's negotiating position is reduced to that of reacting to the proposal and trying to convince the investor to modify those terms that are unacceptable. This can prove difficult, especially when a company's need for money is acute and there are no other offers on the table. Therefore, one good strategy for improving management's bargaining position is to begin the search for money early and to approach several investors simultaneously. Companies who wait until their need for money is immediate and severe before they approach investors, reduce their ability to negotiate effectively.

Another good strategy is to convince the investor that the company presents an exceptional and extremely rare opportunity. (This too is usually best done before the investor makes his funding proposal.) The care management takes in preparing its plans and presentations to investors pays off in better financing packages and easier negotiations. An investor's impression of the company and his judgment as to its value usually have more to do with the value he places on the company, which translates into the price he expects to pay for his stock, than all the persuasion attempted during the negotiation of the actual financing agreements. As a result, much of management's most effective negotiation occurs when it is selling its concept to the investor, long before formal negotiation of the terms of that financing begins.

That is not to say, however, that management should relax once a funding proposal is made and accept whatever price and structure an investor proposes. Most investors are interested in getting the best deal they can and will propose a price and structure favorable to themselves. Management should expect this and analyze the investor's proposal carefully, using the analysis as the basis for its negotiation with investors.

Most investors expect a reasoned, issues-oriented negotiating approach from management in which management and the investor openly address the concerns of both parties and search creatively for solutions that build a workable deal. Negotiating effectively in this context requires an understanding of venture capital deals and structures, of the needs and concerns of the company and its management, and of the perspective of the investor.

A major purpose of this book has been to provide entrepreneurs with more knowledge about the venture capital deal structuring process so that they can understand better the compromises and concessions they are asked to make. A better understanding helps management identify and articulate its concerns with objectionable parts of an investor's proposal, which, in turn, makes it easier for the parties to discuss the open deal points and arrive at acceptable compromises.

Understanding a proposed deal and its short-term and long-term effects involves more than just reading one book and looking closely at the investor's proposal. It also involves getting qualified professional help from someone who has done venture deals before and can give management an independent appraisal of the proposed deal. This person should be able to guide management in suggesting effective solutions to many of the problems identified in the deal proposal. He should be conversant with the applicable securities laws so he can direct the deal's structure in a way that avoids securities problems for management and the company.

In most cases this person should be a lawyer. It simply is not true for most entrepreneurs that they can negotiate a commercially reasonable financing package without the help of a qualified professional. In most cases, the professional investor has vast deal-making experience, while the entrepreneur has little or none in structuring a funding. This, coupled with the far-reaching and often prejudicial effects of many common venture deal provisions, makes it almost foolhardy to complete a venture deal without qualified professional help.

And, while it is true that most venture investors use a reasoned analysis approach in their negotiations, entrepreneurs should not be so naive as to believe that investors will not also use deceptive tactics and pressure strategies to get the deal they want. While most effective deal-makers find that an open, analytical approach makes for the best deals, some also view games and pressure tactics as a legitimate part of the negotiating process. Many of these investors mix these tactics into an otherwise straightforward negotiation. They may include delay, refusals to discuss reasons, and last-minute demands for concessions to get the deal done. An adviser who is practiced at venture deal making usually can distinguish these tactics from the heart of the negotiating process so they can be dealt with effectively.

The discussion in the *Equity Penalties* entry describes one last-minute demand tactic that occurred in an otherwise open negotiation with one of the senior fund managers of a nationally prominent venture capital firm. In that case, the entrepreneur received a phone call late Friday night from the fund manager saying he could not close the deal on Tuesday unless the entrepreneur agreed to give him significantly more stock if the company did not meet its plan. The deal had been negotiated at length and was ready to be closed. The investor had numerous opportunities to raise this issue before but waited, instead, to bring it up at the last minute, to couple it with a threat not to fund, and to do so in a manner that made it difficult for the entrepreneur to get his counsel's advice.

The entrepreneur should have called his lawyer at home. Instead, he worried all weekend about his deal dying. On Monday morning, when he called his lawyers, he had convinced himself to make the concession to get the deal done.

The investor's proposal was absurd, particularly in view of the manner in which it was made. It smacked of bad faith. The entrepreneur's lawyers counseled him to reject the proposal in a way that showed how ludicrous it was. The entrepreneur contacted the fund manager and told him he could not go forward with the equity penalty proposed, that it was unfair, and that if an equity penalty was critical, the parties would also have to discuss an equity bonus to management (and corresponding dilution of the investor's interest) if the company met its plan. The investor promptly dropped his demand and closed the next day.

There are several good books on negotiation. Two good examples are *Getting to Yes by Roger Fisher and William Ury* and *Getting Together - Building a Relationship that Gets to Yes by Roger Fisher and Scott Brown*. Both books are a result of research conducted by the Harvard Negotiation Project and describe a constructive, issues oriented approach to negotiation. *See: Deal Breakers, Financing Agreements, Golden Rule, K.I.S.S., Letters of Intent, Lawyers, Pricing, ROI (Return on Investment), Shopping, Structure.*

## *Practical Strategies for Negotiating with Investors*

*Completing a successful fundraising involves hard work, planning, attention to detail, and an understanding of both the fundraising process and the interplay of the deal structure* terms. The following strategies can improve the odds of negotiating a favorable deal.

1. *Start early*. It takes time to put together the proper presentation, identify likely investors, and make contacts that lead to meaningful discussions about investing. Starting late creates pressure to get done quickly and limits the number of prospects that can reasonably be pursued. With an early start and enough prospective investors, an attractive company can sometimes create competition for their deal that leads to better pricing and more favorable terms. A late start that leaves the company strapped for cash invites interested investors to hold out for lower valuations and stricter terms.

2. *Line up the inside investors*. It is important for companies with existing venture investors to be able to tell the market of potential new investors that existing investors will participate in the new round of funding. This is best done during the planning stage by getting verbal commitments from the existing investors to invest in the new round at the price and on the terms negotiated by the new investor. While the amount inside investors are willing to invest may vary depending on price and terms, most venture capital investors with the ability to make follow-on investments understand the importance of participating in later rounds.

3. *Build a convincing plan*. Ultimately it's the quality of a company's opportunity combined with the ability of its management team to capitalize on that opportunity the makes an investor want to invest. The stronger the plan and the better articulated it is, the more eager investors will be to participate. Strong plans and attractive businesses that attract more than one potential investor, or that investors realize can attract more than one investor, create more bargaining power for company management. This can result in higher valuations and better terms.

4. *Get qualified help*. Start with your lawyer and accountant. Be sure the lawyer is qualified to assist you in understanding and negotiating the transaction. Do your best

to engage an accountant who understands your business and can help you identify meaningful metrics to manage and measure your business. These metrics and what they say about management's understanding of its business can add measurably to company's prospects for a successful fund raise. These professionals can often help with introductions to fundraising sources including, when appropriate, professional investment bankers to help market a plan.

5. *Know your strengths and weaknesses*. Know your company's strengths and weaknesses in detail and be prepared to respond to intensive questioning by interested investors. Be ready to discuss your market and your competition and to state your value proposition clearly. Keep your accounting and reporting systems up to date and timely. Demonstrate your ability to understand and respond to how your business is doing in all its key areas by developing meaningful measures of progress and reporting on them regularly to the company's decision makers.

6. *Do your homework*. Do not try to raise money from anybody. Some investors make better partners than others. Investigate the background of prospective investors to find out about their success rate and their reputation for being constructive. Most private company investors have preferences and constraints on how they invest their money. If the company is an early stage medical device company do not waste its time or the time of investors by pursuing investors who invest only in later stage investments or investments in the information processing industry.

7. *Gauge your company's realistic value*. Get help if you need it but spend time analyzing your company's realistic range of valuation so that pricing negotiations can be productive. Professional valuation experts can be hired but usually it's enough to have a general range. The entries on *Discounted Cash Flow* and *Pricing* elsewhere in this book can help you get a handle on your company's value.

8. *Make connections*. Reach out to your network and the networks of your advisors. A personal introduction to a prospective investor can get a company plan more attention and adds credibility to management.

9. *Attend to details*. Getting qualified help can be very important here. Negotiate constructively but with close attention to detail. Get help from legal counsel to understand the ramifications of the various deal structure provisions investors seek in private company financings.

10. *Be ready for the unexpected*. Keep your guard up until the money is in the bank. Even in negotiations that appear constructive and well meaning, misunderstandings and just plain old tactics can result in unpleasant surprises. Despite protestations from investors that "we all have the same agenda," it just is not true that an investor's interests are perfectly aligned with management. See the *Equity Penalties* entry earlier in this book for a description of one unexpected last minute demand.

11. *Have another plan*. Realistic alternatives to raising equity investment on a fixed schedule leave management with the flexibility to negotiate better financing terms. Whether it is managing growth at a slower pace or reconfiguring company operations to improve cash flow and reduce research funding, always have a realistic alternative plan.

See: *Auctions, Deal, Deal Breakers, Deal Flow, Discounted Cash Flow, Negotiation, Networking, Pricing, Venture Capital Deal Structures.*

**Networking** refers to a method many investors use to identify viable companies and syndicate investments. Networking refers to sharing information and prospects with other investors and persons involved in the venture capital process. Networks can be as informal as loosely knit associations among investors and their consultants or as formal as a trade association or networking organization. Many venture capital clubs provide regular opportunities for investors, and sometimes entrepreneurs, to meet and discuss mutual opportunities. Incubators and technology development centers also provide a base of networking for entrepreneurs.

Networking is important. Many investors will not consider an investment proposal unless they receive it with a recommendation from someone they know. Business plans that come unannounced through the mail have less chance of being read than plans that are accompanied and preceded by a call from a friend or acquaintance.

Entrepreneurs should recognize the existence and importance of networking when they solicit funding. Whenever possible, entrepreneurs should use an introduction of an acquaintance to help them get the attention of an investor. Often the best way to become a part of a community's venture network is to join an incubator or attend chamber of commerce or local development authority meetings. Sometimes, the right banker, accountant, or attorney (one who deals regularly with venture capital) can introduce the entrepreneur to the area's network. *See: Deal Flow, Incubators, Shopping, Technology Development Centers, Venture Capital Conferences.*

**Noncompete Agreements** are contracts in which one party, often an individual employee, agrees to refrain from competing with another party. They are used regularly in growing companies to encourage key employees to remain employed and to prevent them from working for competitors after they leave. Most venture capitalists require noncompete agreements from top management as a condition to funding. Investors often combine stock vesting agreements and stock bonus plans with noncompete agreements to better insure management loyalty. Trade secrecy and confidentiality agreements are also commonly included in noncompete agreements.

To be enforceable, noncompete agreements need to be drafted carefully. Courts dislike noncompete agreements because they interfere with a person's ability to earn a living. As a rule, courts will enforce them only when their provisions are carefully limited. The types of restrictions these agreements must contain to be enforceable vary from state to state. Some state courts will not enforce any employee noncompete agreement. Others will, but only if they are entered into in connection with the sale or financing of a company. All states require noncompete agreements to be tightly drawn in compliance with the particular requirements of local law.

Although the rules vary from state to state and different states apply similar rules with different emphasis, a few principles of noncompete agreements do have general applicability. All states require noncompete agreements to be in writing and supported by valuable consideration. Most require them to be restricted as to territory and time. That is, an employee cannot be prevented from competing everywhere forever.

Many states require that the competitive behavior that is restricted include only the types of activities the employee undertook for the company. Some states will not enforce a noncompete agreement that is signed after the employee joins the company unless the employee receives something significant from the company at the time. Most states are more lenient about enforcing noncompete agreements entered into between management and a company buyer or financier. Most are also more lenient when the noncompete agreement is matched with significant severance payments that prevent the employee from being economically disadvantaged during the noncompete period.

It is difficult to draft an enforceable noncompete agreement, especially one that is not entered into in connection with a company financing. Only an attorney who is knowledgeable about his state's noncompete laws can insure that a noncompete agreement is drafted properly. When noncompete agreements are important, management should be sure to enlist the aid of a qualified attorney to either draft the agreement or consult with management as to the agreement's scope and enforceability.

Noncompete agreements are also used to protect company interests in other situations. Consultants or companies engaged to assist in developing technologies are often required to refrain from completing similar development strategies for company competitors for a period of time. Companies that participate in joint ventures or strategic partnerships routinely agree to refrain from competing with the business they jointly form. Management teams and owners of companies that are sold are routinely required not to compete for as long as five years with the business they sold. *See: Confidentiality Agreements, Golden Handcuffs, ISOs (Incentive Stock Options), Options, Think Capital, Vesting Schedules.*

**Nonrecourse Debt** is an obligation that entitles the holder to collect if the payor fails to pay only against assets pledged to that debt as collateral. A promissory note that permits the holder to take the collateral in payment of the note but not to collect from the maker personally in the event of a default is a nonrecourse debt. Sometimes investors use the term more broadly to refer to company debt that is not guaranteed by management in order to point out that the investor cannot look to the personal assets of individual management members to satisfy the loan. This type of debt is still recourse debt as it relates to the company borrowing the money. *See: Collateral, Personal Guarantees, Promissory Notes.*

**NASVF** refers to the National Association of Seed and Venture funds, a national network of private, public and non-profit organizations facilitating investment in entrepreneurs. The organization fosters the development of best practices for the seed and early stage investing community. It host annual events where education and networking promote the organizations goals. Their web site can be accessed at www.nasvf.org. *See: NVCA (National Venture Capital Association), NASBIC (National Association of Small Business Investment Companies).*

**NVCA** is the acronym for the National Venture Capital Association, national trade association of venture capital industry. Its members consist of venture capital firms and other managed pools of equity capital that invest in growing companies at all investment stages. A listing of the NVCA's members can be found on its web site at www.nvca.com. *See: NASVF (National Association of Seed and Venture Funds), NASBIC (National Association of Small Business Investment Companies).*

# O

## Off Balance Sheet Financing refers to ways
companies raise money or finance operations that do not
appear as loans or injections of capital on their financial
statements. Joint ventures, R & D partnerships, and leasing
(rather than purchases of capital equipment or real property)
are examples of off-balance sheet financing.

Joint ventures work by combining the know-how of one
party with another party's money and resources. The
company contributing know-how may receive royalties or a
share of the profits as the venture succeeds. The money
partner may also receive a share of the profits or ownership in
the venture. The know-how partner may retain significant
control over how the venture operates or share that authority.
The arrangements can also permit the know-how partner to
purchase the business of the joint venture or its product at a
future date. By using a joint venture instead of funding the
project out of its own funds, the know-how company can
accomplish an important objective while preserving its cash
for other purposes.

R & D partnerships work in much the same way.
Generally, a company contributes know-how about a certain
product to a limited partnership whose other partners
contribute money to fund further development of the product.
In this way the company gets its development funded without
affecting its balance sheet. If the development succeeds in

producing a marketable product, the company may either pay the partnership a royalty or purchase the product for a price that nets the contributing partners a fair return on their investment.

Leases preserve company funds by enabling a company to use equipment or property without having to purchase it. In so doing, the company can avoid the cost of a substantial down payment and does not show the leased equipment as an asset on its balance sheet. As with other off balance sheet financing techniques, leases can benefit a company by permitting it to accomplish a company goal with less cash.

Off balance sheet financing often depends on the ability to transfer some tax benefit to an investor or requires a company to part with more control or ownership of its product or know-how than it would otherwise. Sometimes the trade-off is in the upside potential to the company, with the company having to share more of the potential profit from a project to obtain off balance sheet financing than it would if it financed the activity in another way. But sometimes off balance sheet financing is the best or only alternative to keep a company project alive. When this is the case, the ability to keep a project going without depleting a company's other assets can mean more profits for the company and a better deal for the investor. *See: Cash Flow, Joint Ventures, Licensing, R&D Partnerships. See also: Joint Venture Checklist.*

**Offering Memos**, or memorandums, refer to written descriptions of securities offerings used to raise funds for company operations or expansion. They are usually prepared by management and company counsel and contain descriptions of the amount and type of security offered, the terms of the offering, the company's background and prospects, and the risks associated with purchasing company securities. Offering memos are sometimes referred to as private placement memos when they are used in private offerings of securities. The term prospectus is used to refer to an offering memo used in a public offering. *See: Private Placements, Prospectus, Public Offerings, Reg D, Restricted Securities, Safe Harbors, SEC (Securities and Exchange Commission), 10b5, 33 Act.*

## Operating Covenants

refer to agreements between an investor and management that outline undertakings management agrees to perform after the investor provides funding. Operating covenants are typically imposed on management at an equity or loan financing, where they are required as conditions to the receiving funding.

Sometimes called "affirmative covenants" and "negative covenants," these agreements commonly include the obligation to provide the investor with regular financial reports, to maintain the company's corporate status, and to continue pursuing the company's main business objectives. Operating covenants can also require management to achieve specified goals or to refrain from engaging in specified activities. *See: Affirmative Covenants, Loan Covenants, Negative Covenants, Reps and Warranties, Take Away Provisions.*

## Opinion Letters

are statements of legal counsel in correspondence form provided at the request of a party to a transaction. They contain counsel's opinion as to the manner in which the law applies to various aspects of the transaction being closed.

Venture capitalists usually require an opinion letter from the company's lawyer as a condition to funding. Commonly, these letters opine that:

- the company is duly incorporated and qualified to conduct its business,
- the number and character of company shares outstanding are as represented in the financing documents,

- the company has the authority to enter into and perform its obligations under the financing agreements,
- the financing agreements are valid, binding and enforceable against the company, and
- the company has no other agreements that conflict with the financing agreements.

Many of these opinions cover matters warranted to the investors by the company or management in the financing agreements. Venture capitalists usually require these opinions to provide an independent check of business law issues warranted by the company and management.

By contrast, venture investors rarely provide legal opinions to the companies they invest in. While some company counsel may ask for legal opinions, investors say their circumstances are different from the companies they invest in and opinions are not warranted. For one thing, investors put up cash and receive in return only promises and an opportunity to participate in a company's success. As a result, investors have good reason to be concerned about the details that insure him the company's representations are correct. By contrast, the company usually has more than the venture capitalist's promise in hand when the financing agreements are signed. It also has the venture capitalist's cash or, at least, a portion of the cash that has been promised.

This is not to say, however, that management should always forgo the opinion of investor's counsel. Depending upon the way in which the financing is structured, an opinion of investor's counsel on certain matters may be the best or only way management can protect itself from risk or liability. Company counsel can usually be the best judge of whether an opinion of investor's counsel is needed. *See: Financing Agreements, Reps and Warranties, Structure, Vesting Schedules.*

**Options** are contractual rights that entitle but do not obligate their holders to purchase company securities in the future for a predetermined price. Because they do not obligate the holder to purchase shares, they are not effective tools for raising capital. Options are effective at helping companies attract and retain qualified people. They are also used in connection with some loans and to reward outstanding performance.

The authority to grant options is vested in a company's board of directors. They are typically granted by a company's board of directors or a committee designated by the board. Shares that can be purchased through an option are referred to as the option shares. The purchase price for option shares is referred to as the exercise price or strike price. Options with exercise prices higher than the fair market value of the company's shares are considered to be "out of the money." Options with exercise prices lower than the fair market value of the company's shares are considered to be "in the money."

Option grants are usually for a fixed number of shares at a fixed price per share. Often, the option only becomes exercisable in the future or becomes exercisable as to progressively more shares as time passes. Exercise, or purchase of the shares, is effected by paying to the company the purchase price for the shares after the option becomes exercisable.

Options are effective in attracting and retaining employees because they give them the opportunity to share in the value created by a company's growth. For example, a company's board might grant a prospective executive employee an option to purchase 40,000 shares of company common stock at an exercise price of $.10 per share as an inducement to join the company. The right to purchase the option shares might be conditioned on the executive remaining employed by the company and might be staggered so that he would have to wait one year before purchasing the first 10,000 shares, with another 10,000 shares becoming available for purchase on the following three anniversaries.

Investors sometimes bargain for options when they fund a company. They do so because options enable them to increase the upside potential of their investment without obligating them to purchase additional shares. Options are sometimes used to provide investors with a measure of protection against future dilution of their ownership percentage. They do this by giving the investor the right to purchase securities in the future at today's price or another bargain price. Lenders sometimes request options, or warrants, in consideration of making a loan or granting an interest rate or term concession. *See: Equity Kickers, First Refusal Rights (Company), Golden Handcuffs, ISOs (Incentive Stock Options), Qualified Stock Option Plans, Warrants.*

# P

**Participating Preferred Stock** is a form of convertible preferred stock that entitles the holder to receive back his purchase price for the stock and, possibly, some guaranteed return before any funds are distributed to other shareholders and then to participate pro rata with the common shareholders in the remaining sale or liquidation proceeds.

The following example illustrates how a participating feature in a convertible preferred stock affects the investor's and management's return on investment. The example assumes the investor purchases 1 million shares of convertible preferred stock for $5 million when management owns 4 million shares of common stock and that the participating feature entitles the holder to receive back the purchase price of his preferred stock and then to participate pro rata in the remaining proceeds of a company sale as if he had converted his preferred stock into common stock.

The illustration shows the investor's and management's return if the company is later sold for $10 million, $20 million or $100 million.

| | Non-Participating | Participating |
|---|---|---|
| Preferred Purchase Price | $5 million | $5 million |
| Number of Shares | 1 million | 1 million |
| Other Shares - Common | 4 million | 4 million |
| | | |
| **$10 Million Sale Price Distribution** | | |
| Preferred | $2 million | $6 million |
| Common | $8 million | $4 million |
| | | |
| **$20 Million Sale Price Distribution** | | |
| Preferred | $4 million | $8 million |
| Common | $16 million | $12 million |
| | | |
| **$100 Million Sale Price Distribution** | | |
| Preferred | $20 million | $24 million |
| Common | $80 million | $76 million |

Like convertible preferred stock that does not have a participating feature, participating preferred stock provides the holder with defined preferences over the holders of the company's common stock. These preferences typically include enhanced voting rights, liquidation and dividend preferences, the option to convert into common stock, and antidilution protection.

Because of the extraordinary sale and liquidation preference in participating preferred stock, companies usually agree to sell participating preferred only when they receive a meaningful price or other concession in return. Whenever possible, managements negotiate sunset provisions into the preference that make it inoperative after a passage of time or in a sale or liquidation that generates an agreed upon minimum return.

For example, a participating feature could be made to apply only when the holder would receive less than three dollars for every dollar invested without the feature. Alternatively, the provision could have a catch-up feature that allows common shareholders not protected by the participating feature to receive a catch-up payment from remaining sale proceeds before the participating stock begins pro rata with common. The chart below illustrates the effect including the three-dollar condition or a catch-up provision where the amount of the catch-up is equal to the total dollar amount of the preference.

| | $3 Condition | Catch-Up Provision |
|---|---|---|
| Participating Preferred Price | $5 million | $5 million |
| Number of Shares | 1 million | 1 million |
| Other Shares - Common | 4 million | 4 million |
| | | |
| $20 Million Sale Price Distribution | | |
| Preferred | $8 million | $7 million |
| Common | $12 million | $13 million |
| | | |
| $100 Million Sale Price Distribution | | |
| Preferred | $20 million | $23 million |
| Common | $80 million | $77 million |

As is apparent from the charts, the details of a participation provision can have dramatic effects on the ultimate return to the preferred investor and other investors not protected by the participating provisions. The inclusion of a participating feature or a limitation on its application can redirect millions of dollars of proceeds from a later sale by the company. *See: Antidilution Provisions, Convertible Preferred Stock, Convertible Securities, Preferred Stock Umbrella.*

**Patents** refer to limited government monopolies bestowed on inventors who create a sufficiently novel product or process and file the necessary applications. A grant of patent enables the inventor to prohibit others from making his invention in the United States for up to twenty years. Other countries provide similar patent rights.

To obtain a patent, an inventor must file a patent application, which describes the best form of the invention and why it is an improvement on the existing state of the art. The application is made in confidence to the U.S. Patent Office, where it is examined for novelty. If a patent is issued, the invention is made public by the patent office, and the inventor relies upon the patent to prevent others from copying his invention. If a patent is not issued, the patent office makes no public disclosure, and the inventor is left to rely on the trade secrecy of the invention to protect it from being copied.

Only individuals can be inventors, and only inventors and their assignees are entitled to patent protection. As a result, it is important for companies to take steps to insure that they obtain the patent rights to inventions developed by their employees and others hired to conduct research. Employee inventions often become the property of the employer by operation of law, but there are exceptions to this rule that depend on the scope of the employee's job responsibilities and the manner in which the invention is developed. To be certain of acquiring the patent rights to which they are entitled, companies should require their employees and consultants to enter into written agreements that clearly set out the company's rights to inventions. In many cases, these agreements can be included as part of an employment or secrecy contract.

Patents are not always the best way to protect an invention. This is because they require a high degree of inventive novelty before they are available, they require the inventor to disclose his invention to the public, and their issuance does not guarantee their validity (and thus enforceability) against a challenge by a competitor. The high degree of novelty required means that many inventions may not qualify for patent protection even though they may qualify for trade secrets protection. Even for a sufficiently novel invention, the patent disclosure may enable others to reconstruct the invention and help them design around the scope of the claims in the patent. Also, patent disclosures allow others to examine the invention's patent for weaknesses that might enable them to challenge its validity. If they succeed, the inventor's patent protection will be lost, and he will be unable to protect his invention as a trade secret.

There are many situations in which a company might choose to forgo patent protection in favor of trade secrecy protection. For example, if the new product cannot be reverse engineered or reinvented (that is, a competitor cannot duplicate it once it appears in the marketplace), trade secrecy protection, which is not limited to a term of years, might serve the company's interests better.

The formula for Coca-Cola® is one example of a product that was better protected by keeping secret its ingredients than it would have been by applying for patent protection. If Coca-Cola had secured patent protection, its formula would now be available to everyone as a matter of law. By keeping it secret instead of securing a patent, Coca-Cola has managed to retain the exclusive rights to the formulation long after its patent monopoly would have expired.

Sometimes a new product does not warrant the cost or time necessary to secure patent protection. A newly invented process that is only one of many cost-effective methods for obtaining a certain result may not give the inventor a sufficient competitive advantage to warrant the expense of preparing and filing for a patent. If the patentable portion of a new product does not add significantly to its commercial value, or the application for the patent would require disclosing other proprietary methods that are valuable but cannot be protected by a patent, reason may suggest that the patent process is better ignored. Sometimes a company simply cannot afford to apply for patent protection in every country in which it needs it and so forgoes it in the United States to avoid disclosing its invention to the world and losing its ability to claim the protection of secrecy elsewhere.

Any inventor who is concerned about protecting an invention should consult with an experienced attorney. An attorney who specializes in patent law can provide a complete explanation of the patent process and the advantages of choosing patents or trade secrecy to protect an invention. There are many pitfalls in the patent process, including strict time limits during which a patent application must be filed in order to qualify. Foreign patents must be timely filed also, or the ability to secure them can be lost. Only an experienced patent attorney can guide an inventor through the process without the inadvertent loss of protection. *See: Employment Contracts, Licensing, Trade Secrets.*

**Pay-to-Play** refers to conditions imposed by lead investors in venture financings that motivate investors to invest more money in future fundraisings. The motivation to reinvest is the prospect of forfeiting value in their existing shares if they do not participate in future investments. The value forfeiture is frequently built into terms of the security they purchase. The feature might reduce the value of the security purchased by reducing the number of shares of common stock that their security stock can convert into if the investor does not "play" in the future round or it might reduce other preferences.

Pay-to-pay also refers to conditions imposed in down round financings by the new investor that cause existing investors to forfeit value if they do not reinvest in the current down round. The lead investor imposes the conditions by refusing to fund unless the conditions are met. The new investor's conditions work with the issuance of large numbers of shares in the new funding to remove much of the value from existing shareholdings. The company and prior investors concede to the conditions because other funding opportunities are unavailable and funding is needed to continue operations.

Pay-to-play financings of the this second sort typically involve the issuance of large numbers of shares at low prices to new investors that effectively dilute the percentage ownership of existing investors to very small percentages. The incentive for existing investors to reinvest in the new round is the ability granted to those who reinvest to convert the stock the purchased earlier into a new class of stock with preferences that give it greater value. The provisions have the effect of punishing existing investors who do not participate in the new financing by further reducing the value of their existing shareholdings.

One pay-to-play approach has the company amend its charter to create a new series of convertible preferred stock into which shareholders who invest in the down round may convert their existing convertible preferred stock. The amended series of stock allows holders to convert their shares of preferred stock into more shares of common stock than the preexisting preferred stock. Existing investors who participate purchase stock with the new investors in a convertible preferred stock created for their investment and obtain this additional right convert their existing shares of preferred stock into the new enhanced preferred stock. Existing investors who do not put new money into the company are left with their original, now devalued, convertible preferred stock.

For example, participating investors in a new Series B round might be allowed as a part of their purchase of Series B stock to convert their existing Series A into a newly created preferential Series A-2 stock. The preference might be a revised conversion formula that increases the number of shares of common stock they are entitled to receive on conversion by a factor of five, where the new conversion more closely resembles the value afforded in the subsequent Series B down round. Nonparticipating investors are left with the original Series A stock.

In the example, two Series A investors who invested $1 million each for 500,000 shares at $2.00 each representing a total of 40% of a company each might see the value of their investment largely wiped-out by a new Series B investment. If the Series B investor invests $4 million at $.10 per share, he will receive 40 million shares for his investment, dramatically reducing the ownership percentage represented by the Series A stock. By participating in the Series B round, a Series A investor might not only receive $.10 stock but also be allowed to convert his Series A stock into a newly created Series A-2 stock that converts into 4 million shares instead of 500,000. The resulting capitalization of the company before and after the down round might look like this.

| | Share Class | Common Share Equivalents After A Round | Common Share Equivalents After B Round |
|---|---|---|---|
| Nonparticipating Investor 1 | Series A | 500,000 | 500,000 |
| Participating Investor 2 | Series A | 500,000 | 0 |
| Participating Investor 2 | Series A-2 | | 4,000,000 |
| Participating Investor 2 | Series B | | 5,000,000 |
| Common Stockholders | Common | 1,000,000 | 1,000,000 |
| Employee Option Plan | Common | 500,000 | 500,000 |
| New Preferred Investor 3 | Series B | | 40,000,000 |
| Fully Diluted Shares | | 2,500,000 | 51,000,000 |

In the foregoing example, the Series B down round effectively dilutes the ownership of the nonparticipating preferred investor 1 from 20% to less than 1% of the fully diluted outstanding shares. The second preferred investor who participates by investing $500,000 in the Series B round sees his Series A investment convert into a Series A-2 stock that converts into 7.8% of the outstanding stock and acquires new stock representing 9.8% of the outstanding stock for a total holding of 17.6%. Common shareholders see their 20% holding reduced to less than 2%, with employee option holders falling below 1%. *See: Antidilution Provisions, Convertible Preferred Stock, Dilution (Percentage), Dilution (Value), Down Round, Convertible Securities, Follow-on Fundings, Participating Preferred Stock, Preferred Stock Umbrella.*

**P/E** is a commonly used abbreviation for the price-earnings ratio. It refers to a multiple applied to a company's earnings (net operating profit after tax) to estimate its value. For example, a company with earnings of $500,000 and a P/E of twelve would have an estimated value of $6 million (or twelve times $500,000). Dividing that value by the number of outstanding shares gives an estimated value for each share of company stock. *See: Price-Earnings Ratio, Pricing.*

**Penny Stock** refers to publicly traded stock that trades for $5 or less per share. Often, the phrase penny stock is used to indicate shares that actually trade for pennies. Penny stock also refers to an alternative form of venture financing, in which money is raised through a public offering of company stock at prices as low as ten shares for a dollar. Usually, the penny stock offering is underwritten by a professional underwriter who, for a fee, structures the financing and uses his best efforts to sell the shares.

In most cases, the underwriter charges a fee up front for conducting the offering. The underwriter receives additional compensation if he successfully completes the offering. Often, the charges are steep. They reflect the level of risk the underwriter accepts in agreeing to put together the offering. As with all initial public offerings, the other costs associated with completing an offering are high as well. These include the cost of management's involvement in the public offering, the cost of preparing an offering circular and complying with federal and state securities laws, and the costs of engaging independent accountants and lawyers to complete the project.

Entrepreneurs who attempt penny stock offerings often do so in lieu of trying to raise money from private investors. Many do so because they are unable to attract funds from private investors. Others believe they can raise money more cheaply in the public market even after paying the high transaction costs associated with a public offering. Still others enter the penny stock market to increase the liquidity of their shareholdings by creating a public market for shares they may hold personally.

Whatever the reason, management should consider carefully the potential ramifications of a penny stock deal before rushing into one. Many professional investors view a penny stock offering as an indication of weakness and hesitate to participate in later rounds of funding. The large number of shareholders a penny stock offering creates can discourage later investments by venture investors. This is because a large class of unsophisticated and unrepresented (by virtue of their inability to elect a representative to the company's board of directors) shareholders exposes directors to greater potential liability for shareholder suits claiming the directors have not fulfilled their fiduciary responsibilities. A sophisticated investor willing to provide significant funding may want a voice in management but not potential liability to a large class of investors.

Some observers believe that selling penny stock depresses the trading value of the company's stock over the long term. These observers contend that investors always will think of the company as a bargain-basement company whose stock price reflects its low value (as compared to companies with higher-priced stocks). Others contend that penny stock attracts speculative investors whose frequent trading on small price gains makes it difficult for a company to sustain a long-term increase in share price. Overcoming these market disadvantages can be difficult and make it harder for the price of the company's stock to increase significantly.

On the other hand it may be true for a given company that a penny stock offering to the public can command a better price per share than a corresponding offering to private investors because the liquidity of publicly tradable shares adds to their value. If the liquidity adds enough value to offset the high costs of conducting the offering, a penny stock offering may be the least expensive way to raise money.

When alternative sources of funds are not available at reasonable prices, a penny stock offering may be a company's only real alternative for raising money. When this is the case, comparing the relative advantages of conducting a public offering to private funding may be irrelevant.

However, in every other case, management should consider other alternatives carefully before engaging an underwriter and initiating a penny stock offering. In their analysis, management should consider whether the liquidity created by a public offering will create enough extra value to offset the high transaction costs associated with such offering and whether this extra value is worth the extra hassle and expense associated with being a public company. In making the decision, management should also evaluate how likely it is that going public with a penny stock will depress the growth of market value for the stock and, thereby, make future financings more costly to the company than they might otherwise be. *See: Going Public, IPOs (Initial Public Offerings), Mezzanine Financing, Private Placements, Public Offerings, Reg D, Underwriters, Unit Offerings.*

**Performance Options** are options to purchase company stock that become exercisable only when the option holder, usually an employee, meets a predefined performance objective, such as obtaining sales of $1 million in a fiscal year. Employers like performance based incentives when they motivate employees to achieve a measurable objective.

Performance options are used sparingly, however, particularly in companies that plan to go public. This is because of accounting issues that can force a company to record a charge against earnings when a performance option matures and becomes exercisable. This reduction in earnings, if great enough, can make a company a less desirable candidate for a public offering. It can also cause a company to violate a financial ratio covenant in its loan agreements.

Current accounting standards can require a company to book a charge against its earnings when the option becomes exercisable (when the performance is achieved) if the fair market value of the option shares is greater than the option's exercise price. Growing companies usually plan for increasing valuations and set exercise prices in their qualified options at fair market value at the time of option grant. If the company's value increases as planned, a charge to earnings is certain when the performance is achieved at a later date. The accounting rules applicable to performance options are complex. A qualified accountant should be consulted before granting performance options. *See: Going Public, ISOs (Incentive Stock Options), Options.*

**Personal Guarantees** are promises made by an individual to personally repay debts defaulted upon by another party. Often, the other party is a business owned or managed by the guarantor. The guarantee is usually granted only because the lender requires it as a condition to making the loan. Entrepreneurs are frequently asked to guarantee payment of company debt or lease obligations. Sometimes, personal guarantees are supported by the granting of security interests or mortgages on the guarantor's personal assets.

Not all personal guarantees are equal. Entrepreneurs should be aware of the concessions lenders sometimes make so that they can negotiate to reduce their personal exposure under their guarantees. For example, when two or more company officers are asked to guarantee a single loan each officer may be liable to repay the entire amount of the loan or just a pro rata portion. Also, the availability of company assets to secure part of a loan can sometimes be used to limit a guarantee to a portion of the dollar value of the loan. On long-term loans, provisions can sometimes be negotiated that cancel the guarantee upon the happening of some future event, such as the passage of time, the infusion of new equity into the company, or the payment of a portion of the loan.

Another way to reduce exposure under a guarantee, when there is more than one guarantor, is with a contribution agreement. Most guarantees enable the lender to collect the entire default amount from any of the guarantors. A contribution agreement among the guarantors can give the guarantor who is called upon to pay under a guarantee the contractual right to require the other guarantors to contribute money to cover part of the guarantee payments.

Personal guarantees are not required in equity financings. Many venture financings, however, are made up of debt and equity. As a result, investors that fund companies with both debt and equity sometimes ask management to guarantee the debt portion of the financing. A personal guarantee in such a situation, however, may not be appropriate. If the funding is essentially a debt financing with attached stock rights given as a bonus, a guarantee may be unavoidable. When a financing is essentially an investment of equity with a portion characterized as debt to sweeten the deal for the investor, management is justified in objecting to guaranteeing the debt portion of what is really an equity financing. *See: Buy-Sell Agreements, Nonrecourse Debt.*

**Phantom Stock Plans** are employee benefit plans that give participating employees many of the benefits of stock ownership without actually giving them company stock. Instead of giving key employees stock or stock options, the company adopts a phantom stock plan and credits each key employee with a number of units of "phantom" stock. Each unit increases in value as the company's shares of common stock do and as dividends are declared but no unit entitles any holder to any stockholder rights.

When a participant retires or his rights in the plan otherwise vest, he receives an amount equal to the appreciation in value of a share of the company's common stock plus the amount of any declared dividends for each of his vested units. For example, if the company's common stock is worth $5 a share when the units are distributed and worth $10 a share when the employee's right to draw against the plan vests, the employee will receive $5 per unit. He will also receive an amount equal to any dividends declared on the common stock while he held the unit. The total amount the employee receives will be taxable at ordinary income tax rates.

Phantom stock plans have certain advantages over actual stock plans. For one thing, they permit company employees to participate directly in the increased value of the company stock without giving them voting rights. Also, they do not dilute the ownership percentages of the company's stockholders. For cosmetic purposes, management can design phantom stock certificates that closely approximate actual stock certificates in appearance so that the units the employees receive look very much like company share certificates. *See: Compensation and Bonus Plans, Golden Handcuffs, ISOs (Incentive Stock Options), Qualified Stock Option Plans.*

**Piggyback Rights** are contractual rights that entitle investors to register and sell their shares of company stock whenever the company conducts a public offering. Unlike demand rights, piggyback rights do not entitle investors to require a company to conduct a public offering but, rather, allow them to include shares in a registration that is initiated by the company.

Piggyback rights usually appear as provisions in a financing agreement, an investor rights agreement, or a registration rights agreement. Piggyback rights are common in venture financings. Because share registration is often necessary to permit the sale of stock to the public, registration rights give investors a way to cash out all or a part of their investment. Venture capitalists routinely require piggyback registration rights as a condition to providing funding.

Piggyback rights should be evidenced in a written agreement to be sure an underwriter will honor them. If management wants piggyback rights, these too should be reflected in a written agreement. Except for certain fees required by various state securities law administrators to be shared by all selling shareholders, companies usually bear the cost of investors exercising piggyback rights. *See: Cashing Out (or In), Demand Rights, Exits, Registration Rights, Registration Rights Agreements, Shareholders' Agreements.*

## PIPE (Private Investment in Public Equity) refers to a method public companies use to raise capital, often when the public offering market is unreceptive and other easier or more attractive fundraising avenues are unavailable. A PIPE involves the sale of the public company's unregistered securities, frequently common stock or a convertible debt or equity security, to a limited number of accredited investors pursuant to a private placement exemption. The company typically agrees, as part of the sale, to register the privately sold shares for resale in the public markets after a brief period of time. After the sale, the company registers the shares with the SEC, enabling the investors to sell the shares into the public market.

The security can be sold in the PIPE at a fixed price or at a price that floats based on the public price of the company's securities. The price charged to the PIPE investor is typically discounted when compared to shares freely traded in the company's public market. This is because the shares are not freely tradable at the time of their purchase and are, therefore, less valuable. Sometimes, the PIPE investor also receives warrants to purchase company stock in the future as part of the transaction.

Qualified investment bankers frequently assist in structuring and completing PIPEs. Company securities counsel are routinely involved in structuring and documenting the transaction and the security registration that follows.

PIPEs typically unfold in the following manner. Company management reviews the possibility of conducting a PIPE with their counsel and interviews one or more qualified investment bankers to assist and act as the placement agent in the private placement. The agent solicits interest from a select and limited group of accredited investors. These investors may be institutions or wealthy individuals. The solicitation may or may not include the use of a traditional private placement memorandum.

The company then negotiates and completes a stock purchase and registration rights agreement with the interested investors. Once the sale is complete, the company announces the sale to the public and begins preparation of the documents needed to register the investors' stock for resale into the public market. The company later files the registration statement and the PIPE investors are free to sell their shares into the public market. This registration occurs only after the sale of the PIPE is complete so that the private offering is not integrated into the later public offering.

The principal disadvantage of a PIPE when compared to a public offering of company securities is the price obtained for the securities, which are routinely sold to the PIPE investor at a discount to reflect the liquidity risk the investor takes until the securities are actually registered for resale. The advantages of a PIPE include:

- *Speed and lower cost.* Because the investment documents are not reviewed by the SEC and no general solicitation is involved, PIPEs can be completed more quickly and cheaply than public offerings. It is not uncommon for a PIPE offering to be completed in less than a month. Registered public offerings take much longer.
- *Price.* Even though PIPEs are sold at a discount to current public market price, this discounted price can still be higher than what the public offering price would have been. Public markets can be unpredictable and company stock prices sometimes fall after a secondary public offering of securities is announced. The PIPE price is typically discounted against the company's public security price determined before announcement of the PIPE.
- *Confidentiality and reduced volatility.* Because the sale by the company is completed before public announcement, the transaction is confidential until closed. The limited number of accredited investors permitted in a PIPE makes the PIPE offering less subject to volatility than a registered public offering.
- *Reduced time consumption.* PIPEs are less time consuming to complete than public offerings.

Notwithstanding their advantages, PIPEs are usually entered into cautiously and carefully structured. Care must be taken by the company and the investment banker to conduct the offering in a way that complies with applicable securities laws. The very existence of a PIPE program, when it involves raising substantial capital and is kept confidential, constitutes material insider information that should keep company management and investor prospects out of the public market. If information leaks out before the transaction, short sellers can enter the company's public market and drive securities prices down.

The PIPE program also increases the company's need to make full public disclosure of relevant material information so that the information available to the public and the PIPE investors about the company's operations is equivalent. The increased disclosure can sometimes tip off savvy short sellers to the fact that a PIPE is being conducted and lead to downward pressure on the company's public securities prices. As a consequence, PIPEs need to be carefully managed to accomplish management objectives. *See: Going Public, Integration, Investment Bankers, IPO, Private Placement, Public Offering, Reg D, Restricted Securities, SEC.*

**Poison Pill** refers to an anti-takeover device employed by public companies. It usually appears as part of a stockholders rights plan that grants existing shareholders the option, triggered by an attempted hostile takeover, to purchase additional shares of common stock at a significant discount. The discount is not available to the party attempting the hostile takeover. The options become exercisable when the acquirer purchases a predefined percentage of the company's outstanding stock, such as 5% or 10%. The exercise of the options dramatically increases the number of shares of stock that must be purchased to obtain control, thereby discouraging the acquirer from attempting to purchase control without negotiating directly with the company's management and board of directors. In a friendly acquisition, the board of directors can disable the poison pill, making it easier to purchase the company. *See: Shark Repellents.*

**Pool** is a term frequently used to refer to venture capital and other private equity funds. The term comes from the investors in the fund pooling or commingling their investments to create the fund. Typically, these pools are managed by professional managers who receive a small percentage of the funds under management as an annual management fee. They also commonly receive a share of the partnership's profits, called "carried interest", as well. This carried interest portion provides an incentive for the venture managers to invest wisely. Typical venture fund investors include pension funds, insurance companies, corporations, and individuals. *See: Venture Capitalists.*

## Post-Money Valuation

refers to the value of a company after an investor's money is invested. It is usually contrasted with the term "pre-money valuation" that refers to the value of the company before the investment is made. For example, a company with a post-money valuation of $15 million after receiving $5 million in investment would have a pre-money valuation of $10 million consisting of the $15 million post-money value of the company minus the $5 million to be invested. *See: Discounted Cash Flow, Fully Diluted, Pre-Money Valuation, Pricing, Valuation.*

## Preemptive Rights

are entitlements that existing shareholders have to purchase new shares of stock issued by a company. In some states, these rights automatically exist unless the company's articles of incorporation specifically waive them. In other states, they do not exist unless they are specifically granted in the company's articles of incorporation. Preemptive rights can also be created by contract and are frequently requested by venture capital investors.

Preemptive rights can complicate future fundraisings. By forcing a company to offer its shares to existing shareholders before it offers them to outside investors, these rights can postpone the sale of company shares to outsiders. Because the share offering needs to be offered pro rata among existing shareholders, preemptive rights can even delay funding from an existing investor by requiring the company to first offer a percentage of the shares the investor wants to purchase to the other existing shareholders.

When companies with preemptive rights fail to follow the necessary procedures, they can complicate future fundraisings and create rights in shareholders who have not waived their rights. This can make it difficult to determine what preemptive rights each shareholder is entitled to receive and to whom the company is entitled to sell shares. Untangling such a mess can be costly and time-consuming.

*See: Antidilution Provisions, Charter, Dilution (Percentage), First Refusal Rights (Shareholders).*

**Preferred Stock** is a form of equity ownership in a corporation that contains preferences over common stock. Typically these preferences include rights to receive dividends at a fixed rate or the right to receive dividends before holders of common stock. Sometimes they include preferences in voting, rights to veto certain company actions, or rights to cause their shares to be redeemed. In a liquidation of the company, preferred stockholders with liquidation preferences are paid their preference amounts before common stockholders but after creditors.

When used in venture capital transactions, preferred stock often includes a convertibility feature. That is, it is exchangeable for common stock at the will of the investor or upon the happening of some event. When preferred stock has this feature it is referred to as convertible preferred stock. *See: Common Stock, Convertible Preferred Stock, Convertible Securities, Debentures, Preferred Stock Umbrellas.*

**Preferred Stock Umbrellas** refer to a common form of venture capital financing in which the investors are issued convertible preferred stock while management and founding shareholders hold common stock. The structure is frequently used when management receives its shares at or about the same time as the outside investors but it is also commonly used in other situations.

The preferred stock terms give their holders significant preferences compared to management and other holders of common stock. These preferences make their convertible preferred shares more valuable on a share for share basis than the common stock held by management and others.

These preferences also establishes the basis for selling common stock at lower prices. The need for this arises when management desires to issue cheaper shares to attract or retain important employees or when management shareholders purchase less expensive shares of common stock at or about the same time the preferred stock is sold. Without a real value difference between the convertible preferred shares issued to outside investors and the common stock issued to management, the IRS might treat the difference in share prices as "hidden income" to management and tax management on the amount of that difference times the number of shares purchased by them at the lower price.[*]

This result can be avoided, however, to the extent the preferences granted to the convertible preferred shareholders convey real value. The preferences granted can include the rights to receive dividends and distributions in liquidation before holders of common stock, voting preferences, management influence, stock registration rights, preemptive rights, and rights of first refusal and cosale with management shareholders. To the extent additional value is given to the shares purchased by the outside investor, management can reasonably contend that a lower price per share is justified for their common shares. When this is the case, management can issue common shares at lower prices without the risk of hidden taxable income.

Another way to reduce the likelihood of hidden income is to have management purchase their shares long before the

---

[*] Note, though, that if a tax is charged to the management shareholder, this hidden income may be deductible by the company if it withholds taxes from other payments to the shareholder.

investors buy their shares. The longer the period of time between the two purchases, the easier it is to argue that the company's stock was worth less when purchased. Neither the preferred stock umbrella nor the passage of time between purchases, however, can guarantee that management shareholders will not be taxed on hidden income - they only reduce the likelihood of being taxed and, then, only to the extent they create distinctions that reflect real differences in value.

Structuring a financing so that outside investors receive preferred stock while insiders receive common stock can also make it easier for management to use common stock to attract and retain key personnel. This is because shares issued to employees must be issued at their fair market value, or the IRS may claim that the recipient must pay taxes on the difference between the fair market value of the stock and the purchase price. If only one class of common stock has been issued, the best evidence of the fair market value may be the price per share paid by the outside investors. If little time has transpired since the outside investors bought shares or the company is growing or becoming more profitable, a lower valuation is unlikely. In other words, the issue price of the shares used to attract a new key employee will probably have to be as high or higher than the price paid by the outside investors.

If, instead, the outside investors purchase convertible preferred stock with preferences that add real value, the company may be justified in issuing common stock to new employees at prices that are lower than that paid by the venture investor. This can make it easier for new employees to purchase shares and make the purchase more attractive. The justifiable difference in prices, of course, depends on a real difference between the value of the preferred shares and the common shares.

As a practical matter, most venture investors insist on acquiring convertible preferred stock as a condition to funding because of the preferences and rights they give to their holders. One of the most common venture investment vehicles is the convertible, redeemable preferred stock instrument. Because complex issues are raised when preferred stock is issued, management shareholders should review their situation carefully with experienced legal counsel before proceeding. *See: Convertible Preferred Stock, Convertible Securities, ISOs (Incentive Stock Options), Participating Preferred Stock, Preferred Stock, Pricing, Unit Offerings.*

**Pre-Money Valuation** refers to the value of a company before an investor's money is invested. It is usually contrasted with post-money valuation that combines a company's pre-money valuation with the value of the money invested. For example, a company with a pre-money valuation of $10 million that receives $5 million in investment would have a post-money valuation of $15 million consisting of the $10 million pre-money value of the company plus the $5 million invested. *See: Discounted Cash Flow, Fully Diluted, Post-Money Valuation, Pricing, Valuation.*

**Price-Earnings Ratio** is the relationship of the market value of a company's stock to its after-tax earnings expressed as a fraction, with the current share price as the numerator and the current per share after-tax earnings as the denominator. For example, if a company's stock sells for $10 a share and its per-share earnings for the year is $1, the company's price-earnings (or P/E) ratio is ten to one, or ten. Companies in industries that boast high P/Es make attractive investments for venture capitalists because they require fewer dollars of earnings to support a high company valuation and stock price. *See: Emerging Growth Companies, P/E, Pricing.*

**Pricing** refers to the process of determining the cost of new money to a company and its shareholders. In pure equity investments, like a venture capital preferred stock investment, the pricing process determines how many shares of stock an investor receives for his investment.

**Factors involved in pricing.** How much equity must a company sell to attract an investor? Unfortunately, there is no easy answer. Venture capitalists weight many factors when deciding how much equity they want in return for their investments. The amount of equity (or price) they want for their money depends on:

- when they think the company can attract a profitable buyout or go public at an attractive price,
- what they expect the total value of the company to be at that time, and
- how likely the company is to reach that goal on schedule.

Investors also consider:

- how much of its own money management has invested in the company,
- how much more money the company will need before it can support a profitable exit like a public offering, and
- how likely the company is to fail to achieve its goals and how much of the investment they will recoup if the company does fail.

Other factors affect pricing as well. For instance, if a venture capitalist invests all of his money in stock, he will probably expect a higher percentage of equity than if he puts part of his money into stock and the rest into a senior security or debenture. An investor who puts his money into a company in stages instead of all at once can afford to take less equity since a portion of his money is invested only after the company has met goals that reduce the risk of later investments. The availability of collateral can also reduce a company's cost of funding by reducing the downside risk of the investor.

The stock market affects pricing too. If the initial public offering market is supporting high price to earnings (P/E) ratios for businesses in the company's industry, investors are more likely to be enthusiastic and use a higher P/E when evaluating the company. This higher P/E means the company can raise its funding with fewer shares of stock. By contrast, if the market is doing poorly, investors will tend to think in terms of lower P/Es and require more shares to do the same funding.

**Arriving at a pricing proposal.** Despite all these variables, venture capitalists do make concrete funding proposals to companies that are specific about price. How do they do it? Most often, the process goes something like this: After reviewing the company and its business, the venture capitalist determines what rate of return he thinks he needs to justify the investment. He knows the return he normally requires in similar-stage investments, but in making this one he will determine whether the risks are greater than normal. If he usually requires a 40 percent compounded annual rate of return and this investment is riskier, he may require a higher rate. If the company's success is more certain, he may take less.

Having arrived at an appropriate rate of return, the investor next analyzes the company's projections and its own ideas about how the company is likely to progress to determine when he thinks the company will be ready for a profitable exit and how the company should be performing by then. In this exercise, investors frequently discount the projections of a company by adding costs they believe have been under estimated or postponing revenues they believe are too aggressively assumed. The sooner the venture capitalist thinks the company will be ready for a profitable exit, and the greater he believes its after-tax earnings will be, the lower his price for providing the funding.

*Investors, Deal Structures, Legal Strategies - 285*

After this, the investor investigates the P/Es of publicly traded businesses in the same industry as the company. To the extent the information is available, the investor also will look at the P/Es paid for companies in the same industry that have been sold. Usually, this means that the venture capitalist compares the P/Es of several of the company's competitors in the present market. If there have been any recent sales or public offerings by competitors, he will be most interested in those transactions. Although the investor is interested in estimating an appropriate P/E for the company when it is ready to go sell or go public, the present P/Es of the company's competitors usually make the greatest impression on the investor. If the stocks of the industry leaders are selling at 20 times earnings, and smaller competitors are selling at between 15 and ten times earnings, the venture capitalist will probably pick a number between 15 and ten depending on when he expects the company to be ready to go public.

Once these decisions are made, the investor computes what percentage of the company's stock he needs to acquire in order to give him his rate of return based on his assumptions of value, timing, and P/Es. After this, he may adjust his percentage up or down depending on whether he feels he has adequately considered his downside risk or the likelihood that the company will not make its projections.

**Pricing example.** For example, an investor who needs a 38 percent annual rate of return may determine, that the company he is considering will be ready for to be sold or to conduct its initial public offering in five years when, he estimates, its sales will reach $8 million and its after-tax earnings will be $800,000. A company of that size with those earnings, he believes, should support a P/E of 15. If he invests $600,000, and no additional equity funding is needed before the company is sold or goes public, the investor would compute his price proposal by multiplying the company's projected earnings of $800,000 by the P/E of 15 to project a value for the company of $12 million in five years. In order to obtain a 38 percent rate of return in the fifth year, the investor must receive five times the amount of his $600,000 investment, or $3 million. To do this, the investor must own 25 percent of the company's equity when it goes public in five years with a $12 million valuation.

This is a simplistic example and it only one way of arriving at a valuation. The actual process can be less analytical or more so. The investor can employ a number of different techniques that evaluate not only the prospect of success but also the probable value of his equity if the company is only moderately successful or unsuccessful. He may also place more emphasis on other methods of valuation, such as the discounted cash flow method described elsewhere in this book. Factors such as the need for additional funding and the structure of the funding can complicate the pricing analysis. Nonetheless, this example portrays the fundamentals of venture capital pricing and provides management with a yardstick it can use to evaluate an investor's funding proposal.

**Evaluating a pricing proposal.** How does management a funding proposal and negotiate a better price (that is, reduce the percentage of equity the company must sell) or improve the terms of the offering? First, ask the investor how he arrived at his price. Sometimes the investor will give a detailed explanation of his assumptions and method of pricing so that management can evaluate its fairness. Even if the investor is vague, often he will explain when he thinks the company will grow to a size large enough to support a public offering and what size and how profitable he thinks it will be then. He might also tell management what he thinks will be an appropriate P/E for the company.

Even without this information, management can still analyze a funding offer and respond with intelligent proposals for reducing the company's cost of capital. Consider the following scenario: Zano Co. develops and markets specialty materials. It has current sales of $500,000 and is looking for $700,000 to fund expanded activities, which management asserts will position the company for an exit in three years. At that time, management forecasts sales of $20 million and after-tax earnings of $500,000. At present, the stock market is sluggish, and Zano's publicly held competitors support P/Es of between five to 20 times earnings. Publicly held competitors with sales and earnings similar to Zano's projected sales in three years are supporting P/Es of between ten and 15. Six months ago, when the market was bullish, similar companies were supporting P/Es of between 20 and 30.

The venture capitalist says he thinks the company's projections are unrealistic and that it will probably not be able to support a public offering until its fourth year. At that time he thinks the company may have reached $20 million in sales and $500,000 in earnings. He offers to fund the $700,000 needed in return for 56 percent of the company's outstanding common stock.

Is the offer fair? What assumptions is the investor making? To answer these questions, management needs to conduct its own analysis of pricing.

The first thing for Zano's management to do is pick a P/E for the purpose of estimating company value. The P/Es for similar companies range from a high of thirty in the best markets to a low of ten in sluggish ones. Assuming a P/E of ten in the worst case, the investor is asking for 56 percent of ten times the $500,000 earnings he projects the company will make in its fourth year. In other words, the venture capitalist expects a return equal to 56 percent of $5 million in four years. Assuming the lowest P/E, this means that in four years the investor expects to hold $2.8 million worth of company stock in return for making a $700,000 investment today. Stated another way, he expects to receive a return of $4 for each $1 he invested four years earlier. In percentages, this is a compounded annual rate of return of 41 percent.

Assuming a P/E of twenty makes the investor's return much higher. At this rate, the company's $500,000 earnings will be worth 20 times $500,000, or $10 million, and the investor's 56 percent will be worth $5.6 million, or eight times his original investment four years earlier.

Now management should evaluate the company based on its own projections and a fair but conservative P/E. These projections assume the company will generate $500,000 of profits in its third year. If management splits the difference between the best and worst possible P/Es and uses twenty, then Zano could be worth $10 million in three years. To give the investor a 44 percent compounded annual return on his investment would triple his money in three years. In other words, the investor's stock should then be worth three times $700,000, or $2.1 million. The percentage of stock necessary to generate this value would be 21 percent. This is much less than the 56 percent originally proposed.

**Pricing negotiations.** Despite all the computations of management and investors, the price the venture capitalist will receive for his investment will be the one the parties agree on. The foregoing illustration, however, does give management some clues as to how to negotiate to reduce the percentage of equity the venture capitalist will be willing to take and still do the deal. To reduce the price, management must convince the investor that some of his assumptions are unrealistically conservative or that his return on investment is too high. (The latter may be close to impossible to accomplish.) As one might expect, these discussions usually go best for management when the investor believes the company has other investors or sources of funds giving him competitive reasons to revisit his analysis.

Several pricing assumptions are always open to further analysis and refinement. These include the following:

- *The P/E employed by the investor.* A higher P/E ratio would reduce the cost of the company's funding. How did the investor arrive at the P/E he chose? Have higher P/Es dominated the industry? Is his P/E based on current P/Es in a sluggish market? Does the investor really believe the low P/E he chose will prevail when the company is ready to sell its stock to the public?

- *The return on investment the venture capitalist expects to make.* Does the return his pricing proposal generates reflect the rate of return he usually requires, or is it significantly higher? Is the return on investment in line with those commonly quoted within the venture capital industry? If not, why not?

- *The future valuation of the company assumed by the investor.* How does it compare with the company's projections? Certainly, it will be less optimistic. But should the valuation be a higher number that is closer to that projected by the company?

- *When the investor expects to be able to cash out.* Most likely this will be later than when the company projects. After all, things never go according to plan. But if the company's projections were well done, they should have provided for some of the unexpected contingencies. If they have, perhaps the investor should move his projected exit date forward.

- *What the investor thinks his downside risk is.* This may be difficult to quantify, but it plays an important role in the investor's pricing. Is his analysis of the downside realistic? Does he think company failure is more likely than it is? (Certainly, he will think it is more likely than management does.) What does he think his likely loss will be if the company fails? Should his expectations be mitigated by factors he did not adequately consider?

The cost of a fundraising can also be reduced by decreasing the amount of money raised. Raising $10 million from outside investors will be cheaper and easier when a company needs $15 million if the other $5 million can be provided by bank loans made possible by the company's improved balance sheet. Changing deal terms to reduce risk can reduce funding cost as well. For example, if collateral can be given, the investor's downside risk will be reduced. Issuing senior securities to the investor can give him priorities in the case of liquidation and thereby reduce his risk. Recasting some of the investor's funding as debt that the company can repay with interest also reduces risk. Raising more of the needed money from other sources does the same, especially if the source is management.

The most effective way for a company to use this information about pricing, however, is for its management to conduct a serious and realistic pricing analysis before it begins the search for capital. Armed with this information and a good plan for raising funds, management can then attempt to attract more than one potential investor and create competition for its stock. Nothing softens an investor's negotiating position over valuation like a little competition from his colleagues. *See: Convertible Securities, Debentures, Discounted Cash Flow, Negotiation, P/E, Preferred Stock Umbrellas, Price-Earnings Ratio, ROI (Return on Investment).*

## Shareholder Value: Premiums, Discounts and More

*If you think you know the value of your common stock shares because your last round of venture capital was at $9 per share, think again. While a venture investor may say a company is valued at $50 million because he bought shares of convertible preferred stock equal to 40% of the company's outstanding shares of stock for $20 million, that does not necessarily mean your 10% is worth $5 million.*

*Not every share in a privately held company has the same value. Some share classes have more preferences and rights than others. And even among shareholders with the same* class of stock, the amount you own or the restrictions on free tradability can make their value different. If you start from the premise that your stock is worth what a willing buyer would pay for it (the classical definition of fair market value), here are some factors that can decrease the value of your shares compared to others.

- _Preferences_. A convertible preferred stock share is generally worth more than a common share. Preferences in liquidation, protections against dilution, and rights afforded to preferred shareholders to influence company decisions all have value. Participating preferred stock goes so far as to guarantee the holder receives a preference amount and then shares equally, on a pro rata basis, in the remaining value of the company in a liquidation event. The sale of Series A convertible preferred stock for $10 a share does not mean the common shareholders shares are worth $10 each. It means their shares are worth less than $10 each.

- _Liquidity discounts_. That a public company's common shares sell for $10 per share does not mean shares of a comparable private company are worth the same. Shareholders pay a premium for the ability to freely trade their shares on short notice. Registered public company shares are freely tradable under the securities laws and have ready-made markets for their shares. Private company shares are subject to trading restrictions and have no ready-made market. Consequently, sophisticated purchasers discount their value and pay less.

- _Control premiums_. Two shareholders with the same class of stock in a private company may own shares that are worth different values. A shareholder who ones a controlling interest in common stock has a security that is more valuable than one who owns a minority interest. This is because he can sell the *ability to control company decisions in addition to the stock itself. The minority shareholder gets a benefit when the entire company is sold in one transaction. Then his shares usually receive the same per share consideration.*

- *First refusal rights. The obligation to give someone the right to match another party's offer to purchase your shares, depresses the value of your shares. The first refusal provision makes it more difficult to attract a buyer because the buyer knows you cannot close the sale without offering someone else the opportunity to buy the stock first.*

- *Splits. Stock splits change the value of a holder's shares but not of his holdings. That is because splits apply evenly across a class of securities and increase the number of shares to offset the decrease in per share value. For example, a two for one stock split decreases the value of each share by one-half but doubles the total number of shares each person holds.*

- *Whole-company sales. When a company is sold, as opposed to the shares of just one shareholder, each holder of a share of stock in a class receives the same per share consideration as every other shareholder. This removes the control premium for the controlling shareholder but, theoretically, delivers a higher price. Whole-company sales can also remove or decrease the liquidity discount because the buyer is likely not looking for a trading security.*

- *Share restrictions. Contractual limitations on the rights of shares reduce their value. Common stock shares that are subject to a voting agreement that leaves the holder without a voice in management can be worth less than shares with voting rights. Contracts that permit a shareholder to sell his stock only if the holder agrees to be bound by the shareholders agreement will fetch a lower price.*

*See: Common Stock, Convertible Preferred Stock, Participating Preferred Stock, Pricing, Valuation.*

## Private Equity Funds

**Private Equity Funds** refer to pools of capital managed by professional investors that invest in private companies or real property. The term usually refers to buyout funds or real estate investment funds. Although technically applicable to venture capital funds that purchase minority interests in growing companies, the term private equity fund usually refers to groups that purchase majority control interests in operating companies or commercial real estate projects. Private equity funds frequently use debt borrowed from third party sources along with equity from their committed capital to complete a portfolio acquisition. When acquiring an operating company, private equity firms are also referred as financial buyers. This distinguishes them from operating companies who are frequently referred to as strategic buyers when they acquire other businesses. *See: Leverage, Leveraged Buyout, Venture Capital.*

## Private Placements

**Private Placements** are sales of company securities that do not involve a public offering and that are not required to be registered with the federal and state securities commissions. In many cases, the exemption calls for the preparation of an offering memorandum that describes the company and the risks associated with investing in it. Sometimes the exemption permits a sale of a limited number or securities to certain qualified investors without a formal offering memo.

Failure to register the sale of securities or to comply with the requirements for an exemption from registration can impose serious liabilities on a company and its management. Experienced counsel should be consulted before any offering of company securities is made, including an offer to a professional venture capitalist.

Whether an offering is a private placement depends upon a number of factors, including requirements and limitations relating to the:

- Number of offerees (not purchasers).
- Experience and knowledge of the offerees in making investments.
- Ability of the offerees to bear the economic risk of the investment.
- Number of securities offered.
- Dollar size of the offering.
- Manner in which the offering is conducted.

The company issuing securities also bears the burden of establishing that each offeree in a private placement has had appropriate access to sufficient information about the company and is capable of fending for himself in analyzing such information to reach an investment decision. To fulfill this burden, the issuing company must document the identity of each offeree, the characteristics that make him an appropriate purchaser, and the nature of his access to company information.

This requirement can be hard to meet with any certainty. This is because it requires the issuing company to make judgments about the nature of the offerees. While this may be relatively easy to do with institutional investors (such as established venture capital funds), which are clearly sophisticated and able to fend for themselves (based, in part, on the fact that they have made many other investments), judging the qualifications of individual investors is more difficult. As a general rule, individuals who are officers of the issuer or who have made similar investments before and are familiar with the issuer's operations will be easier to qualify than individuals who are not involved in the company's ongoing operations or who have not made investments in similar ventures.

Companies must also be sure that the purchasers of their securities are acquiring shares for investment and not for the purpose of redistributing them. If those purchasers, in turn, transfer the securities to others, the company may be deemed to have engaged in a public offering from the outset and to have violated the registration requirements.

In order to prevent such transfers, companies should require each purchaser in a private placement to state in writing that he is purchasing the securities for his own account and without a view to their subsequent distribution. In addition, the company should place a restrictive legend on the share certificate that is delivered to the purchaser. The legend should state that the securities represented by the certificate cannot be transferred unless pursuant to an effective registration statement or an exemption from the registration requirements, which is satisfactory to the company's counsel. The company should also instruct its transfer agent not to transfer any of the securities (containing the legend or not) without counsel's approval.

It is not difficult to see that the general exemption for private placements (Section 4(2) of the 33 Act and corresponding state laws) contains subjective requirements that can be difficult for a company to fulfill with any certainty. Because of this, the Securities and Exchange Commission and the state securities commissions have identified a number of more clearly delineated safe harbor exemptions that companies can use to avoid the registration requirements of the securities laws. These safe harbors set out specific objective requirements that must be followed in order for them to apply. Because of this specificity, companies find them easier and safer to use than the general 4(2) exemption.

The federal safe harbor exemptions include the Rule 504, 505, and 506 exemptions of Regulation D (discussed in detail in the *Reg D* entry), the federal intrastate exemption, and the Regulation A exemption. In general, these exemptions provide for three types of offerings with different requirements for disclosure, investor sophistication, and maximum number of investors. One exemption permits offerings of up to $1 million, another allows offerings of up to $7.5 million, while the third contains no dollar limitation but imposes sophistication requirements on unaccredited investors.

The federal intrastate safe harbor provides a registration exemption for offerings by local companies that are conducted entirely in one state. It provides objective standards companies can follow to be sure of obtaining the more general intrastate exemption contained in Section 3(a)(11) of the 33 Act. The standards are contained in Rule 147. In general, they permit sales only in the state of residence of the issuing company and only to residents of that state. They require that the issuing company derive a substantial percentage of its revenues from the state and limit resales of securities purchased in the offering. Under the rule, resales may be made only to residents of the state for a period of time after the offering. If any resales are made outside the state during the period, the exemption for the entire offering can be disqualified. Because of this resale requirement and the restriction of the exemption to local companies, other exemptions are more commonly used than the intrastate exemption.

The SEC's Regulation A permits offerings of up to $5 million of securities under specified conditions. To meet this exemption's requirements, a company must prepare an offering circular (unless the offering is for less than $100,000) that includes two years of financial statements. The offering circular is reviewed by the SEC, like a public offering circular. Also, as in registered public offerings, there is no limitation on the number of persons the shares may be offered or sold to and no special investor qualification requirements. Nonetheless, the Reg A exemption has been used infrequently compared to other exemption because of the restrictions on the amount of money that can be raised and the expense generated by preparing the offering circular and completing the SEC review. *See: Blue Sky Laws,*

*Investors, Legend Stock, Public Offerings, Reg D, Restricted Securities, SEC (Securities and Exchange Commission), Safe Harbors, 10b5, 33 Act.*

**Procrastination** can be deadly to a company's fundraising efforts. Raising capital effectively and on reasonable terms takes time and planning. Three to six months is not an unusual amount of time to elapse between the beginning of a fundraising effort and the receipt of funds. Once company management decides to raise outside capital, it should begin its efforts in earnest. Delaying the process when funds are needed can make it harder and more costly to raise money. This is especially true when the delay leads to a company's needing funds quickly to survive.

By the same token, delaying the need for funding can actually help management retain more of its company's equity. As a general rule, the longer a successful company avoids selling stock to outsiders the less stock it will have to sell in order to raise needed funding, and the less management's stockholdings will be diluted. Put another way, the more management can accomplish without using outside equity, the better bargaining position it will be in when it eventually does look for venture capital.

There are two reasons for this. First, delaying the company's need for additional investment shows prospective investors that management can make things happen and manage cash flow wisely. Second, and more important, the more the company can achieve without outside help, the less risk an investor must take when he invests in the company. *See: Cash Flow, Dilution (Percentage), Stage Financing.*

**Projections** refer to financial estimates of future company performance contained in a business plan or elsewhere. They are where all the narrative analysis and market research of the business plan are translated into language investors understand best - dollars and cents.

Business plans used to raise funding usually contain detailed projections in the form of prospective financial statements that include pro forma cash flow and income statements broken out on a monthly or quarterly basis. Projections usually appear immediately after the company's historical financial data in the business plan. Most venture capitalists like to see projections carried forward three to five years.

Investors scrutinize projections. If the numbers interest them, they will question management thoroughly about the assumptions underlying the projections. The more rigorous, considered, and realistic the projections are the more likely they are to be achieved, and the more likely they are to withstand an investor's scrutiny.

Projections provide investors with a basis for determining how much equity they will require in return for funding a company. Projections can also help management of a company estimate a reasonable range of value for their company using a discounted cash flow or market pricing methodology, which are discussed in the *Discounted Cash Flow* and *Pricing* entries found in this book. *See: Benchmarks, Business Plan Format, Pricing.*

**Promissory Notes** are written promises to repay borrowed money plus interest. They typically describe the amount borrowed, the interest charged, and the method for repaying the lender.

Promissory notes can be secured or unsecured. If they are secured, property (collateral) is pledged to back up the company's promise to pay. If the note is not paid on time, the lender can foreclose on the collateral and apply the proceeds to pay down the note. Unless they specify otherwise, promissory notes are assumed to be with recourse. That is, the holder of the note can collect it against the maker directly if it is not paid. If the note specifies, however, its holder can be limited to proceeding only against the collateral that secures the note. These are frequently referred to as nonrecourse notes.

Promissory notes can be, and often are, backed up by personal guarantees of key management members. Guarantees are commonly required by banks and lending institutions that lend to entrepreneurial companies. Promissory notes that are not secured or guaranteed are backed only by the company's promise to pay.

Professional venture investors often use more sophisticated debt instruments instead of promissory notes, such as debentures or debt-like instruments like redeemable preferred stock. When they use notes, they often require management to execute guarantees. *See: Angels, Collateral, Debentures, Factoring, Inventory Financing, Nonrecourse Debt, Personal Guarantees, Receivables Financing.*

**Prospectus** refers to the form of offering memorandum used to offer securities for sale in public offerings. These offering memos contain detailed descriptions of the offering, the company making the offering, and the risks associated with investing in the company's securities. The prospectus is typically prepared by the offering company and its counsel but is extensively reviewed and revised with input from the offering's underwriters, underwriters' counsel and the company's accountants. Once completed, the prospectus is filed with the SEC for further review and comment. Most initial public offerings follow the SEC's Form S-1 for their prospectus. *See: Going Public, IPO (Initial Public Offerings), Offering Memos, Public Offering.*

**Public Offering** refers to an offering of company securities that is registered with the federal Securities and Exchange Commission (SEC) and state blue sky commissions. The registered offering and sale does not rely on an exemption from the 33 Act's registration requirements. Shares purchased public offerings are freely tradable, except to the extent they might be otherwise restricted by virtue of a purchaser's status as a company insider.

Public offerings generate needed cash but can be expensive and time-consuming to conduct. Initial public offerings are generally the most expensive public offerings to conduct because they involve the creation of a detailed descriptive prospectus and frequently require the offering company to develop and implement new internal controls and procedures or to identify and elect new independent directors. Initial public offerings also subject the issuing company to ongoing reporting and disclosure requirements with the SEC.

The great advantage of a public offering is the market of freely tradable company securities it creates that the company can use to raise capital in the future and that management or employee shareholders can use, with care, to convert their holdings into cash. Subsequent offerings can be easier and cheaper to complete with abbreviated disclosure forms, such as S-3, that incorporate by reference descriptive material contained in other company filings.

Having publicly traded stock makes company shares in employee incentive plans more attractive because the shares are easier to convert into cash. An active market for company shares can make it easier for a company to expand its activities through the acquisition of other businesses. Because they are readily convertible into cash, registered company shares can often be used instead of cash to acquire an attractive business. With the proper deal structure, using company shares for part of the acquisition consideration can also ease the immediate tax burden of the seller and make the acquisition easier to close. *See: Going Public, IPOs (Initial Public Offerings).*

## *Your 'Going Public' Team*

*A successful public offering is a team effort that involves substantial commitment from management and a team of professionals they assemble to complete and file the required documentation. The team typically includes underwriters, attorneys, accountants, financial printers, public relations professionals, and transfer agents, each with a distinct role in the process.*

*Management. Management serve critical roles during the process: they assemble the team and initiate the process; they provide the factual basis for the offering document through interviews and document production; and they assist the sales process through a series of 'road show' meetings with underwriters, analysts and potential investors. They also manage the adoption of internal reporting and governance changes necessary to comply with securities and stock exchange requirements. In concert with the underwriters, who understand market sensitivities and how securities are sold, management also directs the development of the company's 'story' that distinguishes it in the marketplace and is reflected in the offering document. Management's intimate knowledge of the company and its role in creating the success that makes the public offering possible make it the single most important member of the going public team. The 'road show' that follows completion of the offering document offers management the chance to sell the offering by presenting the company's story to the investment community.*

*Underwriters. The underwriters are the next most important members of the going public team. They handle the actual sale of the company's securities and provide direction to the process of drafting and completing the company's offering document. Offerings are typically conducted by a team of underwriters selected by the lead underwriter chosen by the company. Sometimes companies select two underwriters to serve a co-leads. No two underwriters are the same. Some have better research capabilities in a company's industry. Others may have less research expertise but larger sales distribution capability or the ability to sell better to institutional investors. One key role of the underwriter is to price the company's stock for the offering after analyzing the market and making comparisons to other offerings. The going public price is often the subject of extensive discussion between management and the underwriters before a price is fixed. Once a price is agreed, the lead, or managing underwriter, completes putting together the syndicate of underwriters who will market and sell the securities and orchestrates the 'road show' of company executives to sell the securities.*

*Attorneys. Two sets of attorney's are involved in the going public process - attorneys for the company and attorneys for the underwriter. This team of professionals is primarily responsible for preparing the offering memo and assuring company compliance with the many federal and state securities rules and regulations governing the process. They typically prepare the first draft of the offering document and are responsible for completing the document in compliance with applicable securities laws after obtaining detailed input from management, the underwriters and the other professionals involved in the process. Going public and complying with post-offering requirements is a complex and specialized process that requires experienced attorneys to guide and advise company management. Going public also usually involves making extensive changes to corporate governance procedures and to the configuration of the company's board of directors. The company's attorneys also assist in making these changes.*

*Auditors. The company's accountants play an important role in preparing the company's financial statements in the form required by applicable securities laws. This often involves planning in advance of the public offering process to get the company's financial statements in form to meet the strict requirements of the federal securities authorities. The auditors also help the company implement additional accounting procedures and methods required of public companies so that management is prepared to operate in compliance with Sarbanes-Oxley and other public company rules.*

*Financial Printers. The offering memorandum must be printed to specific standards of the Securities Exchange Commission and must be accompanied by an electronic submission to the SEC's Electronic Data Gathering Analysis and Retrieval System (EDGAR). The limited number of firms that specialize in meeting these requirements are experienced at working within the tight time constraints common to an initial public offering and offer facilities that provide confidentiality and working space to accommodate the typical public offering team.*

*Public Relations Agents. Public relations experts are often, though not always, retained to assist management in keeping the public informed and interested in the company after completion of the offering. This often includes planning during the public offering stage and a long-term relationship with the company afterward.*

*Transfer Agents. Transfer agents keep and maintain the company's shareholder records, often taking this role over from an internal company officer. They are required for companies joining the NYSE or AMEX, and are highly recommended for OTC companies. Transfer agents also assist companies with shareholder correspondence and handle stock transfers.*

**Puts** refer to contractual rights that entitle one shareholder to force a company (or other party) to purchase his shares for an agreed-upon price. Puts usually appear in written agreements such as financing or shareholders agreements. Puts provide investors with wanted liquidity but at a significant cost to the company.

When exercised, puts force companies to devote resources to paying off the investor that could otherwise be devoted to operations. For example, an investor who puts 100,000 shares back to the company at $10 per share can force management divert $1 million from other priorities to purchase his shares. Sometimes this diversion can delay important purchases or even create a cash-flow crisis for the company.

Key terms to consider when negotiating a put are:

- *Timing*. When is the investor entitled to exercise his put? Must he wait for a period of years? Are there conditions to the exercise, such as the company's failure to meet a milestone? Can the investor retain some stock or must he tender it all with the put?

- *Payment terms*. What price has to be paid for the stock? When does it have to be paid? One restriction commonly found in these agreements is the limitation that the company cannot pay funds to the investor if doing so would render the company insolvent. Deferred payment terms that permit payment over time gives the company more flexibility.

- *Deferrals*. Are there conditions under which the company can defer the investors right to exercise the put? For example, if the company is actively planning a sale or merger can the board postpone the put for a period of months to allow the company to complete the transaction?

- *Term*. When and under what conditions does the put expire? Does it expire with a public offering or a sale of the business?

- *Reciprocal rights*. Does the company receive any rights to require the investor to sell the stock back to the company? If the company gets such a call right, under what conditions and at what price is it exercisable?

*See: Calls, Cash Flow, Convertible Preferred Stock, Liquidity Agreements.*

**Qualified Stock Option Plans** refer to a form of tax-advantaged incentive stock option plan used by growing companies to attract and retain important employees. See: *ISO's (Incentive Stock Options)* for a more complete discussion of qualified stock option plans.

# R

**R & D Partnerships** refer to research and development limited partnerships, which are used to obtain financing for technology development projects. In this type of arrangement, the company usually contributes its rights to a product or technology platform in development to a limited partnership it manages. One or more third parties provide funding for the partnership to complete the development of the product. During the development period the partnership loses money since it has no source of income and all the expenses of development. The investors expense these losses to reduce their taxable income. The partnership completes the product development and sells or licenses the technology back to the company.

R&D partnerships were once a staple tool of new technology and product development. The usefulness of R & D partnerships as a method for transferring tax benefits, however, has since been limited by the passive loss rules of the Internal Revenue Code that restrict investors in the types of income they can apply their losses against. Generally speaking, investors can only use R & D partnership losses to offset income from other passive investments.

Obtaining tax benefits from an R & D partnership requires careful attention to a variety of complex and interrelated tax laws. Failure to structure the partnership correctly will lose the advantages of the R & D partnership. A qualified tax professional should be consulted before structuring any R & D partnership investment. *See:Limited Partnerships, Off Balance Sheet Financing, S Corporations.*

**Ratchets** refer to a powerful form of antidilution provision investors sometimes request when they invest in private companies. In a ratchet, the investor is given additional shares of stock for free if the company later sells shares at a lower price. The number of free shares the investor receives is enough to make the investor's average cost per share (counting all of his purchased and free shares) equal to the lower price per share given to the later investor. What makes the ratchet so powerful is that the first investor is given these extra shares regardless of the number of shares purchased by the later investor.

For example, if an investor with a ratchet purchases 1 million shares of company stock for $2 million, or $2 a share, and the company later sells another investor 100,000 shares for $1 each, the first investor would receive another 1 million shares for free. The result would be the same if the second investor bought only one share for $1 or 10 million shares for $10 million.

Other antidilution provisions grant investors fewer shares of free stock when fewer shares are sold in the later dilutive sale. These "weighted average" provisions employ formulas that take into consideration the smaller financial impact felt by a protected investor when fewer shares are sold in the later sale. These formulas reduce the number of free shares granted to the investor when the later lower-price sale occurs for a limited number of shares.

Ratchets, and other antidilution provisions, are frequently contained the formulas used to convert convertible preferred stock sold to outside investors into common stock. In other words, they are set up to entitle the investor to receive additional shares of common stock when the investor converts his stock into common stock. Ratchets can also be tied to options or warrants. When they are, the investor receives extra shares when he exercises his option. *See: Antidilution Provisions, Dilution (Percentage), Weighted Average Antidilution.*

**Recaps** refer to any arrangement where investors and company management reorganize a company's capital structure, as by causing the company to take on debt to purchase shares from selected shareholders.

Recapitalizations are frequently undertaken to add stability to a company's capital structure. For example, when an investor's debentures or a lender's debt is converted into company stock in order to reduce the company's repayment obligations to creditors, the transaction would be called a recap. Sometimes recaps occur as part of another transaction, such as a venture capital investment in a growing company where part of the investment proceeds is used to purchase stock directly from a founder. The purpose may be to remove the founder from management or to provide the founder with some liquidity.

A leveraged buyout undertaken by existing management for the purpose to liquidating the founder's ownership interest and changing control would be a type of recapitalization. Recaps are also undertaken by public companies as a tool to discourage hostile takeovers. In this case the company takes on a large amount of debt to issue dividends to shareholders, weakening the company's capital structure and making it less attractive to potential purchasers. Companies are routinely recapitalized when they file for Chapter 11 protection in bankruptcy court as part of the reorganization process. *See: Equity, Leveraged Buyouts, Shark Repellents.*

**Receivables Financing** refers to any borrowing that is secured by a company's accounts receivable. *See: Factoring, Inventory Financing.*

**Reg D** refers to Regulation D of the federal Securities and Exchange Commission (SEC), which sets out certain safe harbor exemptions to the 33 Act's registration requirements. These safe harbors have clearly delineated requirements that enable companies to safely sell their shares in private or limited placements without conducting public offerings. Because of their specificity, Reg D exemptions are easier to rely on than the general private placement exemption contained in Section 4(2) of the 33 Act. Whenever possible, one or more of the exemptions spelled out in Reg D should be followed.

The provisions of Reg D are set forth in six rules, the last three of which contain the exemptions. Because of their importance, each of the rules is summarized below.

*Rule 501.* Rule 501 provides the method of calculating the number of purchasers who can be involved in sales conducted under the exemptions in Rules 505 and 506 and defines the term accredited investor as it is used in Reg D. Under circumstances spelled out in Reg D, sales to these accredited investors can be made without counting them toward the maximum number of allowable investors under the exemption. The accredited investor category consists of persons who fall within, or who the issuing company reasonably believes fall within, one of the categories summarized below.

- A director, executive officer or general partner of the issuing company or a director, executive officer or general partner of a general partner of the issuing company.
- A natural person whose net worth (individual or jointly with his spouse) exceeds $1 million.

- A person who has had individual income of over $200,000 or joint income with his spouse of over $300,000 during each of the last two years and reasonably expects to maintain those minimum income levels in the coming year.
- A qualified bank, savings and loan association, or insurance company.
- A corporation, partnership or business trust with at least $5 million in assets that was not formed for the purpose of acquiring the offered.
- A private business development company that meets the definition contained in the Investment Advisers Act of 1940.
- A 501(C)(3) charitable organization with at least $5 million in assets.
- Employee benefit plans subject to ERISA that have either a plan fiduciary that is a bank, insurance company or registered investment adviser or total assets of at least $5 million.
- A non-business trust with at least $5 million in assets, which is directed by a "sophisticated" person (as defined in Rule 506).
- An entity in which all of the equity owners are accredited investors.

*Rule 502.* Rule 502 describes general conditions that must be met to secure a Reg D exemption. The rule deals with integration, information disclosure, the manner of conducting offerings, and resale limitations.

Integration. The SEC will not integrate (or combine) sales made more than six months prior to or after a Reg D offering so long as within such period the issuing company makes no offers or sales of a same or similar class of securities (other than under certain employee benefit plans).

Information Required. Rule 502(b) provides that no prescribed information need be furnished for offers and sales of up to $1 million under its Rule 504 exemption or where such sales are made only to accredited investors under the Rule 505 and 506 exemptions. For offers above $1 million that include non-accredited investors, the type and degree of disclosure is linked to the size and nature of the offering under Rules 505 and 506. If the offering involves both accredited and non-accredited investors, the issuing company must distribute the information to all investors.

The amount and type of financial and non-financial reporting required varies depending on the size of the offering. Different requirements apply to offerings up to $2 million, between $2 million and $7.5 million and above $7.5 million. Offerings of up to $2 million require disclosure of the type required Item 310 of Regulation S-B. Those between $2 million and $7.5 million require distribution of the kind of information called for in Part I of Registration Form SB-2. If Form SB-2 is unavailable (e.g., if the issuer is a reporting company), the company must supply the kind of information "required in Part I of a registration statement filed under the 33 Act on the form the issuer would be entitled to use." (For most companies this will be Registration Form S-1.) Companies offering more than $7.5 million worth of securities must supply information of the type required in Part I of a registration statement.

<u>Manner of Offering Limitations</u>. Rule 502(c) provides that, with the exception of offerings under Rule 504, the issuing company or anyone acting on its behalf may not publicly solicit or generally advertise in connection with any offer.

<u>Resale Limitations</u>. Rule 502(d) requires issuers to exercise reasonable care in determining that purchasers of their securities are not engaging in illegal private resales. The reasonable care required by the rule includes (but is not limited to):

- Making a reasonable inquiry into whether the purchaser is acquiring the securities for himself or another.

- Providing written disclosure to each purchaser prior to sale that the securities are not registered under the 33 Act and cannot be resold unless registered or exempted.
- Placing a legend on the stock certificate stating that the securities represented by the certificate have not been registered under the 33 Act and setting forth the restrictions imposed on the transferability of those securities.

*Rule 503.* This rule requires a written notice of sale to be filed on Form D. The issuing company must file five copies of the form within fifteen days after the first sale in order to receive a Reg D exemption. (Some states require filing before the first sale.)

*Rule 504.* Rule 504 provides an exemption for companies that are not reporting companies or investment companies, and for certain development stage companies. The exemption applies to sales of up to $1 million in securities made during a twelve-month period. Rule 504 permits issuers to make general advertisements and solicitations in connection with an offering. The Rule requires the filing of a timely notice on Form D but the availability of the exemption is not contingent upon filing of the notice.

*Rule 505.* Rule 505 allows an exemption for offers and sales of securities up to $5 million, subject to offsets for certain types of sales occurring within the past twelve months and throughout the Rule 505 offering. The issuing company, which cannot be an investment company, must meet the disclosure requirements set forth in Rule 502, as well as the offer and resale provisions in Rules 502(c) and (d). Although there may be an unlimited number of accredited investors, Rule 505 requires that the issuer reasonably believe that it has sold securities to no more than thirty-five non-accredited purchasers.

*Rule 506.* This rule provides an exemption for limited offers and sales of securities without regard to the dollar amount of the offering. Like Rule 505, it limits the number of non-accredited purchasers to thirty-five. Unlike Rule 505, however, Rule 506 requires that non-accredited investors (either alone or with their "purchaser representative") be "sophisticated" before they can purchase company securities. The language of the sophistication requirement reads as follows:

> Each purchaser who is not an accredited investor either alone or with his purchaser representative(s) has such knowledge and experience in financial and business matters that he is capable of evaluating the merits and risks of the prospective investment, or the issuer reasonably believes immediately prior to making any sale that such purchaser comes within this description.

*Summary of Reg D.* The safe harbor exemptions contained in Reg D are nonexclusive. That is, companies that rely on them need not rely on them exclusively. They may also rely on other exemptions, such as the general 4(2) private placement exemption, to avoid the 33 Act's registration requirements. Nonetheless, because their detailed requirements make them the safest way for companies to obtain a registration exemption, they should be used whenever possible, even in financings to a single venture capitalist.

The Reg D exemptions do not relieve a company or its management from the need to comply with the provisions of the securities laws in the states in which they offer or sell securities. Also, they do not exempt a company from the federal and state antifraud provisions, such as the 33 Act's Rule 10b5. The antifraud provisions make it necessary for issuing companies to disclose or make available to offerees material information about the issuing company and the offering even in offerings conducted under exemptions that do not require the disclosure of any prescribed information. Failure to comply with state blue sky laws or the antifraud provisions of the federal and state securities laws can impose serious liabilities on a company and its management. It can even impair a company's ability to raise money in the future.

Because of the complexity of the federal and state securities laws and the severity of the penalties for failure to comply, a company should consult experienced counsel before offering or selling any of its securities. Rules also change. Only a qualified professional can assure management that the company's security offering has been conducted in a manner that will not create significant liabilities for the company and its management. *See: Blue Sky Laws, Going Public, Integration, Investment Reps, Investors, IPOs (Initial Public Offerings), Legend Stock, Private Placements, Restricted Stock, 10b5, 33 Act.*

## Registration Rights are contractual rights that entitle

investors to force a company to register investors shares of company stock with the Securities and Exchange Commission (SEC) and state securities commissions. This registration, in turn, enables the investors to sell their shares to the public. Registration rights provide liquidity to investors by enabling them to free their shares from the transfer restrictions imposed on unregistered securities by the federal and state securities laws. Venture capitalists invariably require them as a condition of funding.

Registration rights come in two varieties: demand rights, which enable investors to require a company to register their shares for sale in a public offering any time an investor demands; and piggyback rights, which allow investors to include (or "piggyback") their shares in a public offering the company is already conducting.

Entrepreneurs often treat registration rights as a necessary evil and pay only cursory attention to the details of these agreements. This attitude can prove costly later on.

Management should negotiate the registration rights agreement as it would any other important part of its financing arrangements. Some important issues to address in any registration rights negotiation are

- The number of demand registrations the investor can require (generally, one is enough).
- When the investor can make demand (most will refrain from making a demand for a period of time).
- Who pays for the demand registration.
- The minimum and maximum dollar size of a demand registration (the larger the minimum and smaller the maximum the better).
- Whether management shareholders can participate with the investor in demand and piggyback registrations.
- How often the investor can participate in a piggyback registration and how many shares he can sell.

Most companies have no trouble giving an investor piggyback registration rights as long as his rights are subject to the veto of the company's underwriter. Giving such rights does little to disrupt a company's plans and does not require the special effort of demand registrations.

Demand registrations, however, do nothing for a company after the initial funding but do require it to undertake the expensive and time-consuming effort of conducting a public offering whenever the investor demands. These offerings require significant efforts from management, diverting them from the business of running the company. They also commit the company and management to running the company as a public company, with all of the additional cost and effort associated with complying with public company rules of the SEC and the company's stock exchange.

Demand registrations can also depress the market price of the company's stock if the offering is poorly timed. Premature entry into the public markets before a company can command a sustainable price for its stock or before management can predict operations with public company predictability can result in low and volatile stock prices and difficulty in accessing public markets for additional funding. *See: Demand Rights, Going Public, IPO (Initial Public Offering), Liquidity Agreements, Piggyback Rights, Sarbanes-Oxley.*

**Registration Rights Agreements** refer to the written agreements between a company and its investors that provide investors with registration rights. *See: Demand Rights, Piggyback Rights, Registration Rights.*

**Reports and Records** refer to the monthly balance sheets, income statements, and cash flow statements that most venture capitalists require of the companies in which they invest. Investors expect these reports to be provided promptly and regularly after a funding is completed. A typical venture capital investment term requires a company to provide reports on a monthly, quarterly and annual basis, with the annual statement being presented in an audited format. Often, the reporting requirements of the investment documents require the statements to contain comparative data from prior periods or comparisons to budget.

Well-kept records tell investors and management what the company has done and how it is proceeding toward accomplishing its goals. The types of records a company generates (beyond balance sheets and income statements) tell investors a lot about how much control management exercises over the company and how well informed management is about its company's performance and challenges. In fact, an important role many active investor director nominees seek to play on a company's board of directors is to help management identify key, measurable factors (sometimes referred to as "metrics") that can be monitored to help management better understand its business and anticipate future problems.

Maintaining well-maintained books with appropriate and well-considered reporting mechanisms is important to attracting investors. Without these fundamental reports investors cannot properly evaluate the history of a company or the prospects for its success. *See: Audits, CPAs (Certified Public Accountants).*

## Reps and Warranties refer to the statements of facts,

opinions, and estimates investors ask companies and managements to put into writing as a condition of funding. These representations (reps) and warranties usually appear in the financing or stock purchase agreement. Some of the more common ones are:

- *Organization and corporate power.* The company is duly organized, in good standing, and is qualified to conduct business in the manner and at the locations it is conducting business.
- *Authorization.* The company has the power and authority to enter into the financing agreements and to perform its obligations under them. The agreements have been duly authorized by the company's board of directors and by all other necessary corporate action.
- *Capitalization.* The company's outstanding shares of capital stock consist of only those disclosed in the representation. No person has any rights to acquire any capital stock in the company except those that management has described. If the company owns shares in any other companies, that ownership is disclosed as well.
- *Financial statements.* The financial statements delivered by the company to the investor are accurate, complete, and prepared in accordance with "generally accepted accounting principles."

- *Undisclosed liabilities.* The company is not subject to any material claims or liabilities that are not disclosed on its most recent balance sheet.
- *Absence of changes.* There have been no material adverse changes in the company or in its operations since the date of the last balance sheet delivered to the investor.
- *An accurate business plan.* To the best of management's knowledge, neither the company's business plan nor any other information delivered to the investor contains any untrue or misleading statements. The business plan projections were prepared based upon the assumptions disclosed therein, which management believes to be reasonable.
- *Properties.* The company has good and marketable title to all of its properties.
- *Compliance with laws.* The company has complied with all laws and regulations that apply to it.
- *Taxes.* The company has filed all of its tax returns on time and has paid its taxes.
- *Contracts and laws.* All of the company's material contracts have been disclosed to the investor. The company is not in default under any of its agreements. The financing agreements do not conflict with or cause a default under any of the company's other agreements, its charter, or any laws.
- *Intellectual property.* The company has sufficient title to its patents, trademarks, copyrights and other intellectual property to conduct its business. To management's knowledge, the company's business does not infringe upon any patents or intellectual property rights of others.
- *Litigation.* Except as has been disclosed to the investor, there is no litigation or other claim pending or threatened against the company.

Other representations regarding cost estimates, market research conclusions, and revenue projections may also be requested. Reps and warranties should be made carefully. If they are inaccurate, they should be corrected. If they are over broad, they should be narrowed. Otherwise, they may create a default that releases the investor from his obligations and subjects management and the company to liability.

The phrase "reps and warranties" is also used to refer to the representations made in other types of transactions, including mergers and acquisitions. The content and extensiveness of reps and warranties are always negotiated matters and can vary dramatically depending on the type of transaction involved. *See: Boilerplate, Investment Reps, Operating Covenants, Opinion Letters.*

**Restricted Stock** refers to shares of company stock that have not been registered in a public offering and consequently cannot be resold or transferred until certain events occur that exempt the resale from registration or fulfill the registration requirements. Usually, the certificates for restricted securities bear legends identifying the limitations on their transferability. Hence, the other name used to refer to restricted stock – legend stock. When issuing restricted securities, prudent management requires its investors to represent in writing that they are purchasing the shares for investment purposes only and do not intend to resell them.

Venture capital investors usually buy restricted stock from companies that rely upon exemptions from the 33 Act registration requirements when selling their shares. As a result, the venture investor cannot resell the shares without first causing the company to either register the shares with the Securities and Exchange Commission (SEC) and state securities commissions or complying with an exemption to those registration requirements. Because of this, venture investors negotiate registration rights agreements that give them limited rights to force registration of their shares.

Restricted shares can also be sold by public companies. PIPEs, described earlier, are a form of restricted stock offering conducted by public companies. Initial public offerings and other share registrations that enable free tradability only apply to shares included in the registered offering.

Even registered shares can have resale restrictions in certain circumstances. Company officers and directors who hold shares in their public companies have special limitations that restrict their ability to freely trade even registered shares, especially while they are in possession of insider information. Unregistered shares held by these insiders are usually sold, when other rules permit, under the provisions of SEC's Rule 144. This rule identifies circumstances under which restricted securities may be sold by affiliates. In general, it allows affiliated holders of restricted securities who have held their securities for 12 months after they have paid for them to sell in any three-month period a number of their shares no greater than the larger of

1 percent of the total number of shares of their class of stock then outstanding or, if the security is listed on a national exchange or quoted on the National Association of Securities Dealers Automated Quotations (NASDAQ), the average weekly trading volume of their class of stock.

To qualify as a Rule 144 sale, there must be adequate public information available about the company at the time of the sale and the sale must be handled by a broker.

After three years, most resale restrictions lapse for persons who are not significant shareholders or members of company management. State securities laws and other rules relating to insider trading and certain SEC reporting requirements must be complied with before any restricted security is sold. Because of the complexity of these laws, any holder of restricted securities should consult an attorney before transferring ownership of his stock. *See: Exits, Going Public, Investment Reps, IPOs (Initial Public Offerings), Legend Stock, Liquidity Agreements, PIPE (Private Investment in Public Equity), Private Placements, Reg D, Registration Rights.*

**Risk Capital** refers generally to any money invested in a business venture but, more specifically, to money invested by venture investors in undercapitalized private companies. These investments of capital are risky because of the early stage of the companies, the lack of collateral to secure the investments, and their illiquid nature. This is why private company investors look for high rates of return and a degree of participation in company management. *See: Pricing, ROI (Return on Investment), Venture Capital.*

**ROI (Return on Investment)** is the premium an investor receives for investing in a company when he liquidates his holdings. Private equity investors express their return expectations in terms of percentages, much the same way lenders price their loans. By determining what compounded annual rate of return he wants from a given investment, an equity investor can then work with his projections for the company's growth to arrive at the percentage of the company's stock he needs to receive in order to reach his desired return.

What ROIs do most venture capitalists require to fund a company? They vary from company to company. The following chart gives some general ranges, based on an economy supporting prime interest rates below 10 percent.

| *Company Stage* | *Compounded Annual ROI* |
|---|---|
| Seed or start-up | 35% and up |
| First and second stage | 20% to 50% |
| Third stage and mezzanine | 15% to 30% |

How these rates of return translate into cost to a company depends in large part on how long it takes the investor to exit. The following table illustrates this fact.

| Payoff | Compounded Annual ROI |
|---|---|
| Three times investment in three years | 44% |
| Five times investment in three years | 71% |
| Seven times investment in three years | 91% |
| Four times investment in four years | 41% |
| Three times investment in five years | 25% |
| Five times investment in five years | 38% |
| Seven times investment in five years | 47% |
| Ten times investment in five years | 58% |

*See Pricing, Procrastination, Projections.*

# S

**Safe Harbors** refer to registration exemptions that enable companies who comply with their requirements to offer and issue securities privately with assurance that they will not run afoul of federal and state securities law registration requirements. The Reg D private placement exemptions and integration rules are examples of safe harbors. Companies routinely attempt to structure their securities offerings to meet the requirements of a safe harbor. *See: Integration, Private Placements, Reg D, 33 Act.*

**Sarbanes-Oxley** refers to the Sarbanes-Oxley Act enacted by Congress in 2002 to restore investor confidence in publicly traded securities. The enactment followed a series of highly publicized corporate scandals that resulted in large financial losses to shareholders. Following its adoption, the Securities and Exchange Commission, the Public Accounting Oversight Board, the New York Stock Exchange and the National Association of Securities Dealers adopted regulations and rules to conform their practices to the requirements of the Sarbanes-Oxley Act. The net result is adoption of a host of new corporate governance and financial practice requirements applicable to public companies in the U.S.

These new rules require public companies to pay significantly more attention to the details of corporate governance. They also impose significant new duties on company directors and officers. New independence requirements have changed the membership configuration of many public company boards. One significant result of these changes has been to increase the cost of being a public company, causing many smaller public companies to reconsider whether the advantages of being public outweigh the cost. Not surprisingly many public companies have considered and taken their companies private in the aftermath of the statutes adoption. *See: Revolution in Public Company Governance, Going Private, Going Public, SEC (Securities and Exchange Commission).*

## SBA (Small Business Administration) refers to an agency of the U.S. government that facilitates equity and debt financings of small companies. The SBA also administers the U.S. government's small business investment company activities described below under *SBICs (Small Business Investment Companies).*

The SBA's loan guarantees are administered under its 7(a) Loan Guarantee Program. Under the program, participating banks, business development corporations, and other institutional lenders evaluate potential borrowers, set the borrowing terms, and prepare the lending paperwork. They also set the interest rate (but are prohibited from charging more than a fixed percent rate over prime). The SBA then guarantees up to 80 percent of qualifying loans, which decreases the lenders' risks and makes it more feasible for small companies to borrow.

The SBA relies extensively on its participating lenders to evaluate and service the guaranteed loans. Two of its programs demonstrate this reliance. Under the Certified Lenders Program, qualifying lenders are certified by the SBA and promised quick turnaround on loan applications they submit to the SBA. Preferred lenders are authorized to extend SBA guarantees on loans that meet SBA guidelines.

Whichever type of SBA lender a company approaches, management should be prepared to meet numerous requirements. Each lender evaluates loan applications against its own and the SBA's requirements. Borrowers should expect questions relating to the company's capitalization, its ability to repay the loan, and the personal resources of its principals. To meet the SBA's requirements alone, management must show, among other things, that it owns a for-profit business that is not dominant in its industry, and that it does not discriminate in employment practices.

The documentation for SBA guarantees is usually extensive, containing protective provisions that limit the manner in which the company can use the money loaned, require personal guarantees from management, and require regular reporting to the lender. SBA-guaranteed loans are usually collateralized by every available asset, including company real property, receivables, inventory, and equipment. Key management members are frequently required to secure their guarantees of the company's borrowings with liens on their homes.

The SBA guarantee to the lender makes money available under the program to companies that might not otherwise be able to borrow at commercially reasonable rates. The SBA guarantee does not, however, reduce the lender's desire for company collateral or for the personal guarantees and property pledges of management. Nor does it reduce the requirements for covenants and restrictions in the loan documentation. This is because lenders still look to the borrowing company and its management as the parties primarily responsible for the loan. SBA lenders will foreclose against the assets of a company and its management. They will do everything within their power to avoid calling on the SBA guarantee, because in doing so they jeopardize their relationship with the SBA. *See: BDCs (Business*

*Development Corporations), SBICs (Small Business Investment Companies), SBIR (Small Business Innovation Research), SSBICs (Specialized Small Business Investment Companies). See also: the SBA's online web site at www.sbaonline.sba.gov/financing.*

**SBICs** refer to privately owned investment firms, called Small Business Investment Companies, that are licensed and regulated by the SBA that use their own funds and monies borrowed with an SBA guarantee to make investments in qualifying businesses. Under the applicable rules, SBICs can use the SBA guarantee to leverage their capital by up to three times, although most are limited to leverage of two times their capital. For example, a privately owned and operated SBIC with $25 Million of its own capital might issue debentures with SBA guarantees to borrow up to an additional $50 Million to increase its funds available for investment to $75 Million.

SBICs that use the SBA guarantee feature to increase their available investment capital are referred to as leveraged SBICs. Banks who form SBIC affiliates often forgo the leverage afforded by the guarantee program to create self-funded SBIC that enable them to make equity investments they would otherwise be precluded from making under existing banking laws. These are sometimes referred to as un-leveraged SBICs.

Some SBICs limit their activity to making long-term loans to small businesses or invest only in specific industries. Other SBICs provide long-term loans and make equity investments in small businesses of more than one industry.

Only firms that meet the definitional requirements of a small business according to the SBA's rules qualify to receive funding from an SBIC. For most industries, this requires a company to have a net worth of less than $18 Million and average net income over the preceding two years of less than $6 Million. Some industries have other standards. SBICs generally may not invest in finance or investment companies, unimproved real estate, passive operations, farm land, or businesses with less than halfo of their employees or assets in the United States.

In practice, leveraged SBICs usually require that a significant part of their investment in a company be in the form of loans or income-producing securities. This is because the majority of the funds they invest are borrowed moneys on which they have to pay interest and repay principal. For the same reason, may leveraged SBICs avoid earlier stage investments where the risks of nonpayment are greater.

Nonetheless, SBICs, both leveraged and unleveraged, represent a valuable source of funds, particularly for later stage companies whose prospects are more secure. If the prospects are secure enough, an SBIC will sometimes invest in a company that offers a more moderate potential for growth than might be required to attract a more traditional private venture capital firm. *See: CDCs (Community Development Corporations), SSBICs (Specialized Small Business Investment Companies), Venture Capitalists.*

**SBIR** refers to a U.S. governments Small Business Innovation Research program that provides funding for research to for-profit businesses that operate primarily within the United States, have a place of business within the United States and have 500 or fewer employees. The program requires major government agencies to allocate a portion of their research and development funds to small private businesses through the SBIR program. A related STTR program (Small Business Technology Transfer) provides similar funding for research projects that involve substantial collaboration (30% or more) with a non-profit institution. In the right circumstances, either the program can provide valuable funding for an entrepreneur's new product development activity.

Participating federal agencies set aside a portion of their research and development budgets to the program and invite qualifying small businesses to apply for grants. Each agency includes identifies technical topics it is interested in funding. The Department of Energy, for example, might identify research areas such as energy production, energy use, fundamental energy sciences, environmental management and nuclear nonproliferation as areas of interest. Typically, subtopics are also identified such as fossil, nuclear, renewable and fusion energy for the energy production area. Grant applications from small businesses must respond to a specific agency topic and subtopic to be successful.

The Small Business Administration (SBA) oversees the program and produces informational pieces which describe the program and the types of research for which funds are available. Each participating agency establishes its own funding and contract criteria. Participating agencies include the following:

Department of Agriculture
Department of Commerce
Department of Defense
Department of Education
Department of Energy
Department of Health and Human
Department of Homeland Security
Department of Transportation
Environmental Protection Agency
National Aeronautics and Space Administration
National Science Foundation

The SBA periodically issues a listing of research and development projects for which each agency is soliciting proposals. A copy of the listing can be obtained by contacting the SBA. By responding to an agency's request for proposal (RFP), the entrepreneurial company can compete for the funds available to conduct the announced research. Some agencies will accept unsolicited research proposals.

Research grants are typically awarded in phases. The first phase consists of a grant of up to $100,000 to be used to evaluate the feasibility and scientific merit of the proposed research over a six to nine month period . If the first phase is completed successfully, the company can obtain up to $750,000 in the second grant phase to develop the subject technology over a one- or two- year period.  Success ratios recently published by the Department of Energy suggest as many as one in five phase one grant proposals are successful and one in two phase two proposals are funded following successful completion of phase one research.

The funding agency typically retains a limited use license to the developed technology but, otherwise, ownership of the technology remains with the company.  Production contracts with the federal agency sometimes follow successful completion of the second phase. Solicitation and other procedures vary from agency to agency, so companies should investigate the agency's rules carefully before competing for its research funds. *See: SBA (Small Business Administration).*

**S Corporations** are form of corporation that is not taxed by the Internal Revenue Service as a separate entity. Instead, income and losses pass to the shareholders of the company and are taxed on their personal returns. S corporations are often contrasted with C corporations that are taxed as separate entities with no pass through of income or losses to shareholders.

Profits and losses pass directly to the shareholders of S corporations without regard to whether or how much money the company distributes to them. If the company makes a profit and needs it to fund operations, the shareholders will have to show that profit on their individual tax returns and pay taxes on it even if they receive no cash from the company. Because of this, agreements are frequently made among shareholders and S corporations requiring the corporation to make cash payments to shareholders that are at least sufficient to pay taxes.

When individual tax rates are lower than corporate tax rates, S corporations can to be used to reduce federal taxes paid on corporate earnings by giving the company the benefits of its shareholders' lower tax rates. When individual rates are higher, S corporations can still be used to distribute losses generated by the company to individual shareholders. While there are limits on the amount of losses a shareholder can claim on his return, this pass-through can reduce the after-tax cost of investment for investors in companies that are losing money. At the same time, however, this pass-through deprives the company of the ability to use these losses to shelter future income from taxes. This can increase the likelihood that it will need additional funding in the future.

S corporations are not as effective as some other structures when it comes to allocating company losses to outside investors. This is because losses and profits are allocated to S company shareholders on the basis of their percentage ownership in the company. In other words, outside investor who invests $1 million in a company for 40 percent ownership will get only 40% of losses generated by the company's use of his money. If the company loses all of his $1 million, he will only be allocated $400,000 of the loss.

Other company structures, such as limited partnerships and limited liability companies, permit more flexibility in the allocation of losses and profits and consequently are used more often than S corporations to attract investors who want to reduce the after-tax cost of their investments. Limited partnerships and limited liability companies can be structured so that almost all of the company's losses are allocated to the outside investor. This means an investor who purchases a 40% interest in a limited entity could, nonetheless, receive almost all of the losses attributable to the use of his $1 million even though he may only be entitled to receive 40 percent of the profits.

Establishing an S corporation requires strict compliance with a number of IRS requirements, including rules relating to the nature of the company's shareholders and its outstanding securities. It is not available to all entrepreneurial companies. For example, S corporations are available only to companies organized under the laws of a state in the U.S. Foreign corporations, even if they have assets or do business in the United States, cannot qualify. Even some domestic companies defined by the IRS as "ineligible corporations" (e.g., insurance companies, certain financial institutions, and other enumerated companies) cannot qualify. S corporations can have only a limited number shareholders, all of whom must be individuals, estates, or certain qualifying trusts or tax exempt organizations. And only one class of stock can be issued without jeopardizing the S corporation's tax status (although that class can be divided into subclasses with different voting rights). Certain consent and timing requirements must also be met to secure S corporation status.

As you might imagine, the flow-through of profits and losses is not without complications. For one thing, losses can be used by a shareholder only to the extent of his "basis" in his stock. Initially, this basis equals the individual's purchase price for his stock plus his basis in any loans he makes to the company. As the company operates, this basis can fluctuate, however, generally increasing with company income and gains and decreasing with company losses. Also, losses generated to a shareholder may not be used to offset all types of income.

Because of the complexity of S corporations and the peculiarities of the manner in which they and their shareholders are taxed, entrepreneurs should always consult with their accountants and legal advisers before organizing S corporations. Failure to do so could result in unwanted surprises for the company and its shareholders. *See: Limited*

*Partnerships, LLCs (Limited Liability Companies), R & D Partnerships, Structure.*

**SEC** refers to the U.S. Securities and Exchange Commission,s the federal government agency that administers the 33 Act and other federal securities laws. It reviews public offering documents and promulgates rules and regulations interpreting the federal securities acts and establishing safe harbors from the registration requirements of the 33 Act. *See: Going Public, IPOs (Initial Public Offerings), Private Placements, Reg D, Restricted Securities, Safe Harbors, 10b5, 33 Act.*

**Serial Entrepreneur** is someone who has builds more than one business. Investors like serial entrepreneurs because their experience with building new businesses often translates into repeat success. *See: Track Record.*

**Secrecy Agreements.** *See: Confidentiality Agreements.*

**Secured Loans** are loans that are backed by assets of the borrower. The availability of the assets pledged as security reduces the lender's risk in making the loan and can result in lower interest rates or more favorable terms. In some cases, the availability of collateral for a loan is essential to qualifying to receive the loan. Receivables financing, for example, is available only when the company's accounts receivables are pledged to secure the loan. The amount of availability under the financing is typically stated as a percentage of the company's total outstanding receivables. Upon default of a secured loan, the lender is entitled to foreclose on and sell the property acting as security. The proceeds from the sale of foreclosed assets can be applied by the lender to pay the loan balance and lender's costs. *See:*

*Collateral, Credit Lines, Factoring, Security Agreements, Term Loans,*

**Security Agreements** refer to contracts entered into between companies and lenders in connection with a secured loan to create the security interest in the collateral being pledged to secure the loan. The presence of the security interest entitles the lender to foreclose on the collateral acting as security if the borrower defaults on the loan. *See: Collateral, Secured Loans.*

**Seed Capital** refers to financing obtained by a company before it has completed developing a prototype of its product. Sometimes it refers to capital raised after a company has developed a prototype but before it has manufactured any production units. This is the most difficult and expensive money to raise because it is needed so early in the business building process, long before management has proved its ability to even build a product. The entrepreneur's family and friends as well as his personal savings are primary sources of seed capital. Angel investors and a few specialized seed capital funds are also possible sources. *See: CDCs (Community Development Corporations), Stage Financing.*

**Shareholders' Agreements** are contracts entered into between company shareholders, frequently at the insistence of a minority shareholder. They take a variety of forms and serve a number of purposes from protecting a minority shareholder, securing specific rights for a majority shareholder, or providing arrangements for transfer of control or buying a deceased partners stock. Shareholders agreements are usually in writing and often signed by persons who together own a majority of the outstanding shares of the company's voting stock.

Venture capital investors frequently require shareholders agreements with management and major shareholders as a condition of funding. They do this to secure rights to representation on the company's board of directors and rights limit founder and management freedom to dispose of their shares. In early stage companies, these shareholder agreements may also subject management shareholdings to vesting requirement designed to make it more costly for management to become disengaged with the company.

Management that sells a controlling interest in its company's stock will commonly negotiate for a shareholders' agreement to ensure its continued ability to be represented on the company's board of directors. It may also negotiate an employment agreement to preserve some rights to remain active in management.

Shareholder agreements between equal or near equal owners often address questions of influence over company decisions and methods for transitioning ownership. Often, they contain mechanisms such as first refusal or first negotiation rights that insure each partner with the first opportunity to purchase the other partner's stock in the future. Buy sell agreements are sometimes included to provide a mechanism for each partner to force the other to sell his ownership in the company in the event the parties are unable to agree on the management of the company.

Shareholders' agreements are also commonly used for estate planning purposes. In these cases, they are frequently funded by life insurance purchased by the company on the life of the protected party. When the protected manager dies the proceeds of the policy paid to the corporation are used, pursuant to the contractual obligations of the shareholder agreement, to purchase the deceased managers shareholdings in the company.

Shareholder agreements often impact management, its freedom to operate, and its relationship with its investors. Common provisions can limit a manager's ability to sell his shares to outsiders and provide for the disposition of his shares in the event of his death or termination of employment. Management should consider shareholders' agreements carefully. Shareholder agreements should have limited terms and, in most cases, should terminate in the event of a public offering of the company's stock or sale of the company. *See: Benchmarks, Buy-Sell Agreements, Common Stock, Control, Co-Sale Agreements, Cumulative Voting, First Refusal Rights (Shareholders).*

## Shark Repellents

**Shark Repellents** refer to provisions that make it more difficult for an outsider to gain operating control of a company without the consent of the company's existing board of directors. The shark being repelled is the outsider who would change management if he gained control of the company. Shark repellents are common in public companies whose publicly traded stock gives outsiders opportunities to acquire large blocks of company securities.

Common shark repellents include:

- *Super-majority voting.* These are requirements built into a company's charter or bylaws that require more than a majority of the company's shareholders (typically, 67 percent or more) to vote in favor of a company sale before it is approved.
- *Staggered elections.* Also incorporated into a company's charter or bylaws, are rules that specify that only a part of the company's board of directors stands for election each year. These make a forced acquisition less attractive to a buyer because the staggered election process delays the ability to take control of the board. In a company with seven directors, for example, each director might stand for election only once every three years, with two standing in year one, two in year two, three in year three.
- *Nonvoting stock.* Designating more than one class of common stock with different voting rights specified for each class can also make a hostile takeover more

difficult. If the stock traded in the public market does not have the power to elect a majority of the company's board of directors, prospective acquirers can only obtain operating control by purchasing the other privately held shares or negotiating directly with the board of directors.

- *Poison pills.* These are plans adopted by companies that grant extraordinary rights to purchase additional shares of stock at discounts to shareholders other than the party attempting a hostile takeover. The rights are triggered when the acquirer purchases a predefined percentage of the company, making the stock purchased less valuable and dramatically increasing the cost of acquiring the company.

*See: Control, Going Public, Poison Pill.*

**Shell Merger** refers to an alternative method of going public that, typically, does not involve the raising of capital. In a shell merger, a private company merges with a registered public company that has minimal assets and debt. The merger is structured as a 'reverse merger' so that the surviving company after the merger is the public company, which by virtue of the merger contains the business and assets of the private company. The owners of the private company typically own more than 90% of the public company after completion of the merger and change the name of the company to the name of the private company. The management and directors of the private company become the management and directors of the public company, which is now controlled by the shareholders who controlled the private company. *See: Going Public, Public Offering.*

**Shopping** refers to the practice of presenting a company's business plan to several investors simultaneously. Selective shopping when looking for venture capital investment is a fact of life. Most investors take weeks or months to evaluate a

*Investors, Deal Structures, Legal Strategies - 337*

prospective investment and many will invest only when other outside investors participate in a funding. As a result, few successful companies limit themselves to one investor prospect when searching for money.

The most productive private fundraising practice includes an early screening phase designed to identify investors who are most likely to be interested in the company's business and stage of investment. The goal of this phase is to identify likely investors and the company's existing contacts with those investors. Investors have preferences and investment policy limits. Showing a plan for a seed investment, for example, to a mezzanine investor is a waste of time for both the company and the investor. Sharing plans for a blockbuster medical product to an electronics industry fund indicates to the investment community that the company's management team has not done its homework.

Investment bankers and other professionals are sometimes engaged to assist in this process and in process of shopping the company's plan to the identified investors. Even when professional investment bankers are not involved, companies routinely poll their professional advisors for information and contacts with potential investors. Published sources are also available that describe the investments made by venture investors in portfolio companies.

Another method of screening potential investors is to send an inquiry letter to a pool of qualified investors. This letter should identify the company, its business, the amount of money needed, and the way in which the money will be used. After providing this information, the letter can offer to send business plans to interested investors.

Used in a mailing to investors that have invested in the company's industry and stage of investment before, this process can help management identify those investors who are currently funding companies like theirs. This, in turn, allows management to concentrate its efforts on investors who are interested and more likely to fund.

The following is the body of an inquiry letter that was sent to a number of investors around the country. The investors were selected based on their histories of funding companies in the company's industry. The letter generated significant interest and led to serious funding negotiations.

Dear Investor:

We are seeking first-stage investment capital for our business. Minimum investment requirements are $1 million with a comprehensive package totaling $2.5 to 3 million. We have been in business for one year and can demonstrate rapid growth, achievement, and potential. All of our operating subsidiaries are involved with musical merchandise and high-tech electronic application to this field.

We are interested in taking our company public. Our management team is very experienced and already in place. I have enclosed an issue of *Musical Merchandise Review* (the trade publication) that features our company. This will provide you with some background information. We have made a significant impact on our industry with our merchandising ability as well as our rapid success.

Please contact me personally if you are interested in learning more about our firm.

Entrepreneurs should be flexible in their search for funding and speak with lenders, individuals, family, friends, relatives, and other sources in addition to venture firms. A common mistake many entrepreneurs make when raising capital is limiting their searches to one type of investor before exploring the potential availability of capital from other sources. Many believe (mistakenly) that if they need capital, they must always get it from a venture capital fund.

Another common mistake is to assume that one investor will provide all of the debt and equity financing the company needs. In fact, many venture capital investments involve more than one investor. Many involve a separate lender who receives no equity for lending. To improve the odds of being funded, management can separate its funding needs into debt and equity requirements and approach lenders and equity investors at the same time, asking each to commit to fund a portion of the company's total financing needs.

Getting a commitment for part of a funding is often easier than getting one for all of it. This is particularly true when each investor's commitment is contingent upon the company securing the rest of the financing because each investor knows that his money will not be committed until another investors agrees enough with his positive assessment of the company to invest his money as well. Once a company gets its first commitment using this approach, other investors can become easier to find and more inclined to join in. *See: Networking, Syndication, Venture Capitalists.*

**Software Protection** refers to the fact that copyrights, trade secrets and, in limited cases, patents can be used to prevent others from misappropriating valuable company software. Proprietary software has become important to business in more and more industries as part of what distinguishes their ability to compete in their marketplaces. Often, protecting this proprietary software is essential to the company's success and protecting it adequately is not only prudent but necessary to convince an outsider to invest in the company. Venture investors expect companies to take reasonable steps to protect their proprietary software and other valuable secrets from being misappropriated by their competitors.

Copyrights and trade secrets each protect different aspects of computer software and both require the company to take affirmative action to secure their protections. Copyrights protect the expression of ideas rather than the ideas themselves. That is, copyrights can prevent someone from using (copying) a program but not from using the ideas expressed in the program to produce a new program that does the same thing. Trade secrets protect ideas but only when the owner takes reasonable actions to maintain the idea's secrecy.

Patents provide a government-sanctioned monopoly to commercialize an invention. Patents can be obtained for software when the software code meets exacting standards of novelty required of patents generally. Because patents are published, the option of claiming trade secrecy protection for the portion of a software program that is patented is lost when the patent is published. A more complete description of patents appears in the *Patent* entry earlier in this book.

Copyright protection is governed by federal statute and protects both published and unpublished works. To secure full copyright protection, a company must follow prescribed rules and file with the Federal Copyright Office within five years after the program is developed. Filings with the Copyright Office can be done in object code or source code, and there is a procedure that permits companies to file limited portions of the code. This procedure can help a company preserve its trade secrets in a program while obtaining copyright protection as well.

Trade secrets protect the underlying ideas as opposed to their expression. The availability of trade secrets protection is governed by state law and applies only ideas or code that is kept secret. Protecting a trade secret through litigation involves proving that the trade secret exists, that it was disclosed only in confidence, and the use or disclosure of the information complained about was obtained in violation of a confidence and to the injury of the company.

The existence of a trade secret is a matter of fact. The factors courts generally consider to determine whether a trade secret exists include

- the extent to which the information is known outside the company's business,

- the extent the information is known to employees and others involved in the business,
- the value of the information to the company and its competitors,
- the amount of money and effort expended to develop the information, and
- the ease or difficulty with which the information can be properly acquired by competitors.

In other words, the more valuable the information and the more safeguards the company takes to protect that information, the easier it will be to prove to a court that a given software program should be treated as a trade secret. Both trade secrets and copyrights protection can provide a company with rights to receive money damages and to stop a competitor from using its software.

Often, the best strategy for protecting proprietary software, particularly software that is not mass marketed as a company product, is to claim the protection of both trade secrecy and the copyright laws. Securing both gives a company more ways to stop infringers from stealing its software and gives it access to the federal courts to pursue its claims. In many situations, copyright infringement cases are easier to prove in court than are trade secret infringement cases, giving the company that obtains copyright protection a significant advantage over one that relies solely on trade secrecy.

A good practice when claiming both protections is to mark the software medium and program the software to display at sign-on a message that identifies that the company is claiming both rights. A sample notice claiming both protections follows:

© 2004 by ABC Company
All Worldwide Rights Reserved.
This work contains trade secrets of the ABC Company.
Any unauthorized use, copying, compiling, decompiling,
or reverse engineering is strictly prohibited.

Care must be taken, however, whenever both copyright and trade secrecy protection are sought, to preserve the confidentiality of the software during the copyrighting process. The careless filing of materials with the copyright office or over-reliance on copyright protection in the wrong situation can lead to the loss of important trade secrecy rights in a computer program. A qualified attorney can advise management on the best strategy to follow to obtain the most protection available under both laws. *See: Copyrights, Patents, Trade Secrets.*

**Specialty Funds** are venture capital firms that invest their money only in companies or products that fall within an identified industry or field of endeavor. Often, the organizational documents for the fund specify this focus by limiting the ability of the funds management team to invest more than a limited percentage of its funds outside of its industry focus.

An industry specialty fund might, for example, invest only in businesses that offer a product or service directly, but not necessarily exclusively, related to the needs of the electric and gas utility industry. Another fund might focus exclusively on medical device technologies. Sometimes the phrase specialty fund is used to refer to funds that are not industry focused but, instead, focus on investing in companies when they are at certain business development stages. A seed fund or a mezzanine fund would be an example of a stage specific fund.

Industry specialty funds cater to investors who are interested in specific markets. Their focus, they believe, gives them an edge in identifying the most promising companies in their niche. By specializing, they are able to develop industry-specific expertise that helps them identify industry trends. Their knowledge of the industry players can also help them assist their portfolio companies with recommendations of people to hire and advice on how others in the industry address common business issues.

Identifying specialty funds appropriate to a company's industry or stage of development can make the fundraising process more productive. Even funds that are not specialty funds tend to specialize in industries or stages of financings. Identifying the tendencies of investors can help a company focus its fund-raising activities and increase its changes for success. *See: Venture Capitalists for some sources containing listings of investors. See also: Corporate Venture Capital, Shopping, Value Added.*

**Spin Outs** occur when an established company transfers, or 'spins out', a technology or business activity to a company that was established for the purpose of acquiring the technology or business activity. Often the technology transfer consists of the exclusive right to use the company's core patents and know how in business markets the company does not serve. A company with medical practice scheduling software, for example, might spin out the rights to use its software in transportation industries to a management group with transportation experience and financial backing. The same company might have a business unit unrelated to its software business that it chooses to spin out. Its reasons for doing this might include the lack of internal resources to properly pursue the market, its lack of expertise in the target market, or its desire to focus its resources on other technologies or products.

Spin outs are frequently structured like leveraged buyouts. Often an interested management group, frequently from within the parent company, identifies the proposed technology or business unit for divestiture, obtains company approval to seek funding for a transfer, and, ultimately, creates the new company and negotiates the transfer of the technology or business activity. The company that spins out the activity typically obtains one or more of the following compensations in return for the assets it contributes to the new company:

- stock in the new company,
- royalties from products that use the transferred technology,
- cash or deferred cash payments, or
- rights within the contributing company's markets to technology improvements developed by the new company.

It is not uncommon for the contributing company to obtain a seat on the new company's board of directors or preferential contract rights.

Spin outs require extensive planning and, usually, a financial commitment from the new management as well as the raising of private capital from venture capitalists and banks. Managements of spin outs also have the sensitive task of building consensus for the spin out and raising money for their new business while they remain employed by the contributing company. Internal jealousies and politics of the contributing company often create obstacles to completing a deal on acceptable terms.

The typical steps in completing a spin out, many of which overlap, are as follows:

- *Identify the opportunity.* Internal management members closest to the opportunity often see the opportunity first, put together the management team to lead the deal, and conduct preliminary due diligence and market research to begin quantifying the extent and reality of the opportunity.
- *Assemble advisors.* It is important to obtain competent legal advice early in the process. The spin out

management team must be sensitive to its fiduciary and trade secret obligations to the contributing company throughout the process in order to avoid unnecessary exposure to legal liability. Management's attorneys can help the team determine the optimal timing for alerting the company to management's spin out plan, the limits on management's ability to disclose company information, and the best method for obtaining company approval to pursue the spin out. Counsel can also advise on structure and timing issues relating to the formation of the new company that can minimize management's exposure to tax liabilities from the spin out.

- *Obtain preliminary indications of interest.* Two activities need to proceed here on parallel paths. First, management must determine the contributing company's interest in participating in a transfer and the general terms on which such a transfer is possible. Second, management must identify potential funding sources to complete the acquisition and support the new company's future operations. Those funding sources can sometimes include the contributing company itself.

- *Obtain a letter of intent.* Through a process of persuasion and diligence, the management team must obtain a letter of intent or other formal commitment from the contributing company that spells out the general terms under which the company is willing to make the transfer to a management-backed company. This letter of intent provides management with a period of time during which the contributing company agrees not to pursue alternative transactions for the technology or business activity. Although often difficult to obtain, this formal commitment is critical to the process of completing a spin out because it legitimizes the management's efforts with outside funding sources and makes it possible to have serious discussions of price and terms for financing. As a practical matter, however, preliminary discussions with funding sources, investment bankers, attorneys, and accountants often precede the signing of a letter of intent if for no other reason than for management to get a feel for what terms and conditions will likely be acceptable to the funding sources.

- *Obtain funding commitment.* Once a company letter of intent is obtained, management needs to obtain commitments from lenders and equity capital providers. This process often results in additional negotiations with the contributing company. Management must negotiate deals that create incentives for the contributing company, outside investors, and management. Sometimes, preliminary indications of intent from outside investors are received before the signing of a letter of intent with the contributing company.

- *Complete business planning activities.* All the issues of operating the business after the spin out should be considered and planned for. Additional managers and employees should be identified and space and facility needs addressed.

- *Close the transaction.* Extensive additional negotiation and document preparation follows as the parties prepare for the actual closing. The transfer of the technology or business activity from the contributing company, the investment by management in the new company, and the funding by a bank or equity investor typically occur simultaneously. The resulting new company is ready to open its doors for business.

There are no hard and fast guidelines about the amount or nature of the compensation paid to the contributing company for its contribution or for the amount of stock or other rights given to the venture capital investor in a spin out. Because management is typically perceived as being critical to the success of the new company, however, it is generally true that new investors typically believe that management should be motivated through the ownership of a significant position in the stock of the new company. Nonetheless, management ownership interests in a new spin out company can vary widely, as can the form and amount of consideration flowing to the contributing company.

While all situations are different - company size alone can make a 5% interest in one company worth significantly more than an 10% interest in another - one veteran venture capitalist and investment banker recently summarized his experience by stating that in most situations the key managers receive between 12% and 20% of the equity of the new company for putting together the deal, investing their own funds, and running the company with up to another 10% being made available in a stock plan to motivate other key employees. Whether management falls on the high or low side of this range depends on their perceived importance to the deal, the size of the deal, and other factors.

Of the 12% to 20%, as much as half or more may go to the head of the management team with the rest going to the remainder of the founding managers. A significant portion of managements' stock may be in securities that vest over time to insure that the management team stays with the new company. Outside equity investors and sometimes the contributing company usually expect to receive convertible preferred stock. Management usually receives common stock, at least for the portion of their equity investment that is not issued for equivalent cash investment. *See: Convertible Preferred Stock, Convertible Securities, Earnouts, Earnups, Joint Ventures, LBO (Leveraged Buyout), Letter Agreements, Letters of Intent, MBO (Management Buyout), Negotiation, Venture Capital Deal Structures.*

**SSBICs** refer to Specialized Small Business Investment Companies, government-chartered venture firms that can invest only in companies that are at least 51 percent owned by members of a minority group or persons recognized by the rules that govern SSBICs to be socially or economically disadvantaged. SSBICs borrow government moneys to increase (leverage) the size of their funds just as SBICs do. As a result, most of the investment characteristics of SBICs also apply to SSBICS. *See: SBICs (Small Business Investment Companies).*

**Stage Financing** refers to a method many investors use to reduce their risk when funding companies. Funding a company in stages means providing the money that has been committed in pieces as the company meets pre-established goals. Customarily, the company doles out the shares to the investor as the money is received.

For example, an investor might agree to provide $2 million to a company by paying $1 million down, $500,000 when the company gets its first order, and $500,000 when it receives its first payment from an order. The stock sold to the investor might be issued in increments of 60,000 shares up front, 25,000 shares when the first $500,000 payment is made, and 15,000 shares when the last $500,000 is put in. (The earlier dollars buy more shares because there is more risk at the beginning.) Alternatively, the shares might issue pro rata with the funds invested, giving the investor 50,000 up front, 25,000 when the first $500,000 is paid, and 25,000 when the last $50,000 is paid.

Often, the milestones used for the later stages of funding are tied in some fashion to the financial projections contained in the company's business plan. Sometimes they relate to the completion of specific tasks that reflect success of the management team in meeting necessary objectives. Sometimes, the milestones are no more complicated than the passage of time. Often performance related goals have both a performance component and a maximum time component, during which the goal must be met.

While the commitment is to fund the entire amount, the later stages of funding are contingent on the company meeting the milestones. When those goals are more complicated than the simple passage of time, the investor will be relieved of his obligation to provide additional funds if the goals are not met on time. In this way, the investor can cut his losses when a company does not meet expectations. At the same time, the company gets a commitment for its full funding, which it can obtain by meeting its goals.

Stage financing also refers to the fact that growing companies often need funding at various points in their development. At each point, or stage, the company solicits new investors to fund the next phase of company growth.

It is not uncommon for growing companies to go through two or more private rounds of financing before it is large and successful enough to sell its stock on the public market. Each stage of financing can reduce management's percentage ownership in the company. As the company progresses, however, its stock should command a higher price in each successive stage. The reason for this is that the investor's risk decreases as the company succeeds and meets its goals. As a result, if management gave up 30 percent of its company's stock to attract $2 million in venture capital the first time around, it may only cost an additional 15 percent of the company's stock to raise $5 million in the second round of financing.

The first stage of financing is commonly called seed financing. This is money raised to make an idea for a product into a working prototype. Quite often, seed money is obtained from the company's founders and their family and friends.

Seed money is the hardest to find, and the most expensive (in terms of the percentage of the company's ownership that is sold). Because it is so expensive, many entrepreneurs try to forestall asking for equity investments from outsiders as long as possible. Investing his own savings is one way for an entrepreneur to delay or avoid this stage of financing. Borrowing against the equity in his house is another.

Start-up capital usually refers to money raised to modify a working or almost-working prototype product into a product that can be manufactured at a cost that allows the company to make a profit. It can be the first or second stage of a company's financing. Start-up capital is used to test-market products and prepare companies for their first round of product sales. This money is more readily available than seed capital.

Second- and third-tier financings come next if they are needed. These are traditionally used to finance inventory and company expansions. If a second- or third-tier financing is used to fund a company expansion that enables the company to later conduct a public offering, it is referred to as a mezzanine financing.

In the dynamic world of venture capital and start-up companies, no two companies have the same capital needs or grow in the same way. If management delays the need to acquire seed money until its prototype is almost ready, one venture capitalist might consider the proposed investment a seed investment while another might consider it an early start-up financing. There is no magic to the labels. They are conventions that are casually observed in the industry to describe financings. *See: Benchmarks, Mezzanine Financing, Pricing, Procrastination, ROI (Return on Investment), Seed Capital, Start-Up Capital.*

**Start-Up Capital** refers to money raised to help a company get the working prototype of its product into production and to make initial marketing efforts. This money typically less expensive to companies than seed capital, but more expensive than later-stage financings. *See: Mezzanine Financing, Seed Capital, Stage Financing.*

**Stock Committee** refers to a group of company officers or directors designated by a company's board of directors to decide when and how shares of the company's stock should be issued to employees or others. Stock committees of growing companies often allocate a pool of shares to be granted to key employees as part of an incentive plan.

Many venture capital investors believe an effective plan for including key employees in company ownership is important to building a successful company. Consequently, venture capitalists routinely consent to the reservation of a pool of shares to be issued to employees after closing of a funding even though the issuance of those shares will dilute the percentage interest of the investor. Sometimes, the investor will want to participate in the allocation of these shares. One way for an investor to do this is to require representation on the company's stock committee. *See: Board Committees, ISOs (Incentive Stock Options), Qualified Stock Option Plans.*

## Strategic Partnerships. *See: Joint Ventures.*

**Structure** refers to the combination of debt and equity an investor receives for funding a company as well as the terms and conditions under which the funding is made. Sometimes called deal structure, it covers the timing of the funding and the protections, management participation rights, liquidation rights, and other agreements the investor obtains in return for his investment.

For example, one structure may call for $5 million to be invested in a company in return for 20 percent of the company's outstanding stock. The deal might require all of the money to be invested at once and might include piggyback registration rights and a right of first refusal. Another structure might call for the money to be invested in stages as the company meets certain benchmarks and might

*352 – Growth Company Guide 4.0*

require preferred stock or convertible debentures to be issued to the investor. That investor might also receive demand and piggyback registration rights, rights of first refusal, puts, and options to purchase additional shares. Both might contain antidilution protections for the investor, but the degree of protection provided might vary substantially.

Most negotiations in a venture financing revolve around the price and structure of the proposed deal. Revising a structure can turn a bad deal into a good one, or vice versa. To negotiate effectively, management and its advisers must understand the ramifications of the various deal structuring devices employed by investors and the concerns of investors those devices are designed to address. Those devices and concerns are summarized in the *Venture Capital Deal Structures* entry of this book. Employing qualified professional advisors such as attorneys, accountants, and investment bankers early in the deal making process can be critically important to getting structure that makes sense for the company and its management. *See also: Antidilution Provisions, Benchmarks, Buy-Sell Agreements, Calls, Convertible Securities, Co-Sale Agreements, Debentures, Earnouts, Earnups, Equity Penalties, Exits, First Refusal Rights (Company), First Refusal Rights (Shareholder), Fully Diluted, LBO (Leveraged Buyout), Leverage, Liquidity Agreements, Negative Covenants, Negotiation, Personal Guarantees, Preferred Stock Umbrellas, Pricing, Projections, Puts, Registration Rights, Reps and Warranties, Revenue Participations, Shareholders' Agreements, Stage Financing, Take-Away Provisions, Weighted Average Antidilution.*

**STTR** refers to Small Business Technology Transfer program of the U.S. government program that provides funding for entrepreneurial research and development that expands upon the SBIR program discussed earlier. The program reserves a portion of the federal governments research and development funding for projects jointly conducted by for-profit companies in collaboration with non-profit institutions.

To qualify small businesses must be U.S. owned and based and have fewer than 500 employees. Collaborating non-profit institutions must be located in the U.S., be a nonprofit college or university, nonprofit research organization, or a federally funded research and development center. The program followed the same formula as the SBIR program and provides funding in phases. The following departments agencies participate in the program:

Department of Defense
Department of Energy
Department of Health and Human Services
National Aeronautics and Space Administration
National Science Foundation

*See: SBA (Small Business Administration), SBIR (Small Business Innovation Research).*

## Subordinated Convertible Debentures is a

form of subordinated convertible debt in which the principal and/or interest due under the debenture is convertible at the election of the holder into capital stock of the borrowing company at an agreed upon rate of conversion. These debentures usually do not entitle their holders to any rights to vote on matters that come before company shareholders. Often, however, they contain contractual provisions that entitle the holder to receive financial reports or limit the amount or type of debt to which it will be subordinate. Because they are debt instruments, convertible subordinated debentures have preference over common stock and preferred stock in the event of a company liquidation. Subordinated convertible debentures are sometimes used in lieu of convertible preferred stock in venture capital financings. *See: Convertible Preferred Stock, Convertible Securities, Debentures, Subordinated Debt.*

**Subordinated Debt** is borrowed money that stands to be repaid after other debts but before company shareholders receive consideration in the event the company is liquidated. Subordinated debt is frequently used in venture financings to provide investors with a way to increase their return on investment or to withdraw a portion of it as debt repayment without unduly prejudicing the company's ability to obtain other borrowings. Subordinated debt is a key element in mezzanine financings.

Since it stands behind other debt if the company liquidates, subordinated debt is often treated as equity by other lenders. That is, lenders are willing to extend additional credit to the company as if the debt did not exist, as long as their debt matures and is repaid before the subordinated debt. This usually means that the subordinated debt agreement not only contains specific language subordinating it to other debt but that its maturity date occurs after that of the company's other debt. Therefore, the later the payback on subordinated debt, the easier it is for a company to borrow additional funds.

Subordinated debt provides a company with cash, usually with a long-term payback, and gives the investor the ability to withdraw his invested capital without adverse tax consequences. Sometimes subordinated debt contains a convertibility feature that allows the investor to convert it into shares of stock. This gives the investor the flexibility to withdraw his funds as debt repayment or to convert to share ownership if the company's stock is selling for a good price. *See: Cash Flow, Convertible Securities, Debentures, Mezzanine Financing, Structure, Subordinated Convertible Debentures, Venture Capital Deal Structures.*

**Summary** refers to a synopsis of the key points of a business plan. Sometimes referred to as an executive summary, it appears at the beginning of a business plan and highlights key aspects of the company's plan that are particularly important to prospective investors. It is one of the most important parts of a business plan. Sometimes summaries are delivered separately to investors as part of a screening process. Investors interested in the company from the summary description are then provided with the more complete plan as the company attempts to seek funding.

The importance of the summary can be illustrated by a simple fact: Few venture capitalists will spend more than five or ten minutes on a business plan before deciding whether they are interested enough to study it seriously. The two portions of the business plan most venture capitalists focus on during this critical first reading are the summary and the financial information, which includes the company's projections. If the summary does not heighten their interest, few investors will turn to the financials or consider the company further.

Because of its importance in getting investors to investigate further, the summary should be prepared with particular care. It should be short (two to four pages is ideal), concise, descriptive, well organized, and enticing.

A lot to ask of a summary? Maybe, but while no professional investor is likely to invest in a company on the basis of two pages of reading, many will decide against investing just that quickly. To ensure that the potential investor does not discard the company's business plan after reading only the summary, the plan writer should be sure it provides the investor with the right information about the company.

An effective summary should include the following information:

- *Company identity and contact.* Give the name, address, and telephone number of the company. The name of the person the investor should contact and how he or she may be reached should be prominently displayed.

- *Business of the company*. A short description of the company's business should be given here. How did it get started? What is its market niche, and why will it succeed?
- *Management.* What are the strengths of the company's key management personnel? A short itemization of the relevant accomplishments of key management members should be given.
- *The product*. This paragraph should contain a short description of the company's product and what makes it unique. A brief analysis of the company's competition and why management believes its product will succeed in the marketplace should also be included.
- *Funds required*. How much money does the company need? Does management have any preference as to equity versus debt? If the funds are requested on a staged basis, this should also be set forth. If there is collateral available, it should be described.
- *Use of funds*. How the company plans to use the funds should be detailed here.
- *Financial history*. A short financial history of the company should be provided here. This can be done in a narrative or in a chart listing four or five key figures such as revenues, income or loss, assets, liabilities, and net worth for each year of the company's operation.
- *Projections*. This section should contain a summary of the key elements of the company's projections for the next three to five years.
- *Exits*. Any plans the company has to go public or to provide the investor with other exits in the next three to five years should be spelled out. The investor wants to know how he will get his money out.

*See: Business Plan, Business Plan Format, Negotiation.*

**Sweat Equity** is the hard work, long hours, worry, and fatigue that a founding entrepreneur invests to make his company succeed. The stock initially issued to the entrepreneur usually costs a great deal less than stock later sold to investors who take less risk. This difference between the higher price paid for shares of the company's stock by investors and the price paid by the company's founders is sometimes referred to as the founder's sweat equity. *See: Bargain Stock.*

**Syndications** refer to investments that are shared among several investors, with each providing part of the total funding. Such a funding is sometimes referred to as having been syndicated with the group of investors who make up the syndicate. The investor who takes the largest position in the investment is referred to as the lead investor.

Syndications are popular among venture investors because they allow them to spread their money over more deals and diversify their risks. They also allow them to share information with other investors. A lead investor's inclusion of another investor in an attractive deal is also a form of collateral between investors that makes it more likely the lead investor will be invited to participate in attractive investments sourced by the other investors in the deal. This can be valuable to the lead investor by providing him with a source of pre-screened deals to consider.

A key factor in completing many successful fundraisings is finding an investor who is willing to play the role of lead investor. Some investors are willing to invest but unable or unwilling to take the lead in putting together the syndicate necessary to provide all the money needed. Such an investor is less attractive to a company than one who is willing to help find all the capital a company needs. A good question to ask any interested investors early on in the fundraising process is whether he is able to provide all the funding needed by the company and, if not, whether he will take the lead in syndicating the deal.

A problem that sometimes accompanies a syndicated funding is the desire of each investor to have a seat on the company's board of directors. As a rule, management should try to limit its outside investor group to the same number of board seats management would have given one investor had he provided all of the funding. Usually, this means one or two board seats for the investor group with the investors choosing among themselves who will represent them on the board. Others may attend board meetings and consult with management, but only the ones serving on the board will be entitled to vote.

This encourages the syndication members to cooperate among themselves so that management is not distracted by disagreements among its investors. At the same time, it preserves a small working board of directors and gives management the ability to tap into the expertise and contacts of each investor. *See: Clubbing, Lead Investor, Shopping, Underwriters.*

# T

**Tag-Along Provisions** are agreements that require one or more party, usually company management, to include another party, usually an outside investor, in future opportunities they receive to sell their stock. They are also referred to as co-sale agreements. Tag-along provisions are frequently pared with first refusal rights agreements in venture financing agreements to protect investors. See: *Co-Sale Agreements, First Refusal Rights.*

**Take Away Provisions** are agreements between an investor and management that entitle the investor to penalize management when the company does not achieve agreed upon results. The penalty is often the reduction in management's shareholdings or in its ability to operate the company independently. Take away provisions are most prevalent in financings where the company sells a controlling interest to outside investors and management contracts with the investors to maintain operating control so long as company results are acceptable. They are also common in earnups, leveraged buyouts and other transactions where management's participation is predicated upon it achieving certain results. See: *Earnouts, Earnups, LBO (Leveraged Buyout), Management Agreements, Operating Covenants, Shareholders' Agreements, Structure, Voting Trusts.*

**Take-Out Funding** refers to any company financing undertaken, at least in part, for the purpose of paying off an existing debt or equity investment in the company. The term is frequently used to refer to an investment in company stock whose proceeds are used to replace company debt. *See: Bridge Loans*.

**Technology Development Centers** are facilities with programs designed to help entrepreneurs create viable businesses from their technology innovations. Many state and local governments, often working through their universities, sponsor centers to promote the development of new businesses. Often the motivation is job creation or general economic development. Centers attached to universities often serve to facilitate the commercialization of inventions made by faculty members. Other centers are privately sponsored or associated with venture capital funds or angel investors. Technology development centers are often referred to as accelerators, incubators, or innovation centers.

The types of services offered varies from facility to facility. Some centers provide inexpensive space or month to month leases with access to specialized equipment or facilities, such as clean rooms. Others provide access to university research facilities or consulting services on a reduced-fee basis. Many provide outreach programs to help managers access community resources or general training in business building. Some provide seed capital investment or assistance in raising money. Others assist in company promotion and in obtaining government permits and licenses.

The qualifications for entering an incubator also vary from center to center. So do the costs and commitments. Some are fee based only. Some are limited to companies in which the center sponsor has an ownership interest. Others require companies to transfer a percentage of their capital stock as part of the compensation requirement. Parties considering joining a technology development center should consider carefully both the advantages and the costs before joining a particular center. *See: Incubators.*

**10b5** is a shorthand term lawyers and others use to refer to a provision in the federal securities laws (Rule 10b-5) that prohibits fraudulent and misleading activities in securities transactions. State securities acts contain similar prohibitions. All of these provisions prescribe severe penalties for violators. The use of fraudulent or misleading material, the making of misstatements, or the existence of material omissions in a securities offering can have serious consequences to a company and its management.

The text of the 10b5 provision reads as follows:

> It shall be unlawful for any person, directly or indirectly, by the use of any means or instrumentality of interstate commerce, or of the mails, or of any facility of any national securities exchange,
>
> 1.　　to employ any device, scheme, or artifice to defraud,
>
> 2.　　to make any untrue statement of a material fact or omit to state a material fact necessary in order to make the statements made, in the light of the circumstances under which they were made, not misleading,
>
> 3.　　or to engage in any act, practice, or course of business which operates or would operate as fraud or deceit upon any person, in connection with the purchase or sale of any security.

The securities laws and regulations are complex, and courts have been expansive in their interpretations of section 10b5 and other antifraud provisions of the securities laws. The combined effect of 10b5 and similar state laws is to make it very risky, and potentially costly, to deal in company securities in a way is not honest, straightforward, and in strict compliance with the law. To avoid problems, legal counsel should always be consulted before offering securities for sale. *See: Going Public, Lawyers, Private Placements, Reg D, SEC (Securities and Exchange Commission), 33 Act.*

**Term Loans** refer to a common type of business loan that has a fixed maturity, typically between one and ten years. Term loans can have fixed or floating interest and can be secured or unsecured. The principal portion of the loan is often amortized over the term of the loan. Term loans where the principal is not amortized over the term, but instead paid at maturity, are called balloon notes. Term loans are often used to fund capital acquisitions, with the principal being drawn down upon lending. They are the debt instrument of choice in leveraged and management buyouts. *See: Bridge Loans, Debt Service, Factoring, LBO (Leveraged Buyouts), Secured Loans, Security Agreements*

**Term Sheet** refers to short writing that sets forth the main business points of a proposed deal. Term sheets are usually written to be non-binding except as to terms dealing with confidentiality or exclusive dealing, where they are made expressly binding. They are almost always written as precursors to completion of the actual deal agreements, which tend to be more detailed and often follow completion of extensive due diligence investigations. Term sheets serve the same purpose as letters of intent and are used frequently by investors to fix the terms of a financing agreement before they complete their due diligence. Like letters of intent, term sheets should be reviewed and negotiated seriously before they are signed. The business terms reflected in a term sheet are often very difficult, if not impossible, to change during the negotiation of the definitive deal agreements. *See: Due Diligence, Financing Agreements, Letter Agreements, Letters of Intent.*

## Negotiating Phrases to Watch Out For

*A constructive, reasoned negotiation works best for most deals. But even in the most reasoned of discussions, parties strategize and employ tactics to work the process to their advantage. Consider the following phrases as wake up calls if you hear them in your negotiation.*

- *It's only a non-binding term sheet. True, but term sheets and letters of intent should be treated as seriously and with the same level of attention to detail as binding financing agreements. They set the tone for future negotiations and place practical limitations on the more detailed provisions of the binding agreements. Provisions expressly addressed in the term sheet can be next to impossible to change unless there is a demonstrable change in circumstances or a material concession from the other side.*

- *We never exercise our rights under this provision. This phrase often follows "we always do it this way" and begins with "don't worry." It is designed to comfort management when the investor insists on an onerous provision. Sometimes the phrase is different: "We don't expect to have to use this provision," or "We never use this provision, but we always require it." Management should be careful when someone asks for something they insist they will never use. If they really will not use it then they do not need it.*

- *It's only boilerplate. These more standardized and routine provisions in agreements are just as binding and important as the rest of the contract. Failure to address them seriously and with a view to their impact on the company can be a costly mistake.*

- *You can get your lawyers involved later. If the company's lawyers are not already involved they should be closely consulted when a term sheet is being negotiated. Engaging counsel during the term sheet phase before the final financing agreements are created is the best money a company can spend with counsel. The time it takes to review and discuss a term sheet is miniscule compared to the time and effort it takes to complete the formal deal documents. While the cost may be relatively small, the benefit of counsel's advice during the term sheet discussions can be enormous.*

- *We always do it this way. Companies sometimes get this from an investor or his lawyer after management has negotiated the main deal points and the parties are putting that deal onto paper. Suddenly, the investor's lawyer presents the company with forty-five pages of representations and warranties he wants management to sign. The explanation that investor always does it this way probably means the company has been presented with the lawyer's standard form, which he always uses as a starting point in negotiations. Like all standard forms, much of what it contains will not apply to the company's deal. "We always do it this way" implies that the way the investor did his deals in the past is the way the current deal should be done. But this company and its needs are different from all those other deals. And, while it may be unrealistic to expect an investor to abandon the deal structure or basic deal documents that have worked well for him, it is realistic to expect him to deal openly with management and to change provisions when appropriate.*

- *Let's use the projections from your plan for the benchmarks. The financial projections in a company's business plan usually make poor benchmarks. Since plans are often used to attract investors they may tend to be optimistic. In fact, most venture capitalists routinely discount company projections when they price a deal and do not really expect a company to meet all the goals stated in their projections.*

- *You need to stand behind your plan. No investor has ever seen a growing business unfold in exactly the way it was detailed in its fundraising plan. Real life contains too many variables to reasonably expect a company to meet all the objectives or projections contained in its plan. Few, if any, sophisticated investors price their investment proposals off the numbers contained in a company's plan without applying some discount to account for the uncertainties inherent in growing a business.*

- *We all have the same goals. Companies sometimes hear this from investors. Yes, it is true that investors, like management, are concerned with seeing the company progress. But beyond that, the interests of investors and company diverge in many meaningful ways. For one thing, investors are more diversified in their investments and, frequently, have investors of their own they have to satisfy. Their time horizon for liquidating their investment can be quite different from management's and their perspective on company direction and management often differ from management's.*

- *We are not interested in controlling the company. In general, this is true of venture capital investors who purchase a minority interest in a company. One of the key attractions to investing in the company in the first place is the perceived strength of the management team. The mistake that is made with this statement is when management interprets it to mean the investor is not interested in control under any circumstances. The reality is that if the company fails to meet expectations or if an investor's goals change, investors frequently get more interested and involved in company management. If management was not careful in preparing the financing documents, the outside investors may have the ability to effect serious change at the company or even take control.*

*See: Benchmarks, Boilerplate, Control, Deal, Projections, Reps and Warranties, Stage Financings, Venture Capital Deal Structures.*

**Think Capital** refers to a company's technology and the brainpower of key employees who supply the company with its technological edge. In high tech companies, the protections taken to preserve this think capital are very important to prospective investors. These protections include securing the company's title to important technologies through careful documentation, safeguards to prevent the theft or loss of company secrets, agreements to prevent competition by employees, and incentives to keep key personnel employed with the company. Written confidentiality agreements with employees and others who have access to company secrets and inventions are key to maintaining a company's think capital. Invention disclosure and assignment agreements that secure to the company the exclusive benefits of discoveries and new technologies developed by employees and other are also critical. Where patentable inventions are created, an active patent protection plan should be in place. *See: Confidentiality Agreements, Copyrights, Golden Handcuffs, Noncompete Agreements, Patents, Software Protection, Trade Secrets.*

**33 Act** refers to the federal Securities Act of 1933. Whenever a U.S. company offers or sells its securities, it becomes subject to a variety of laws regulating its activity. The most important of these are the 33 Act and the various State blue-sky securities acts. These laws make it unlawful for any person to offer, sell, or deliver any security unless an effective registration statement for the securities is in effect or an exemption to the registration requirements applies.

The securities these laws apply to have been broadly defined by the statutes and courts. They include corporate stock and debt instruments as well as similar interests issued by individuals, partnerships, and joint ventures. They also include other types of investment contracts that businessmen may not normally think of as securities. For example, a simple promissory note issued by an early stage company can be classified as a security under the right circumstances.

Detailed disclosure or ready access to information must be given to investors in connection with a securities offering. This is generally true whether the offering is registered or exempt from registration. This disclosure is usually made through the use of a registration statement and prospectus (also referred to as an offering circular) that contains pertinent information concerning the offering, the nature of the securities being offered, and the history and nature of the entity issuing the securities. In limited circumstances involving sales only to sophisticated investors, such as to venture capital firms or certain specially accredited investors, the information may be made available in other ways that do not involve the preparation of an extensive offering memorandum. *See: Going Public, Investment Reps, IPOs (Initial Public Offerings), Private Placements, Reg D, Restricted Securities, SEC (Securities and Exchange Commission), 10b5.*

**Track Record** refers to the past experience and business history of a person, management team or company. When used by an investor, it is usually refers to the business background of a company founder or manager. The best track record management can have is to have created a successful company before in the same or a similar business. Next to that, success in starting and growing a business in another industry is most relevant. Experience in working in the company's industry or in other entrepreneurial companies is also helpful, as is management experience with a larger company. Academic degrees or success outside of business can also be relevant to predicting success of managers in growing a business but is, generally, not considered as relevant.

All business experience contributes to a track record. The better the track record management has, the easier it is to attract capital to the company, and to attract it at a favorable price. When combined with a compelling business plan and demonstrable success, a strong management track record can help attract expansion funds when needed. *See: Entrepreneur, Five Factors, Management Team, Turnarounds.*

**Trademarks** are symbols, words, phrases, or design elements that identify a company product and distinguish it from others. Service marks identify and distinguish a service. Businesses can prevent others from using their marks within the United States on competitive products by following federal and state laws that govern trademarks and service marks. Other nations and international treaties provide similar protections and registration procedures.

Trademarks and service marks can provide valuable protections and branding to companies as they build their business and the reputations of their products and services. By providing legal name monopolies in a given fields, trademarks and service marks help companies distinguish their products and services from their competition. Securing a mark involves registration and using the mark in commerce to identify a product or service.

When used in commerce, marks are usually accompanied by a designation that identifies they are registered as trademarks or service marks or that the user is claiming protection for the mark pending completion of a registration. The appearance of an ® designation near a mark indicates that the mark is a registered trademark or service mark. The symbol <sup>TM</sup> or <sup>SM</sup> indicates the mark is being claimed as a trademark ™ or service mark <sup>SM</sup>.

Descriptive words and phrases are harder to register and protect than words and phrases that are not descriptive. For example, a poor choice for a widget that works fast would be "Speed Widget." It would be difficult to obtain registration and, if it was obtained, ineffective in preventing competitors from confusing the market by describing their widgets as speedy or fast, since those characterizations would be descriptive of widget functions. A company with a less expensive widget would likely be able to get away with using the name 'Speedy Widget,' rendering the mark ineffective in distinguishing the company's product.

Companies can usually determine whether a mark is available before they use it to identify their product or service by conducting searches of available databases and public records. The first search most companies conduct is of the records of the U. S. trademark office. A search of these records can determine whether anyone has already registered the mark or a mark that would be confusingly similar to the proposed mark.

If no registration is found, a broader search can be conducted using a private service bureau. This search reviews other public records and product and service listings to see whether the mark or a similar mark is already being used in commerce in an unregistered form. If the mark clears both searches, the chances are good that it can be registered and protected. Company counsel can advise on the best and most appropriate method for conducting these searches. *See: Copyrights, Patents, Trade Secrets.*

**Trade Secrets** refer to the confidential know-how owned by a company or individual. A confidential formula or method can be a trade secret. So can an improvement to an invention. Trade secrets are generally important to growing companies because they give them advantages in the marketplace.

Trade secrets are protected by state law. The availability of protection, however, depends on the party seeking protection first taking reasonable precautions to protect them from unauthorized disclosure. To qualify for protection, information must be confidential to the extent that it is not generally known within its industry.

Unlike patents, which entitle the holder to preclude others from using patented technologies, trade secrets protection prevents others from using company technologies only by keeping them secret. If others discover the company's secrets by reverse engineering or by developing the same secrets on their own, they cannot be stopped from using the knowledge. Trade secrets protection can prevent others from stealing company secrets, but only if the company takes appropriate actions to prevent unauthorized disclosure of its information.

Confidentiality and secrecy agreements with company employees, owners, and consultants who have access to secrets are common methods of protecting trade secrets. Investors who put money into companies with valuable secrets usually require the companies to enter into secrecy agreements with their employees. Some also require management members to enter into secrecy and noncompete agreements directly with the investors.

Confidentiality agreements alone will not protect company secrets. Other measures must be taken to ensure the secrecy of the information. These include limiting access to company secrets (only those persons who need to know the secrets to perform their job and who are bound by a secrecy agreement should have access), marking secrets as confidential, and distinguishing between secrets and non-secrets. Material containing company secrets should be stored in a safe place when not in use.

Trade secrecy laws vary from state to state. Some states, for instance, distinguish between technical trade secrets and non-technical confidential information, allowing a company to protect non-technical information only by contract and only for a limited period of time. Some states require stricter definitions of technical trade secrets than they do of non-technical confidential information. Others make no distinction at all. All prescribe definite limits to the availability of trade secrecy protection.

Attempts to extend protection beyond these legal limits, even if inadvertent, can jeopardize the trade secrecy protection a company relies upon. This, coupled with the fact that companies must comply with all of the conditions and requirements set out by their state's laws before they can claim trade secrecy protection, makes it important for companies to have an experienced professional review the precautions they take to protect their secrets and to review the form of any secrecy agreements they use. *See: Confidentiality Agreements, Lawyers, Software Protection, Think Capital.*

**Turnarounds** refer to troubled business situations where new capital or inspired management is needed to improve the business. Turnaround situations are often identified by banks who are unable to obtain repayment on their loans. Sometimes turnarounds involve companies whose management buys out the controlling shareholders and tries to turn around the company and make it profitable. Other times, professional turnaround management is brought in by a bank or other creditor to improve the company's performance. Certain managers excel at turnaround situations because they have the necessary skills and resolve to make the hard decisions required in these cases. These managers are called turnaround specialists. Their track records are far more important than the industry or the company they corrected. *See: LBO (Leveraged Buyout), Track Record.*

# U

**Underwriters** refer to investment banking firms and others who market and sell company securities to the public and provide other services to public and private companies.

Sales of public company securities are frequently conducted through a syndicate of firms that are selected by the company's underwriter. The managing (or lead) underwriter in the syndicate attempts to select the right combination of underwriters to achieve a distribution of the company's shares among private individuals and institutional purchasers that will assure a good price in the offering and adequate trading in the shares after it is completed. The underwriters usually support the company in the financial community after the offering by making a market in the company's stock, providing research and analysis on the company for investors, organizing communications with investors and potential investors, and generally helping the company create a following in the investment community.

Because of the variety of services they provide and because their ability to provide those services efficiently can affect not only the offering price of the company's shares but also their continuing strength in the public marketplace, the selection of the right underwriter is important. Among the characteristics management should consider when selecting an underwriter to conduct an offering are:

- *Stature within the financial community.* The underwriter's professional reputation as an investment banker can determine, in large part, his ability to put together a strong syndicate to sell the company's shares. The strength of the syndicate can, in turn, influence the quality of the investors attracted to the offering.

- *Experience in the company's industry.* Underwriters develop reputations within industries. An underwriter who is experienced at taking businesses public in the company's industry can enhance the credibility of the company's offering. Experience can also help an underwriter price a company's shares properly so that the company's shares hold their price or increase in price after the offering is sold.

- *Research reputation.* The company's managing underwriter will be a primary source of information about the company to the financial community. It is helpful, therefore, to select an underwriter whose analysts are experienced and follow the company's industry closely. An underwriter's reputation for reliable research in a company's industry can help sustain investor interest in the company's stock.

- *Ability to support the market.* Once issued, the company's stock will be traded on the over-the-counter market. The ability of the underwriter as a "market-maker" to support the market is important. By purchasing and selling the company's stock in the market, the market-maker gives the company's stock needed liquidity, which helps stabilize trading prices.

It is a good practice to interview several underwriters before selecting one to conduct a public offering. Accountants, bankers, lawyers, and other entrepreneurs can make introductions to underwriters. A good deal of information about underwriters and the types of deals they do also can be obtained by watching the financial press, particularly the *Wall Street Journal*. Underwriters regularly run advertisements (called "tombstones" by the trade) that show public offerings they have done and the syndicate members who participated. *See: Going Public, IPOs (Initial Public Offerings), Investment Bankers, Syndications.*

**Unit Offerings** are sales of company securities when more than one type of security is sold as a single unit, or when investors are required to purchase securities in blocks of shares. The term is frequently used to refer to private placements or public offerings where investors are offered the opportunity to purchase units that consist of a share of stock and a warrant to purchase more stock in the future. *See: Going Public, IPOs (Initial Public Offerings), Penny Stock, Private Placements.*

**Unlocking Provisions** refer to contractual mechanisms that enable investors to disengage their financial arrangements with management. One typical unlocking provision is a buy-sell agreement, which allows an investor to force management either to buy the investor's shares at a price he sets or sell its own shares to the investor for the same price. Another provision, the tag along agreement, creates a mechanism through which either management or the investor can force the other to sell its interest in the company to a third party or buy the stock of the other party. Typically, this arrangement empowers the receiving party to accept an offer to buy the company's assets or the stock of both shareholders in the company. *See: Buy-Sell Agreements, Exits, Liquidity Agreements.*

**Unvested Stock** refers to capital stock of a company that has been granted or sold to an investor, typically an employee, but is subject to forfeiture in the event certain

*Investors, Deal Structures, Legal Strategies - 375*

predefined events occur or fail to occur, such as the employee leaving the company before the vesting date. *See: Vested Stock, Vesting Stock Grants.*

**Upside** is the potential profit an investor hopes to receive from his investment under ideal circumstances. It is what the venture capitalist measures against the downside when evaluating a company. For venture investors, the upside represents the potential for their shares to appreciate significantly. This can be achieved by company growth and can be supplemented by the market increasing the stock's P/E ratio. *See: Downside, P/E, Price-Earnings Ratio, Pricing, ROI (Return on Investment), Vested Stock, Vesting Schedules.*

**Valuation** refers to the value an arms-length purchaser would pay for all of the outstanding stock and stock rights of a company. In a public company, valuation is also referred to as a company's market capitalization or market cap, which is the value generated by multiplying the company's outstanding stock by its trading value. For example, a company with 10 million outstanding shares trading at $22.50 would have a valuation, or market cap, equal to $225 million (10 million shares multiplied by $22.50).

Determining the valuation of a privately held company is more difficult because of the absence of an active market in private company securities. Methods frequently used to value growing private companies include the discounted cash flow method and the market price method, discussed elsewhere in this book.

As a shorthand method, entrepreneurs and investors frequently refer to the valuation of a venture capital backed company by reference to the amount of money the venture investor paid for the percentage of ownership acquired in the investment. For example, when a venture capitalist purchases 1 million shares of a company stock for $1 million, the parties may refer to the company's valuation as $5 million if there are 5 million shares outstanding after the investment.

This would also reflect the company's post-money valuation. The pre-money valuation, in this case $4 million, is determined by subtracting the investors investment from the post-money valuation. *See: Discounted Cash Flow, Market Price Method, Post-Money Valuation, Pre-Money Valuation, Pricing.*

**Value Added** refers to the knowledge, management advice, connections, and related non-monetary contributions investors sometimes offer a young company. Many venture investors provide more than money to their portfolio companies. They provide management with the benefit of their experience with emerging growth companies. They also help management by using their contacts in the company's industry and with other financial sources. *See: Consulting Agreements, Geography, Management Agreements.*

## *Does Your Investor Contribute More Than Money?*

*In the stress of searching for expansion capital, it can be easy to forget that the right investor can add more than money to a company's resources. Successful investors with good reputations and broad ranging contacts can help in many ways. As directors and counselors, their experience can help management avoid costly mistakes. They can help direct management develop useful metrics for measuring and directing company activity. Their knowledge of industry practice and the activities of competitors can give management fresh perspective on their business. Their good reputations and finance industry contacts can make future fundraising easier and less costly. Contacts they have can help management find qualified executives to fill important functions.*

*While management's first objective in a fund raise is to obtain capital on favorable terms at the least cost to the company, a strong investor's other contributions can, in the long run, have much more to do with the company's ultimate success than the money they provide in first investment. But how does management know, in advance, that a given investor can or will provide meaningful non-financial value to their company? There can be no guarantees, but inquiries into the following matters during the fundraising process can help management know more about what type of investor they are getting.*

- *Portfolio company success. Success attracts money and good people. It usually follows from good decisions and successful implementation. The more successful your investor has been, the more helpful he is likely to be to the company. In gauging this factor, managements should include discussions with managers of the investor's other investments, past and present, and inquire to what degree their goals and aspirations were met. Investor and management goals are not always the same.*

- *Reputation in the company's industry. Is the investor active in the company's industry? If he is and his reputation is solid, his contacts can help management identify and attract important management members to strengthen its team. Investor knowledge about the industry can supplement management's background, providing more experience for critical company decisions.*

- *Working relationships with portfolio companies. Direct conversation with managers of other companies the investor has been involved with is the best way to determine whether the investor will be helpful or distracting. Any investor should be willing to provide management with a list of companies in which it has invested. Appropriate questions include whether the investor supported the company through difficult times, whether he made constructive contributions as a board member, and whether he was helpful in identifying and attracting investors to later investment rounds.*

- *History of investing in later rounds. Not all investors have the capability or interest in investing in later rounds of company financings. Those that do can make it easier to raise money by committing to provide part of the funding on terms negotiated by new investors when the fundraising process begins. Questions about an investor's ability, willingness and history of investing in later rounds of other companies can help management determine whether they have identified an investor who will invest in their subsequent financings.*

- *Reputation in the finance industry. Is the investor known as a player in the national or regional venture capital industry? Is the investor respected in the investment banking community? Have they backed companies who have conducted successful public offerings or sales at attractive values? The answers to these questions will help management evaluate the degree to which their investor may be able to assist the company in attracting later investment or a quality investment banker to assist in its sale or public offering.*

*See: Due Diligence, Value Added.*

**Value Proposition** refers to the characteristic or quality that gives a business the opportunity to succeed and distinguishes it from its competition. A company's value proposition is the essence of why the business expects to be successful. A medical device company's value proposition might be its ability to deliver treatment options that are safer, cheaper and more effective. Another company might rely on its ability to improve productivity for distribution companies through inventory control improvements. *See: Business Plan, Business Plan Format, Due Diligence, Market Research.*

**Venture Capital** refers to money invested in privately-held businesses at high risk to the investor, usually when the company is unable to secure needed funds from traditional lending sources, such as commercial banks or factors. Typically, the venture investor purchases a minority interest in a company with illiquid securities using a variety of structural devices and contractual agreements to insure his participation in the company's board of directors and access to information about the company's progress.

Venture capital investors look for companies that have prospects for generating very high rates of return to their stockholders. This usually translates into companies with good prospects for rapid growth. Turnarounds and leveraged buyouts are also good prospects for venture capital. *See: Adventure Capitalists, Angels, BDCs (Business Development Corporations), CDCs (Community Development Corporations), Corporate Venture Capital, Emerging Growth Companies, LBO (Leveraged Buyout), P/E, Pools, Pricing, ROI (Return on Investment), SBICs (Small Business Investment Companies), Specialty Funds, Turnarounds, Value Added, Vulture Capitalists.*

**Venture Capital Clubs** are informal groups of venture capitalists, entrepreneurs, financial strategists, accountants, and lawyers that meet regularly to discuss matters of interest, exchange ideas, and share opportunities. They provide a common meeting ground for persons interested in entrepreneurial activity. There are many of these clubs across the United States. If one exists nearby, management should explore the opportunities it provides to become acquainted with the venture capital infrastructure of the area. *See: Networking, Venture Capital Conferences.*

**Venture Capital Conferences** are forums at which venture capitalists meet to exchange information and hear presentations from companies seeking funding. Typically, the sponsor of the conference screens applicants who want to present their companies' funding needs. The applicants who pass the screening then describe their opportunity in short oral presentations to an audience of investors. Interested investors can follow up with the entrepreneurs later in the conference.

The best sources of information about upcoming venture capital conferences are local accounting or law firms, which may cosponsor them, local venture firms, which may participate as plan screeners, and local colleges and universities with entrepreneurship courses, which may provide professors as speakers. *See: Networking, Shopping.*

## *Mistakes Made at a Business Plan Forum*

*The opportunity to present my entrepreneurial business idea to the New Ventures Workshop at the Harvard Business School was too great to pass up. I thought of the exposure to a roomful of investors eager to pour hundreds of thousands of dollars into my venture and the tremendous profits their dollars would initiate. I thought of the feedback I would get from the panelists - surely they would be impressed with the idea, and with me as an entrepreneur. No doubt they would be equally impressed with my wife [the company's cofounder] and her ability to handle the public relations aspects of the firm. Certainly people would be thrusting Offers To Purchase at me before the presentation was over. I made a note to have Offers To Purchase with me.*

*Judging by the process of getting scheduled, how bad could the experience be? Mr. Burt Alimansky, Chairman of the Workshop, was patient and thorough as he explained the ground rules of the workshop and the costs involved. I would need to submit my complete business plan to the panelists at* least ten days before, and have handouts ready for the audience. To be most effective, he recommended that I accompany my talk with a slide show, highlighting certain key aspects of the business. He provided me with a suggested outline and asked for my suggestions for panelists. For $350, I would benefit from the candid business advice of four panelists, all of whom would be familiar with the industry in which I hope to operate. And one of the panelists would be a venture capitalist - so if the deal looked good, I'd make contact right there.

I began working on the presentation months in advance. For a public talk, I thought I would omit a lot of the routine financial information, and instead include more industry background. Instead of pie charts and pro formas, I decided to include color slides depicting the problems the industry is having, and how the new company expects to solve them. Instead of iffy sales projections, I listed the product benefits and hinted at possible unit sales. I wrote jokes into the script here and there to provide comic relief.

Wrong, wrong, wrong. The first comment from the first panelist was, "Mr. Cohen, when it comes to investments of this magnitude, you shouldn't be joking." The first comment from the second panelist was, "Mr. Cohen, instead of providing sales projections, you've given us conjecture. We need solid sales projections, for every product, for ten years, in order to properly analyze your chances for success."

The third panelist said, "Mr. Cohen, your slides are very nice, but you haven't shown us a single slide of your product, nor have you provided a Sources and Uses Statement. As investors, how will we know where our money is going?" And the fourth panelist said, "Mr. Cohen, you've wasted your time and ours. Without detailed financials, including projected profit and loss statements and balance sheets for each of the first ten years, the industry background you've provided is nothing but interesting reading. You've got a lot of work to do."

*And so, $350 and many late nights working on the plan later, I learned to heed the advice I had been hearing from venture capitalists for many years: Don't go looking for capital until the plan is complete, and answers the questions investors are bound to ask. The Plan Forums . . . aren't places for theatrics or creativity. Just stick to the basics, and make sure all your homework is done. Don't agree to be a presenter unless you are certain your plan is complete, including all financials and the shareholder's agreement. Because, like the Emperor and his new clothes, if you're naked up there, somebody will notice.*

> *From an editorial by Steven M. Cohen, which appeared Venture's Capital Club Monthly.*

**Venture Capital Deal Structures** vary from investment to investment but most venture capital deals are structured using the same concepts, many of which are described in detail throughout this book. The following provides a summary of a typical venture capital deal structure where the investor purchases less than a controlling interest in a growing privately held company.

- *Investment Security.* Venture investors usually prefer using convertible preferred stock or convertible debentures when investing in privately held companies. These securities give them preferences over other stockholders and are typically convertible, at the investor's option, into common stock. Usually, conversion is mandatory when the company goes public. *See: Common Stock, Convertible Debentures, Convertible Preferred Stock, Convertible Securities, Fully Diluted, Preferred Stock Umbrellas.*

- *Pricing and Valuation.* The amount invested and the number of shares of common stock into which an investor's security is convertible determines, in the common parlance of the industry, the value of the company receiving the investment. Investors often phrase their investment proposals in terms of purchasing a percentage of a company's fully diluted stock ownership for a given amount of money. For example, a term sheet may express that the investor will invest $2 Million to purchase 1 Million shares of convertible preferred stock which is to be convertible into 1 Million shares of common stock representing 25% of the company's fully diluted capital stock, after investment. This would price the deal, in terms of company valuation, at $6 million pre-money and $8 million post-money. *See: Discounted Cash Flow, Fully Diluted, Post-Money Valuation, Pre-Money Valuation, Pricing, Valuation.*

- *Full Disclosure.* The financing agreements prepared by venture capital investors are detailed and include extensive representations by the company and, sometimes, individual management members respecting all aspects of the company's operations. Ten to twenty pages of single spaced representations accompanied by an extensive disclosure schedule elaborating on the representations are not unusual. *See: Boilerplate, Due Diligence, Reps and Warranties.*

- *Liquidation and Dividend Preferences.* Investors usually build into the securities they purchase preferences that entitle them to receive a predetermined amount (typically their investment amount plus a predetermined return) before other shareholders in the event the company is liquidated. These same securities typically entitle the investor to receive dividends before dividends are issued to holders of common stock. *See: Convertible Preferred Stock, Participating Preferred, Negative Covenants.*

- *Investor Stock Redemptions.* Investor preferred stock is frequently subject to one or both of two types of redemptions. The first requires the company, usually after a fixed period of time and at the direction of the investor, to redeem (i.e. repurchase) the investor's preferred stock at a fixed price. The other entitles the company to require the investor to either redeem his preferred stock or convert into common stock, usually after a fixed period of time. The first provides a mechanism for an investor to liquidate his investment in a company that is not meeting expectations. The second enables management to release the company from some investor preferences (many of which are contained in the terms of the preferred security) by forcing the investor to redeem or convert into common stock. *See: Calls, Puts.*

- *Conversion Rights.* The investors' right to convert preferred stock into common stock is usually coupled with the company's right to require conversion in the event of an initial public offering or, less frequently, sale of the company. The conversion price is usually equal to the purchase price of the preferred stock but is subject to downward revision (resulting in giving the investor more common shares upon conversion of the preferred shares) after a subsequent sale of stock by the company at lower prices. *See: Convertible Securities.*

- *Antidilution Rights.* Antidilution rights entitle investors to receive extra shares of common stock when they convert their preferred stock into common stock if a company sells stock for lower prices after the investors' purchase or if their has been another diluting event, such as a stock split. The mechanism for creating this right is a charter obligation to reduce the conversion price ratio used to determine the number of shares of common stock into which the preferred stock will convert. Ratchet antidilution rights provide investors with the most extra shares by reducing the conversion price to the lower sale price given to other investors. Weighted average antidilution provisions reduce the conversion price less by using a formula that factors in the number of shares sold at the lower price as well as the lower price. *See: Antidilution Provisions, Dilution (Percentage), Ratchets, Weighted Average Antidilution.*

- *Voting Rights.* Investor voting rights preferences usually include the right to elect one or more representatives to the company's board of directors and to approve certain types of actions such as the amendment of the company's charter, the sale of the business, or the issuance of new or preferential securities. Sometimes the voting preferences extend to other matters as well. *See: Shareholders' Agreements, Voting Agreements, Voting Trusts.*

- *Participation and Information Rights.* The voting rights negotiated by venture investors are frequently supplemented with rights to participate in developing or approving the company's business plan, to participate in certain board of director committees, and to receive regular financial reports from company management. Rights to approve certain types of major transactions or changes in company direction are also common. Venture investors who do not join a company's board of directors often request a separate agreement giving them rights to attend board meetings and confer with management. *See: Control, Negative Covenants, Operating Covenants, Reports and Records, Voting Agreements.*

- *Preemptive Rights and First Refusals.* Preferred stock investors frequently require the preemptive right to buy stock in future rounds of company fundings, typically to the extent needed to preserve their ownership percentage. These rights are usually supplemented with first refusal agreements that entitle them to purchase shares sold by management, frequently at the price management negotiates with a willing outside buyer. *See: First Refusal Rights (Company), First Refusal Rights (Shareholder), Liquidity Agreements, Preemptive Rights.*

- *Co-Sale Rights.* Investor co-sale agreements entitle investors to include some of their shares of stock in a sale of stock conducted by a company manager or founder. The purpose of the agreement is to provide the investor with some protection against a sell out by the company's management. *See: Co-Sale Rights, Liquidity Agreements.*

- *Vesting Agreements.* Sometimes investors negotiate to make the shares of the founders and management subject to future vesting so that they will forfeit shares if they leave the company before the vesting periods expire. *See: Unvested Stock, Vested Stock, Vesting Schedules, Vesting Stock Grants.*

- *Registration Rights.* Venture investors typically negotiate agreements that entitle them to require the company to register their shares for resale to the public. The purpose of the agreements is to provide the investor with a mechanism to liquidate his shares. Investors usually require two types of registrations rights - demand rights that entitle them to force the company to register their shares and piggyback rights that entitle them to include their shares in a stock registration initiated by the company. Management employees typically do not obtain registration rights and the rights granted to outside investors are usually carefully limited. *See: Demand Rights, Piggyback Rights, Registration Rights.*

- *Management Noncompetes.* Founders and management are usually required to enter into agreements that require their full time attention to the company's business and protect its trade secrets.

These agreements typically also prevent the founders and managers from going into competition with the company. When combined with the vesting agreements described above, these agreements can provide powerful incentives to keep management from leaving the business to engage in competitive enterprises. *See: Employment Contracts, Noncompete Agreements.*

- *Information Property Agreements.* All company employees are usually required to sign confidentiality and proprietary rights agreements as a condition to the closing of a venture financing. Many companies already have these agreements in place to protect the company's trade secrets and insure the company's rights to inventions created by company employees. These agreements frequently include provisions preventing employees from soliciting customers or other employees away from the company. *See: Confidentiality Agreements, Patents, Secrecy Agreements, Think Capital.*

See the *Deal* entry for a description of the documents used to complete a sale of stock to a venture capital fund. *See also: Deal, Financing Agreements, Structure.*

**Venture Capitalists** refer to professional money managers who provide risk capital to businesses and to the firms they organize themselves into for the purpose of making investments in growing companies. Venture capitalists come in many forms and specialize in different ways, but all share the common trait of making investments in privately held companies that have the potential to provide them a very high rate of return.

Venture capitalists include private funds, companies funded by public offerings of their securities, bank and corporate subsidiaries charged with investing budgeted funds, and private individuals, who are often called adventure capitalists or angels. Some venture firms, such as SBICs leverage their committed capital using government guarantee programs, but the vast majority of funds are not so leveraged.

Most money invested in venture capital investment firms is invested in private limited partnerships and limited liability companies managed by teams of professional investors. Often, the management team is separately organized in a limited liability company that receives an annual fee plus incentive compensation from the venture capital firm. The incentive compensation is frequently referred to as "carried interest" and consists of a share in the profits generated by the venture capital firm from its investments.

Historically, pension funds, insurance companies, and corporate investors have been the heaviest investors in venture capital funds. The most typical fund structure requires the fund managers to invest the firm's money in qualified investments, provide periodic reports to its investors, and to return funds to investors when their portfolio company investments are liquidated. Consequently, venture capital firms routinely return to their market of investors to raise money for new funds every few years.

Two good sources for learning more about venture capitalists are the National Venture Capital Association, at www.nvca.com, and the National Association of Small Business Investment Companies at www.nasbic.org. *See: Adventure Capitalists, Angels, BDCs (Business Development Corporations), CDCs (Community Development Corporations), Corporate Venture Capital, Limited Partnerships, LLCs (Limited Liability Companies), MESBICs (Minority Enterprise Small Business Investment Companies), Pools, SBICs (Small Business Investment Companies), Specialty Funds, Venture Capital Deal Structures, Venture Books, Vulture Capitalists.*

## Think Like a VC

When planning a capital raise for a privately-held company it can help to understand how a venture capitalist thinks. The more a management team understands about the world of its potential investors the more likely it is to target its efforts effectively. Here is a brief description of some of the factors that influence venture capital fund managers in their day-to-day business.

- _Compensation is based on portfolio company success_. The typical fund management team receives a regular annual payment from the fund of between 2% and 3% of committed capital to cover the expenses of running the fund day-to-day plus a bonus, called the carried interest, of a percentage of the profits it makes when its portfolio investments are liquidated. The opportunity for fund managers to get big payouts comes from the carried interest, which makes the success of the portfolio company critically important to the ability of the fund manager to generate personal wealth.

- _Staffing resources are limited_. The regular annual payment received by the fund managers reduces their available investment capital and has to cover all of their expenses, including salaries, benefits, office rental, travel and fees paid to outside professionals. This limits the number of people they can hire and puts a premium on reviewing investment prospects efficiently. For a fund receiving hundreds of plans a month, this creates the need to employ methods of screening business plans quickly.

- _Fundraising is an ongoing activity_. The vast majority of funds are structured so that they have to return their committed capital to their investors once a portfolio company has an exit. In other words, they *only get to invest their funds once. In practical terms, this means that most venture capital funds are always in full fundraising mode or thinking about their next fundraising.*

- *Many periodically stop investing to raise money. Particularly for smaller funds that may only have a few professionals on staff, the constant need to refresh available capital often translates into the periodic need to focus all efforts on fundraising and monitoring existing*

- *Good investments generate returns more slowly than bad investments fail. A fund may have to return to the market for new funds every 4 to 6 years but the good companies it invests in may not be ready for profitable exits until later, depriving the managers of an attractive track record with which to attract new investment. To compound this problem, those companies in a fund's portfolio that do not succeed tend to fail earlier on average than the successful ones tend to liquidate and generate a tangible investment return. This is a function of proper fund management and the illiquidity of private companies as a class.*

- *Some shift their focus as their fund matures. A related phenomenon is that many funds limit their investments to later stage companies as they approach the need to replenish their pool of capital. This is because earlier stage companies are less likely to create a liquidation event in time for the return it generates to be used to demonstrate the fund manager's ability to generate attractive returns. Funds who have just raised their money are often more willing to invest in earlier stage companies.*

- *Their results are measured carefully. Venture capitalists are measured by, and their ability to raise additional funds to support future activities depends upon, how successful they are at returning their investors money with a healthy profit. Results are compared on an annual rate of return basis giving the pension funds and others who invest in venture capital funds a ready comparative measure to use when deciding which venture capital funds will receive its money.*

- *They have lots of competition. Competition is fierce among venture capitalists for the attention of potential investors and for opportunities to invest in the best companies. Despite the flood of unsolicited business plans most venture capital funds receive, only a small percentage of these over-the-transom-plans offer the combination of quality and opportunity venture capitalists are looking for. Many of the best opportunities are secured in other ways that require an affirmative effort to seek out and find the best companies.*

- *Many share investment opportunities. Fund managers do this for many reasons. First, many of the best opportunities they see come from other fund managers. Second, sharing spreads the risk between more than one fund and leads to relationships that lead to more sharing. Finally, sharing is often necessary because of practical limits on the amount of money a fund is comfortable investing in one opportunity. Sharing, when it involves a syndication put together by one of the investors, also makes it easier for the investors to dictate terms.*

- *They have to be actively involved in monitoring their investments. Because of the rules that provide them exemptions from otherwise onerous regulation, venture capital funds have to maintain an active involvement with a majority of their investments. This translates into the need to sit on boards of directors, obtain regular reporting from portfolio companies,* and the inclusion in financing agreements of covenants that give funds that do not have board rights, the right to attend board meetings and participate in discussions.

- *They can be personally liable for mistakes*. Fund managers routinely sit on the boards of the companies in which they invest. Like other board members, they have fiduciary duties to the company's shareholders by virtue of their position. Consequently, they can be sued by disgruntled shareholders and held personally liable for their malfeasance. Directors and officers insurance and indemnifications from the company help to mitigate this risk. Fund managers who serve as directors can be more at risk than other directors when the best interests of their fund conflicts with their director duty to all shareholders.

- *Illiquid investments can be riskier than liquid investments*. A minority investor in common stock of a privately held company has little influence and little ability to liquidate his investment. This basic truth has led to the development of sophisticated investment instruments and deal structures that contractually attempt to mitigate the venture capitalists risk. Many of the components of these deal structures constrict management's freedom and reduce the value of their common stock shareholdings.

- *They are only human*. They make mistakes in the companies they choose and in the ways they organize and manage their businesses. They do not expect perfection in the management teams they back but they do expect them to deal openly and to address their mistakes when they are made.

See: Deal, Financing Agreements, Venture Capital Deal Structures. See also: Ten Strategies for Negotiating with Investors, Seven Deadly Sins of Fundraising.

**Vested Stock** refers to capital stock of a company that is held by an investor and is not subject to forfeiture. It is often contrasted with unvested stock that is subject to forfeiture in the event of the occurrence of certain predefined events. *See: Unvested Stock, Vesting Stock Grants.*

**Vesting Schedules** refer to a method used to make a person's stock ownership contingent upon some future event. Vesting schedules in venture-backed companies often tie an employee's rights to retain shares to employment longevity or some other factor such as company earnings or sales. Often, they are used with noncompete agreements and employment incentives to encourage effort and loyalty from important employees.

When a vesting schedule applies, an employee is granted the rights to a specified number of shares of the company's stock, but those shares are subject to forfeiture until certain defined events have occurred. For example, an employee may be granted 10,000 shares of the company's common stock subject to vesting. Those shares may vest upon his remaining employed with the company for five years. Each year, for instance, 2,000 of his shares may vest if he remains employed by the company. If he remains with the company for the full five years, he will become fully vested in all 10,000 shares. If he leaves after three years of employment, he will forfeit 4,000 shares and receive certificates for only 6,000 shares.

Because of the complexity of the Internal Revenue Code and certain technicalities it contains, anyone who receives stock subject to a vesting schedule should consult with an attorney or accountant to determine the tax effect of receiving it and the advisability of filing an 83(b) election. *See: 83(b) Election, Golden Handcuffs.*

**Vesting Stock Grants** refer to shares of stock granted or sold to an important employee or other party that are subject to a vesting schedule. Until the stock is vested, it remains subject to forfeiture or repurchase by the company on specified terms. Growing companies frequently use vesting stock grants, together with employee elected 83(b) elections, to attract and retain important employees. Sometimes vesting stock grants are made to supplement options issued to a key employee under a qualified stock option plan.

Vesting stock grants work like this. A company whose common stock fair market value is $5 per share may feel compelled to grant rights to 50,000 shares per year for three years in order to attract the level of executive it needs. Any qualified stock option plan grants that exceeded 20,000 shares (with an aggregate exercise price of $100,000) in any year, however, would not receive qualified option treatment under the current Internal Revenue regulations. By granting the prospective employee qualified options for 20,000 shares each of the three years supplemented with a grant of an additional 30,000 shares of stock which vests 10,000 shares per year the company could put together a package that meets its needs.

The employee would need to consider whether or not to file an 83(b) election on the vested share grant. Without a filing, the employee might be taxed at ordinary income rates at the time the vesting requirements are met. The tax will be assessed on the difference between the then current fair market value of the stock becoming vested at that time and his purchase price. With a properly made 83(b) election, the employee could defer his tax until he sells the stock by choosing to pay taxes, instead, on the unvested shares when they are granted. *See: ISO's (Incentive Stock Option Plans), 83(b) Election, Qualified Stock Option Plans, Unvested Stock, Vesting Schedules.*

**Voting Agreements** refer to agreements to vote company shares that are often included in the stock purchase agreement, investor rights agreement, or shareholders' agreement of a venture capital financing. These are contracts that are signed by two or more shareholders and govern the manner in which those shareholders will vote their shares of company stock for the election of directors.

In most situations, if shareholders holding a majority of the shares of voting stock agree to vote their shares together, they can control company management by electing the company's board of directors. Voting agreements are frequently used to protect minority shareholders. In these cases, the minority shareholders use the agreements to assure themselves of having a representative elected to the company's board of directors or to restrict the issuance of additional shares of a company's stock. *See: Board of Directors, Control, Minority Shareholders, Shareholders' Agreements.*

**Voting Trusts** are agreements used to transfer control from management to an investor if the company does not meet its goals. They work by placing management's stock in a trust with the investor's shares. The trustee is instructed to vote the entrusted shares as the venture capitalist directs if the company fails to meet its goals. Voting trusts are not routine in venture fundings. *See: Benchmarks, Control, Take Away Provisions, Voting Agreements.*

**Vulture Capitalists** is a derogatory term used to refer to venture capitalists. Sometimes the source of the phrase is a disappointed entrepreneur describing an investor who refused his deal or who took an action the entrepreneur disagrees with - such as firing management.

Entrepreneurs should keep in mind that venture capitalists do not invest in companies to make friends. They invest to make money. Without profits, the venture capitalist's investors will not participate in later funds of the venture capitalist, forcing him to go out of business.

Understandably, venture capitalists are picky about the companies they invest in and how well they perform. They do not want their portfolio companies to fail. As a consequence, they can be expected to exercise any contractual rights they have to prevent a portfolio company from failing, even if doing so makes them a vulture capitalist in the eyes of the entrepreneur. *See: Deal Flow, Golden Rule, Venture Capitalists.*

# W

**Warrants** are a form of stock option that entitles an investor to purchase shares of company stock in the future at a price fixed by the warrant. When granted, warrants are usually granted in connection with a loan or equity investment in a company. They are also commonly included in the compensation paid to an investment banker for successfully completing a company funding. The holder can exercise the warrant by paying cash for the share price on the warrant or, if given with a loan, by canceling a portion of the debt equal to the warrant exercise price. When they are issued in connection with a loan, they are often called equity kickers to refer to their ability to give debt investors an opportunity to share in the company's capital appreciation. *See: Brokers, Equity Kickers, Options.*

**Wash Outs** refer to circumstances that reduce shareholder value to zero or near zero. Wash outs can occur when a company liquidates its business or files for bankruptcy protection. They can also occur selectively to early-stage investors and common stock holders in a down round financing. *See: Down Rounds.*

**Weighted Average Antidilution** refers to a form of antidilution provision that grants its holders rights to obtain additional shares of stock if the company later sells shares at prices lower than the investor's price. The weighted average provision is less dilutive to management and holders of common stock who are not protected by the provision than its alternative, the ratchet. The weighted average method uses a formula to determine the dilutive effect of a later sale of cheaper securities and grants the investor enough extra shares without charge to offset that dilutive effect.

Weighted average antidilution formulas work by changing the conversion price applicable to a class of convertible preferred shares. The change increases the number of shares of common stock the shareholder is entitled to receive when he converts his preferred shares into common shares but does not increase the number of convertible preferred shares held by the investor.

A common provision adjusts the at which the preferred shares are later converted into common shares by multiplying the number of shares of company stock outstanding, including the protected venture investor's outstanding preferred shares, by the price the new investor is paying for his shares, adds to that product the dollar amount of the new investment (number of new shares bought by the new investor times his price per share) and divides the sum by the total number of shares outstanding after the new investment. The result of this calculation gives a new conversion price for the protected venture investor that is then divided into the dollar amount he invested when he purchased his preferred shares to determine the total number of common shares he will receive when he later converts his preferred shares into common stock. The difference between this number and the number of shares the venture investor already owns is the number of new shares the venture becomes entitled to receive for free when he later converts.

The weighted average antidilution method is usually more favorable to management shareholders than the ratchet method described earlier. Under that method, the protected investor is entitled to get enough free shares to reduce his price per share to the same price paid by the later investor regardless of the number of shares sold to the later investor.

The following example illustrates how great the difference can be between the operation of a ratchet and a weighted average antidilution provision.

Assume that an investor bought 300,000 shares of convertible preferred stock last year for $2 per share when management owned 700,000 shares. A later investor buys 200,000 shares of a new class of convertible preferred stock from the company for $1 per share. A ratchet would adjust the conversion formula of the convertible preferred stock purchased by the first investor to give the first investor 300,000 new shares for free when he converts his shares into common, thereby reducing his as-converted price per share from $2 to $1.

The weighted average method issues far fewer new shares to the protected investor. Under that method, the first investor's 300,000 shares are added to management's 700,000 shares and then multiplied by $2. The $2,000,000 product of this calculation is then added to the $200,000 paid by the second investor giving a sum of $2,200,000. This amount is divided by the total number of shares outstanding after the second sale, 1,200,000, to give the new average price for the first investor. That price is $1.83 per share. When divided into the $600,000 invested by the first investor (300,000 shares x $2) this yields 327,869 total shares to which the first investor is entitled, requiring the company to issue him 27,869 free shares.

The chart below compares how the two antidilution methods fared in the example. The difference in results from the two methods would be even more dramatic if fewer shares were sold to the second investor.

| Comparison of Antidilution Methods | | |
|---|---|---|
| | Weighted Average | Ratchet |
| Shares bought by investor | 300,000 | 300,000 |
| Free shares to investor | 27,869 | 300,000 |
| Total investor shares | 327,869 | 600,000 |
| Total outstanding shares | 1,227,869 | 1,500,000 |
| Average investor share price | $1.83 | $1.00 |
| Percent owned by investor | 26.6 | 40.0 |
| Percent owned by management | 57.0 | 46.6 |
| Percent owned by 2nd investor | 16.4 | 13.4 |

Note, however, that weighted average antidilution provisions differ. Each must be considered on its own merits. *See: Antidilution Provisions, Dilution (Percentage), Ratchets.*

**Windows** is a phrase used in two distinctly different contexts, but in both cases the aspect of timing is crucial.

First, venture capitalists are very sensitive to the timing of the introduction of a company's new product into the market. If the product is too revolutionary, the cost of creating a market for the product may be prohibitive. On the other hand, if the product does not have enough to distinguish it from its competition, it may be too late for the product to gain a profitable market share. That period when the company's technology is new enough to distinguish its products in the marketplace but not so new that no one is ready to purchase it is sometimes called "the window of opportunity." Introducing the product "while the window is open" can be critical to a company success.

The phrase "window" is also used to describe the period during which the public stock markets are receptive to new issues of stock. When one company conducts a successful initial public offering in medical devices, for example, other device companies will often rush to complete their offerings while the window is open. *See: Five Factors, Going Public, IPOs (Initial Public Offerings), Market Research.*

# Z

**Zeal** is a quality investors look for in entrepreneurs. Growing a successful business is a challenging endeavor where long hours and extraordinary challenges are the norm. Even success, as in expanding sales, challenges the resources of a business by calling for more and more cash to support inventories and payment terms. No one should start a business without understanding the effort and risk involved. A zeal for the business can help management get through the challenges that inevitably await their endeavors. A demonstrated and informed zeal for the company's prospects can help convince third party investors to back the company with needed funds. *See: Commitment, Entrepreneur.*

# Appendix

## Annotated Sample
## Series A Stock Purchase Agreement

# SERIES A PREFERRED STOCK PURCHASE AGREEMENT[1]

This Agreement is made as of the 30th day of September, 20XX, by and between Newco Incorporated, a Delaware corporation (the "Company")[2], and Venture Fund LLC, a Delaware limited liability company (the "Investor").[3]

---

[1] *This is an example of the principal investment agreement for a first round investment by an institutional venture capital investor. The agreement contains the venture capitalist's binding commitment to invest in the company in exchange for a new class of convertible preferred stock. The investor's obligation is conditioned on the company making extensive representations (section 2) about its business and is subject to conditions (section 4) the company must meet before receiving funds. The investment obligation is also conditioned on the investor receiving commitments from the company about specific operational matters. These are contained in separate agreements and charter documents referred to in section 4. For its part, the investor commits to purchase stock and makes representations (section 3) needed to qualify its investment as a private placement under state and federal securities laws. The terms contained in this agreement frequently conform to and expand upon business terms contained in a non-binding term sheet negotiated earlier by the parties. All of the contracts needed to complete the investment are identified in this document. A sophisticated individual angel investor might use a similar form.*

[2] *This is the operating company that receives the funding. It is headquartered in Georgia but incorporated as a Delaware corporation.*

[3] *This is the venture capital fund that provides the funding. It is headquartered in California but organized as a Delaware limited liability company. When there is more than one investor, each investor and the amount of its investment can be identified by reference to an exhibit attached to the agreement.*

*406 –Growth Company Guide 4.0*

**1.  Purchase and Sale of Stock.**

1.1.  <u>Sale and Issuance of Series A Preferred Stock.</u>[4]

(a)  The Company shall adopt and file with the Secretary of State of the State of Delaware on or before the Closing (as defined below) an Amended and Restated Certificate of Incorporation[5] in the form attached hereto as <u>Exhibit A</u> (the "Restated Certificate").[6]

(b)  Subject to the terms and conditions of

---

[4] *The Series A designation identifies this as the first class of convertible preferred stock created by the company. Although not specifically designated in the name, this Series A stock is a convertible preferred stock whose terms entitle the holder to preferences over common stock. The prevailing form of equity ownership held by founders and management of growing companies is common stock. By purchasing a convertible preferred stock, the venture capitalist assures itself of receiving certain economically valuable preference rights. Among these are the rights to receive preferential payment if the company liquidates, to convert the preferred stock into common stock, to be consulted on and approve certain major decisions normally reserved to a company's board of directors, and to be represented on the company's board of directors. It is also common for these rights to include 'anti-dilution' rights that increase the number of shares of common stock the investor receives upon conversion if the company sells stock later at prices lower than the Series A price.*

[5] *Many of the preferences the investor receives are written into the description of the Series A stock contained in the company's certificate of incorporation. Since the preferences are negotiated rights and specific to the transaction, the company usually must create a new class of stock to accommodate the investment. This is accomplished by amending the company's existing articles of incorporation to create the new class of stock. This amendment is filed with the Secretary of State's office in the state in which the company is incorporated.*

[6] *By attaching the amended and restated certificate of incorporation as an exhibit, the parties are agreeing to the precise terms of the preferences granted to the investor's shares.*

this Agreement, the Investor agrees to purchase and the Company agrees to sell and issue to the Investor at the Closing 1,000,000 shares of the Company's Series A Preferred Stock (the "Series A Stock") at a purchase price of $2.00 per share for an aggregate purchase price of $2,000,000.[7]   The Series A Stock will have the rights, preferences, privileges and restrictions set forth in the Restated Certificate.

    1.2.    Closing.

        (a)    The purchase and sale of the Series A Stock shall take place at the offices of the Investor's counsel, at 2:00 p.m., on [Month] [Day], [Current Year], or at such other time and place as the Company and the Investor shall mutually agree, either orally or in writing (which time and place are designated as the "Closing").[8]

---

[7] *This purchase establishes a fair market value for the company's Series A stock of $2.00 per share. Because the common stock held by management and earlier shareholders has fewer rights than the Series A stock, its fair market value will generally be considered to be less than $2.00 per share. Notwithstanding this discrepancy between the fair market value of the Series A stock and the common stock, this transaction also establishes what the venture industry routinely characterizes as a fully diluted fair market value for the company. In this investment where there are 3,000,000 shares of common stock issued and another 1,000,000 shares committed to existing stock plans and issued warrants (see section 2.5), the fully diluted fair market value of the company implied by this investment would be $10,000,000 because the investor's purchase of 1,000,000 shares would represent 20% (1,000,000 out of 5,000,000) of the fully diluted shares after purchase and its purchase price of $2,000,000 for that 20% would imply a value for 100% of five times $2,000,000 or $10,000,000. This value would commonly be referred to as the pre-money valuation. Note that this valuation is a convenient fiction to the extent it assumes that the Series A stock shares have the same value as the common stock, which is untrue.*

[8] *The closing is the event where the agreements are signed, the investor's money transfers to the company and the company*

(b)    At the Closing, the Company shall deliver to the Investor a certificate representing the shares of Series A Stock that the Investor is purchasing against payment of the purchase price therefore by certified check or wire transfer of immediately available funds.[9]

1.3.    Sale of Additional Series A Stock.[10]

(a)    At any time prior to [*a future date agreed upon by the parties*] (the "Future Date"), the Company, at its option, shall have the right to sell to Investor, and upon the exercise of such option, the Investor shall purchase from the Company,[11] up to an additional 1,000,000 shares of Series A Stock as may be designated by the Company at the same price per share as the Series A Stock purchased and sold at the Closing[12] (the "Put Option").  At any time prior to the Future

**(..continued)**

delivers stock to the investor. It is the time when all of the commitments made in the agreements become effective and binding.

[9] *This is the exchange that delivers the stock certificate to the investor and the investment funds to the company. The certified check or wire transfer designation generates same-day funds to the company.*

[10] *This provision provides a mechanism for the company to receive additional investment in the future. This type funding is frequently referred to as a staged funding, because investment funding is received in stages over time.*

[11] *The funding mechanism uses a company put and an investor call to create a scenario in which either party can cause the additional investment to be made once the conditions are met.*

[12] *If this investment is made it will complicate the fair market valuation analysis described above. If the second $2,000,000 is invested, the total investment will be 2,000,000 shares of Series A stock for $4,000,000. In this scenario the investor will own 2,000,000 of 6,000,000 fully diluted shares (the common stock, plan stock, stock subject to warrants and the investor's stock). This one-third interest purchased for $4,000,000 would imply a pre-money, fully diluted, fair market value of $12,000,000. See footnote 7.*

Date, the Investor, at its option, shall have the right to purchase from the Company up to an additional 1,000,000 shares of Series A Stock as may be designated by the Investor at the same price per share as the Series A Stock purchased and sold at the Closing[13] (the "Call Option", and together with the Put Option, the "Options"). The Company shall not have the right to exercise its Put Option as to any shares of Series A Stock which were the subject of the Investor's exercise of its Call Option and the Investor shall not have the right to exercise its Call Option as to any shares of Series A Stock which were the subject of the Company's exercise of its Put Option.[14] The Investor may designate a nominee who shall have the right to exercise the Call Option prior to the Future Date; provided, however, that such nominee shall be subject to the Company's written approval prior to any exercise of the Call Option by such nominee.[15]

       (b)       Within thirty (30) days after the exercise

---

[13] *In general, each series of convertible preferred stock is designed for each of its shares to be sold at a price equal to the initial conversion value specified in the stock description. This is because the anti-dilution protection built into the security is usually contained in the conversion feature of the stock in such a way that only provides equal protection of all class shareholders if those shareholders paid the same amount for the convertible preferred stock. If a higher price is desired for stock acquired at a later date, the company can create new series of convertible preferred stock or use sub-series of an existing convertible preferred stock series. For example, if the parties desired to mimic the features of an existing Series A stock, they could create a Series B stock with similar features or use a Series A-2 stock, using different purchase prices in the later series or sub-series.*

[14] *This provision prevents the shares subject to issuance from being sold more than once.*

[15] *The right of the investor to designate another party to purchase the shares is common. It enables an institutional venture investor to use another fund under its management to make the investment, but only if the company approves.*

*410 –Growth Company Guide 4.0*

by either party of one of the Options, Investor shall tender to the Company the purchase price of $2.00 per share by certified check or wire transfer of immediately available funds for all of the shares to be purchased pursuant to such Option (the "Noticed Shares") together with a written confirmation of the representations set forth in Section 3 of this Agreement and the Company at such time shall deliver a certificate for the Noticed Shares of Series A Stock.[16] Notwithstanding any contrary provision contained in this Section 1.3, in no event shall the Company be obligated to issue more than 1,000,000 shares in the aggregate pursuant to this Section 1.3.

At the time or times of the exercise of the Options by the Company or the Investor and the sale of the Series A Stock to the Investor thereto (each, a "Subsequent Closing"), the Investor's obligations with respect to a Subsequent Closing shall be conditioned on satisfaction, as of the date of such Subsequent Closing, of the conditions set forth in Sections 4.1 to the extent related to Sections 2.1, 2.2, 2.3, 2.4, 2.10, 2.11, 2.12, 2.13, 2.14, 2.16 and 2.19 (each subject to the Schedule of Exceptions attached hereto), 4.2, 4.3 (to the extent related to Sections 4.1, 4.2, or 4.5), and 4.5 hereof. [17] The Company's obligations with respect to a Subsequent Closing shall be conditioned on satisfaction, as of the date of such Subsequent

---

[16] *This section establishes the closing procedure for the second round of funding. The Section 3 representations referred to are the investor's securities law representations relied upon by the company in making the sale.*

[17] *This reference requires the company to re-certify fulfillment of the closing requirements required for the initial closing but does not create new milestones for the company to meet as a condition to receiving this additional funding. In many circumstances, the investor's obligation to provide later funding (that is, the company's right to put) is conditioned on the company meeting agreed upon objectives such as completing development of a product, making a first sale, or hiring a key executive to improve the management team.*

Closing, of the conditions set forth in Section 5.1 and 5.2 hereof.

## 2. Representations and Warranties of the Company.[18]

Except as set forth on a Schedule of Exceptions[19] attached hereto which specifically identifies the relevant subsection(s) hereof, the Company[20] hereby represents and warrants to the Investor that at the Closing:

2.1. <u>Organization; Good Standing; Qualification.</u> The Company is a corporation duly organized, validly existing, and in good standing under the laws of the State of Delaware, has all requisite corporate power and authority to own and operate its properties and assets and to carry on its business as now conducted, to execute and deliver this Agreement, the Investor Rights Agreement, the Co-Sale Agreement and any other agreement to which the Company is a party and the execution and delivery of which is contemplated hereby (the "Ancillary Agreements"), to issue and sell the Series A Stock and the Common Stock issuable upon conversion thereof, and

---

[18] *These representations paint a detailed picture of the company's legal structure, assets, intellectual property rights, liabilities, and business. The investor relies upon these representations and it's other due diligence investigations in making its investment.*
[19] *The statements in the Schedule of Exceptions qualify the representations made in the numbered paragraphs of this section. Each numbered paragraph must be read as if it begins with the phrase "except as set forth on the Schedule of Exceptions." None of the numbered paragraphs can be fully understood without referring to the factual statements contained on the Schedule of Exceptions. The level of detail of this schedule can be extensive.*
[20] *Sometimes others, such as the founding manager, are asked to make these representations as well as the company. When this happens, the individual adding his or her representations risks becoming personally liable to the investor if a representation turns out to be false and the investor suffers damages.*
*412 –Growth Company Guide 4.0*

to carry out the provisions of this Agreement, the Investor Rights Agreement, the Co-Sale Agreement, the Restated Certificate and any Ancillary Agreement.[21] The Company is duly qualified and is authorized to transact business only in the State of Georgia. Failure to qualify and be in good standing as a foreign corporation in other jurisdictions will not have a material adverse effect on its business, properties, prospects, or financial condition.[22]

    2.2.    Authorization. All corporate action on the part of the Company, its officers, directors and stockholders necessary for the authorization, execution and delivery of this Agreement, the Investor Rights Agreement, the Co-Sale Agreement and any Ancillary Agreement, the performance of all obligations of the Company hereunder and thereunder at the Closing, and the authorization, issuance (or reservation for issuance), sale and delivery of the Series A Stock being sold hereunder and the Common Stock issuable upon conversion thereof has been taken or will be taken prior to the Closing,[23]

---

[21] *In other words, the company is a viable legal entity with the authority and power to enter into the investment agreements, fulfill its contractual obligations and issue stock.*

[22] *The company is qualified to do business wherever such qualification is necessary to the conduct of its business. Companies qualify by filing forms and paying fees with the Secretary of State offices in states where their local activity qualifies as "doing business." The question of whether a company is doing business in a given state is often resolved with the help of an attorney, as federal law restricts the ability of states to impose restrictions on interstate commerce. Investors are interested in knowing the company is qualified to conduct business because some states impose serious penalties for not being qualified.*

[23] *Company undertakings of this magnitude require authorization from a duly constituted board of directors. To create the Series A stock required for the closing, the company's shareholders must also approve the Restated Certificate. This representation states that these requirements have been met. In some cases, where the company's articles of incorporation include a "blank check*

and this Agreement, the Investor Rights Agreement, the Co-Sale Agreement and any Ancillary Agreement, when executed and delivered, will constitute valid and legally binding obligations of the Company, enforceable in accordance with their respective terms except (i) as limited by applicable bankruptcy, insolvency, reorganization, moratorium, and other laws of general application affecting enforcement of creditors' rights generally, (ii) as limited by laws relating to the availability of specific performance, injunctive relief, or other equitable remedies, and (iii) to the extent that the indemnification provisions contained in the Investor Rights Agreement may be limited by applicable laws.[24]

    2.3.   <u>Valid Issuance of Preferred and Common Stock</u>. The Series A Stock being purchased by the Investor hereunder, when issued, sold, and delivered in accordance with the terms of this Agreement for the consideration expressed herein, will be duly and validly issued, fully paid, and nonassessable,[25] and will be free of restrictions on transfer other than restrictions on transfer under this Agreement and the Investor Rights Agreement and under applicable state and federal securities laws.[26] The Common Stock issuable upon

(..continued)

*preferred" provision, the company's board of directors may have the authority to create the Series A stock without shareholder approval.*

*[24] The company represents that the terms of the agreements are enforceable against it, except to the limited extent described in these three customary exceptions.*

*[25] Nonassessable stock is stock that has been paid for in full. The company cannot require the holder to pay additional sums for the stock at a later date.*

*[26] The Series A stock being purchased is privately issued stock that may not be readily resold like publicly issued stock. The limitations on its tradability come from securities law exemptions that are used to authorize its sale without a public offering. Separate rights and restrictions can be contained in contracts, such as the Investor Rights Agreement referred to in this section. The stock certificates 414 –Growth Company Guide 4.0*

conversion of the Series A Stock being purchased under this Agreement has been duly and validly reserved for issuance and, upon issuance in accordance with the terms of the Restated Certificate, will be duly and validly issued, fully paid, and nonassessable and will be free of restrictions on transfer other than restrictions on transfer under this Agreement and in the Investor Rights Agreement and under applicable state and federal securities laws.[27]

 2.4. <u>Governmental Consents</u>.[28]  No consent, approval, qualification, order or authorization of, or filing with, any local, state, or federal governmental authority is required on the part of the Company in connection with the Company's valid execution, delivery, or performance of this Agreement, the offer, sale or issuance of the Series A Stock by the Company or the issuance of Common Stock upon conversion of the Series A Stock, except (i) the filing of the Restated Certificate with the Secretary of State of the State of Delaware, and (ii) such filings as have been made prior to the Closing, except any notices of sale required to be filed with the Securities and Exchange Commission under Regulation D of the Securities Act of 1933, as amended (the "Securities Act"), or such post-closing filings as may be required under applicable state securities laws, which will be timely filed within the applicable periods therefore.

 2.5. <u>Capitalization and Voting Rights</u>.[29]  The

(..continued)

*will carry legends reflecting these restrictions. See section 3.8(b) for an example of a legend. The same holds true for the common stock issued upon conversion of the Series A stock.*

[27] *When the preferred stock is converted into common stock, the preferred stock will cease to exist and the newly issued common stock will be properly issued and fully paid.*

[28] *This representation assures the investor that all governmental approvals needed for the issuance of the stock and the company's performance of its agreements have been obtained or provided for.*

[29] *This provision describes how the company is currently owned. In so doing, it enables the investor to determine what percentage of*

authorized capital of the Company consists, or will consist immediately prior to the Closing, of:

        (a)    <u>Preferred Stock</u>.    2,000,000 shares of Series A Stock,[30] par value $.0001, of which 1,000,000 shares are reserved for issuance[31] to the Investor at the Closing and 1,000,000 shares are reserved for issuance to the Investor upon the exercise of the Options.[32]

        (b)    <u>Common Stock</u>.    10,000,000 shares of common stock, par value $.0001 ("Common Stock"), of which 3,000,000 shares are issued and outstanding, 600,000 shares are

(..continued)

*the company is being purchased with the investment. Three concepts are needed to understand the representations made in this section. The first is authorized stock, which is the stock the company has legal authority to sell. The authorized stock of the company is specified in its articles of incorporation. The second is issued stock, which is stock the company has issued (by sale or gift) to a shareholder. The last concept is outstanding stock. This is stock that has been issued and not reacquired by the company. For example, a company may be authorized to issue 5,000,000 shares of common stock (authorized stock) of which it sells 600,000 shares (issued stock) and buys back 100,000 shares. The company's authorized stock, in this example, is 5,000,000 shares. Its outstanding stock is 500,000 shares (600,000 issues less 100,000 reacquired). Company ownership is a function of issued and outstanding shares. In our example, someone who owned 200,000 shares would own 40% of the company because they own 40% of the stock that is both issued and outstanding.*

[30] *These are the shares that have been newly created by amendment to the company's restated certificate of incorporation for issuance to the venture capital investor.*

[31] *Reservation for issuance means the company's board of directors has designated to whom these shares may be issued in the future.*

[32] *These shares are set aside for issuance to the investor pursuant to Section 1.3 of this agreement. The term "options" refers to the investor's right defined in Section 1.3 to purchase an additional 1,000,000 shares at $2.00 per share.*

*416 –Growth Company Guide 4.0*

reserved for issuance pursuant to the Company's Stock Option Plan[33] (the "Option Plan"), 300,000 shares are reserved for issuance to The Partner Group L.L.C., a New York limited liability company ("TPG") upon the execution and delivery of a warrant, the terms of which are currently being negotiated between the Company and TPG (the "TPG Warrant"), and 100,000 shares are reserved for issuance to URC upon the execution and delivery of a Technology License Agreement, the terms of which are currently being negotiated between the

---

[33] *This typically refers to a qualified stock plan established to provide a pool of stock for use in hiring and retaining key company employees. Investors and management are interested in the number of shares that are reserved to the plan because these shares represent the capital of the company that has been reserved to attract and retain qualified people to operate and grow the company's business. Rights to purchase stock from the plan stock are typically granted as options that the employees become empowered to exercise over time. Venture capital investors also take into account the number of shares reserved to a plan pool when they calculate the number of shares they require in return for their investment. Typically, they will assume, when determining the number of shares they will require for their investment, that all plan shares, whether or not they have been made subject to granted options, are eventually issued. They will also assume that all shares subject to other warrants or options not issued under the plan are eventually issued. This is often referred to as being on a fully diluted basis. The practical effect of this is that larger plans increase the number of shares an investor will require and, thereby, decrease the percentage ownership represented by the shares owned by management. For example, if management owns 6,500,000 shares and has a option pool of 1,000,000 shares, an investor wanting 25% of the fully diluted shares would ask for 2,500,000 shares making the total fully diluted shares after investment equal to 10,000,000. If, instead, the pool is twice as large, or 2,000,000 shares, the investor will need approximately 2,833,333 to equal 25% of the total 11,833,333 fully diluted shares after investment.*

Company and URC.[34]

        (c)      The outstanding shares of Common Stock are owned by the stockholders and in the numbers specified in <u>Exhibit D</u> hereto.[35]   The outstanding shares of Common Stock have been duly authorized and validly issued, are fully paid and nonassessable.[36]

        (d)      Except for (i) rights granted in Section 1.3, (ii) the conversion privileges of the Series A Stock, (iii) the rights provided in Section 2.3 of the Investor Rights Agreement, (iv) those certain Stock Transfer Agreements listed in Section 2.5(b) of the Schedule of Exceptions, and (v) the TPG Warrant, there are no outstanding options, warrants, rights (including conversion or preemptive rights and rights of first refusal), proxy or stockholder agreements or agreements of any kind for the purchase or acquisition from the Company of any of its securities.[37] The Company is not a party or subject to any agreement or understanding, and, to the best of the Company's knowledge, there is no agreement or understanding between any persons that affects or relates to the voting or giving of written consents with respect to any security or the voting by a

---

[34] *These two warrants illustrate how companies often use the attraction of their stock, and its potential for growth in value, to acquire rights and services of importance to the company. Warrants are like options in that they entitle their holder to purchase shares of company stock at a future date for a defined price. The Partner Group LLC received its warrant for assistance in raising capital. The shares reserved for issuance to URC (University Research Corporation) are payment for license rights to technology needed by the company.*

[35] *This exhibit identifies the present shareholders and their share ownership positions.*

[36] *Fully paid and nonassessable refers to the fact that the company may not require additional payment for the shares.*

[37] *This identifies all outstanding rights to acquire capital stock in the company.*

*418 –Growth Company Guide 4.0*

director of the Company.[38]

2.6.    Subsidiaries.    The Company does not own or control, directly or indirectly, any interest in any other corporation, partnership, limited liability company, association, or other business entity.[39]

2.7.    Contracts and Other Commitments.    The Company does not have and is not bound by any contract, agreement, lease, commitment or proposed transaction, judgment, order, writ or decree, written or oral, absolute or contingent, other than (i) contracts for the purchase of supplies and services that were entered into in the ordinary course of business and that do not involve more than $25,000, and do not extend for more than one (1) year beyond the date hereof, (ii) sales contracts entered into in the ordinary course of business and that do not involve more than $25,000, and do not extend for more than one (1) year beyond the date hereof, and (iii) contracts terminable at will by the Company on no more than thirty (30) days' notice without cost or liability to the Company and that do not involve any employment or consulting arrangement and are not material to the conduct of the Company's business.[40]

2.8.    Related-Party Transactions.    No employee, officer, stockholder or director of the Company or member of his or her immediate family is indebted to the Company, nor is the Company indebted to any such person (or committed to

---

[38] There are no undisclosed voting agreements or contractual rights to influence voting of shareholders or directors. The existence of such rights could diminish the voting and influence rights granted to the Series A holders.

[39] If the company did own interests in other businesses they would be listed here or on the Schedule of Exceptions.

[40] Although written as an absolute statement, this representation anticipates that the company will provide a detailed listing of contracts to which it is a party on the Schedule of Exceptions. The qualifications in the sentence identify types of contracts that do not need to be listed on the Schedule of Exceptions.

make loans or extend or guarantee credit to any of them), other than (i) for payment of reasonable salary for services rendered over a period not in excess of one (1) month, (ii) reimbursement for reasonable expenses incurred on behalf of the Company in an amount not in excess of $25,000 in the aggregate, and (iii) for other standard employee benefits made generally available to all employees (including stock option agreements outstanding under any stock option plan approved by the Board of Directors of the Company) and disclosed in full to the Investor.[41]  To the best of the Company's knowledge, none of such persons has any direct or indirect ownership interest in any firm or corporation with which the Company is affiliated or with which the Company has a business relationship, or any firm or corporation that competes with the Company, except that employees, stockholders, officers, or directors of the Company and members of their immediate families may own stock in publicly traded companies that may compete with the Company.  To the best of the Company's knowledge, no officer, director, or stockholder or any member of their immediate families is, directly or indirectly, interested in any material contract with the Company (other than such contracts as relate to any such person's ownership of capital stock or other securities of the Company or such person's employment by the Company).[42]

---

[41] *This representation identifies loans and other preferences granted to management and inside shareholders of the company. The purpose is to quantify and limit any special deals between the company and the people controlling the company that might redirect the resources of the company away from the goals common to all shareholders. To avoid making a false representation, all of these types of arrangements need to be listed on the Schedule of Exceptions.*
[42] *These last two representations are directed toward discovering any potential conflicts of interest between the company and its managers, shareholders and directors. Any contracts between any management member and the company will be carefully reviewed*
*420 –Growth Company Guide 4.0*

2.9.    Registration Rights.  Except as provided in the Investor Rights Agreement, the Company is presently not under any obligation and has not granted any rights to register under the Securities Act any of its presently outstanding securities or any of its securities that may subsequently be issued.[43]

2.10.  Permits.    The Company has all franchises, permits, licenses, and any similar authority necessary for the conduct of its business as now being conducted by it, the lack of which could materially and adversely affect the business, properties, prospects, or financial condition of the Company, and believes it can obtain, without undue burden or expense, any similar authority for the conduct of its business as presently planned to be conducted.  The Company is not in default in any material respect under any of such franchises, permits, licenses or other similar authority.[44]

2.11.  Compliance with Other Instruments.    The Company is not in violation or default in any material respect of any provision of its Restated Certificate or Bylaws or in any material respect of any provision of any material mortgage, indenture, agreement, instrument, or contract to which it is a party or by which it is bound, or of any federal or state judgment, order, writ, decree, or to the best of its knowledge, any federal or state statute, rule, regulation or restriction

(..continued)

*by the investor to determine whether it is fair to the company.*
[43] *Registration rights entitle their holders to cause the company to register their shares of company stock in a registered public offering. The purpose of this is to create a market for the shares and make them freely tradable. Because there are practical limits on the number of investor shares a company can successfully register without adversely affecting their value, investors are interested in limiting the number of registration rights that are granted by the company. This representation identifies existing registration rights that might have priority over the rights granted to the Series A holders by the Investor Rights Agreement.*
[44] *The company has all the permits and registrations it needs to conduct its business.*

*Annotated Stock Purchase Agreement - 421*

applicable to the Company.[45]   The execution, delivery, and performance by the Company of this Agreement, the Investor Rights Agreement, the Co-Sale Agreement and any Ancillary Agreement, and the consummation of the transactions contemplated hereby and thereby, will not result in any such violation or be in material conflict with or constitute, with or with the passage of time or giving of notice, either a material default under any such provision or an event that results in the creation of any material lien, charge, or encumbrance upon any assets of the Company or the suspension, revocation, impairment, forfeiture, or non-renewal of any material permit, license, authorization, or approval applicable to the Company, its business or operations, or any of its assets or properties.[46]

    2.12.   <u>Litigation</u>. There is no action, suit, proceeding, or investigation pending or currently threatened against the Company that questions the validity of this Agreement, the Investor Rights Agreement, the Co-Sale Agreement or any Ancillary Agreement or the right of the Company to enter into such agreements, or to consummate the transactions contemplated hereby or thereby, or that might result, either individually or in the aggregate, in any material adverse change in the assets, business, properties, prospects, or financial condition of the Company, or in any material change in the current equity ownership of the Company.[47]

---

[45] *The company is not violating any material contract, statute, regulation or charter provision. Such a violation might result in damages or impair the company's ability to conduct its business in its present manner.*

[46] *The making of this investment will not cause the company to violate the terms of any of its important agreements or cause any of its assets to become encumbered.*

[47] *Investors are interested in two types of company litigation, lawsuits that could question the validity of their investment and lawsuits that could damage the company and diminish its value. When lawsuits are scheduled in response to this representation, investor's counsel will question company counsel about the*
*422 –Growth Company Guide 4.0*

2.13. <u>Disclosure</u>. The Company has provided the Investor with all the information reasonably available to it without undue expense that the Investor has requested for deciding whether to purchase the Series A Stock and all information that the Company believes is reasonably necessary to enable the Investor to make such decision. Neither this Agreement nor any other agreements, written statements or certificates made or delivered in connection herewith contains any untrue statement of a material fact or omits to state a material fact necessary to make the statements herein or therein not materially misleading.[48]

2.14. <u>Title to Property and Assets; Leases</u>. Except (i) as reflected in the Financial Statements (defined in Section 2.15), (ii) for liens for current taxes not yet delinquent, (iii) for liens imposed by law and incurred in the ordinary course of business for obligations not past due to carriers, warehousemen, laborers, materialmen and the like, (iv) for liens in respect of pledges or deposits under workers' compensation laws or similar legislation or (v) for minor defects in title, none of which, individually or in the aggregate, materially interferes with the use of such property, the Company has good and marketable title to its property and assets free and clear of all mortgages, liens, claims, and encumbrances. With respect to the property and assets it leases, the Company is in compliance with such leases and, to the best of its knowledge, holds a valid leasehold interest free of any liens, claims, or encumbrances, subject to clauses (i)-(v) above.[49]

(..continued)
*particulars of the lawsuits to help the investor evaluate the potential impact of those claims.*
[48] *This is a catchall representation intended to protect the investor from the risk of failing to ask the right question that would generate a disclosure of important information.*
[49] *Except for scheduled encumbrances or liens described in the subparagraphs, the company's assets are unencumbered and owned by the company. Except as disclosed, its leases are valid and unencumbered. The company is not in default under any of its*

2.15. <u>Financial Statements.</u>[50] The Company has delivered to the Investor its unaudited[51] financial statements (balance sheet and profit and loss statement, statement of stockholders' equity and statement of cash flows including notes thereto) at December 31, [Last Year] and for the fiscal year then ended and its unaudited financial statements (balance sheet and profit and loss statement) as at, and for the nine-month period ended September 30, [Current Year] (the "Financial Statements"). The Financial Statements have been prepared in accordance with generally accepted accounting principles[52] applied on a consistent basis throughout the periods indicated and with each other, except that unaudited Financial Statements may not contain all footnotes required by generally accepted accounting principles. The Financial Statements fairly present the financial condition and operating results of the Company as of the dates, and for the periods indicated therein, subject to normal year-end audit adjustments.[53] Except as set forth in the Financial Statements, the Company has no material liabilities, contingent or oth-

(..continued)

*leases.*

[50] *This is the single most important representation in the agreement. The company's financial statements provide a quantitative historical snapshot of the company's status and operations. The representations contained in this representation identify which financial statements are being disclosed and the basis on which they were prepared. The last sentence represents that no obligations or liabilities that would be considered to be out of the ordinary have been incurred since the date of the last financial statement described in the representation.*

[51] *When available, audited statements will be required.*

[52] *Also referred to as GAAP.*

[53] *The two key representations about the quality and nature of the information contained in the financial statements are that the financial statements "have been prepared in accordance with generally accepted accounting principles applied on a consistent basis" and that all financial statements "fairly present the financial condition and operating results" of the company.*

*424 –Growth Company Guide 4.0*

erwise, other than (i) liabilities incurred in the ordinary course of business subsequent to September 30, [Current Year] and (ii) obligations under contracts and commitments incurred in the ordinary course of business and not required under generally accepted accounting principles to be reflected in the Financial Statements, which, in both cases, individually or in the aggregate, are not material to the financial condition or operating results of the Company. [54]

2.16.   <u>Patents and Trademarks.</u>[55]

(a)      The Company has sufficient title and ownership of all patents, trademarks, service marks, trade names, copyrights, trade secrets, information, proprietary rights, and processes (collectively, "Intellectual Property") necessary for its business as now conducted, and believes it can obtain, on commercially reasonable terms, any additional rights necessary for its business as proposed to be conducted, and to the best of the Company's knowledge, its Intellectual Property does not, and would not, constitute an infringement of the rights of others;[56]

(b)      There are no outstanding options, licenses, or

---

[54] *There are no unusual obligations or contract commitments missing from the financial statements that would have a material effect on the finances or operations of company.*

[55] *Patents, trademarks, copyrights and trade secrets can provide companies with important advantages when they compete in the marketplace. This representation undertakes to inventory the company's rights in its intellectual property and to describe the extent and limits of the rights it has, including the right to exclude others from commercializing those rights. The company's ideas, science, and inventions provide the proprietary methodologies, products, and services that distinguish the company from its competitors. As such, they are an important part of the value proposition to the investor.*

[56] *The company has sufficient legal rights to use and commercialize the technology it relies upon without interference from others and without infringing rights of others. If it needs additional rights it believes it can obtain them upon commercially reasonable terms.*

agreements of any kind relating to the matters listed in subsection (a) above or that grant rights to any other person to manufacture, license, produce, assemble, market or sell the Company's products, nor is the Company bound by or a party to any options, licenses, or agreements of any kind with respect to the Intellectual Property of any other person or entity;[57]

(c)    The    Company    has    not    received    any communications alleging that the Company or its employees has violated or infringed or, by conducting its business as proposed, would violate or infringe any of the Intellectual Property of any other person or entity;[58]

(d)    The Company is not aware that any of its employees is obligated under any contract (including licenses, covenants, or commitments of any nature) or other agreement, or subject to any judgment, decree, or order of any court or administrative agency, that would interfere with the use of such employee's best efforts to promote the interests of the Company with respect to the Intellectual Property of the Company or otherwise or that would conflict with the Company's business as proposed to be conducted;[59] and

---

[57] *This requires the company to list the licenses it has granted to others. The investor can use the list and copies of the licenses to evaluate whether they were granted in the ordinary course of the company's business, the extent to which they create value or incur cost and, most importantly, whether they grant rights that might impinge upon the company's ability to execute its business plan.*

[58] *The company has not been notified about any potential problems that would interfere with it using its technology in its business. Except as disclosed, no one is claiming the company's technology violates any of their rights.*

[59] *The principal risks being addressed are contracts between company employees and others, such as non-compete agreements or agreements respecting the development or deployment of technology, that might give others the right to interfere with the company's business. These agreements could be with former employers or could be recited in a legal judgment pending against an employee. For employees engaged with the company's*

(e)    Neither the execution nor delivery of this Agreement, nor the carrying on of the Company's business by the employees of the Company, nor the conduct of the Company's business as proposed, will, to the Company's knowledge, conflict with or result in a breach of the terms, conditions, or provisions of, or constitute a default under, any contract, covenant, or instrument under which any of such employees is now obligated. The Company does not believe it is or will be necessary to utilize any inventions of any of its employees (or people it currently intends to hire) made prior to their employment by the Company to which the Company does not have sufficient rights to permit the Company to conduct the Company's business as proposed;[60] and

(f)    The Evaluation Agreement and the Clinical Development Agreement, dated December 31, [Last Year], between Technology Company and the Company (the "TC Agreements") are in full force and effect and constitute valid and binding obligations of Technology Company and the Company.[61] The Company, and to the Company's knowledge, Technology Company, are not in default under the TC Agreements.[62]

(..continued)

*technology or in the sales of company products, confidentiality agreements with former employers should be analyzed to make sure confidential information of those former employers is not being used.*

[60] *This subsection is a more specific elaboration of the preceding representation. The last sentence deals specifically with employee contract restrictions that could inhibit the company from using its technology.*

[61] *This refers to a specific agreement relating to important technology used by the company under a license. The investor, who will have reviewed the terms of this agreement, wants assurances that the contract remains in effect.*

[62] *If either party is in default, whether or not the default has been tendered, the rights granted under the agreement could be in jeopardy.*

2.17.   Manufacturing and Marketing Rights.   The Company has not granted rights to manufacture, produce, assemble, license, market, or sell its products to any other person and is not bound by any agreement that affects the Company's exclusive right to develop, manufacture, assemble, distribute, market, or sell its products.[63]

2.18.   Employees; Employee Compensation.   To the best of the Company's knowledge, there is no strike, labor dispute or union organization activities pending or threatened between it and its employees.   None of the Company's employees belongs to any union or collective bargaining unit. [64] To the best of its knowledge, the Company has complied in all material respects with all applicable state and federal equal opportunity and other laws related to employment.[65]   Except for the Option Plan, the Company is not a party to or bound by any currently effective employment contract, deferred compensation agreement, bonus plan, incentive plan, profit sharing plan, retirement agreement, or other employee compensation agreement.[66]

2.19.   Tax Returns, Payments, and Elections.   The Company has timely filed all tax returns and reports (federal, state and local) as required by law.   These returns and reports are true and correct in all material respects.   The Company has paid all taxes and other assessments due, except those contested by it in good faith.   The provision for taxes of the Company as shown in the Financial Statements is adequate for taxes due or

---

[63] *Any manufacturing rights that have been granted would be described on the Schedule of Exceptions.*

[64] *Labor disputes and misunderstandings can be expensive and distracting to the business at hand. Union and collective bargaining agreements are material. When they exist, investors want to know their terms and conditions.*

[65] *Noncompliance with employment laws can lead to time consuming disputes and expensive remedies.*

[66] *Investors routinely require the company to disclose all employee benefits.*

accrued as of the date thereof.[67]

2.20. <u>Environmental and Safety Laws</u>. To the best of its knowledge, the Company is not in violation of any applicable statute, law, or regulation relating to the environment or occupational health and safety, and to the best of its knowledge, no material expenditures are or will be required in order to comply with any such existing statute, law, or regulation.[68]

## 3. Representations and Warranties of the Investor.[69]

The Investor hereby represents and warrants to the Company that:

3.1. <u>Authorization</u>. The Investor has full power and authority to enter into this Agreement, and that this Agreement, when executed and delivered, will constitute a valid and legally binding obligation of the Investor.[70]

3.2. <u>Purchase Entirely for Own Account</u>. This Agreement is made with the Investor in reliance upon the Investor's representation to the Company (which by the Investor's execution of this Agreement the Investor hereby confirms) that the Series A Stock to be purchased by the

---

[67] *That is, the company is current with its tax obligations.*

[68] *Violations of environmental and safety laws can be expensive and time consuming to correct.*

[69] *The investor representations address issues of the investor's authority and capacity to invest. They also provide assurance of compliance with securities laws exceptions that entitle the company to sell securities to the investor without first registering those shares in a public offering.*

[70] *If an institutional investor does not have authority, the company risks having the investor later attempt to undo the obligations undertaken in the agreement. In this agreement with its investor promise to provide an additional $2,000,000 in the future, it is particularly important to know that the investor is acting with proper authority.*

Investor and the Common Stock issuable upon conversion thereof (collectively, the "Securities") will be acquired for investment for the Investor's own account, not as a nominee or agent, and not with a view to the resale or distribution of any part thereof, and that the Investor has no present intention of selling, granting any participation in, or otherwise distributing the same. By executing this Agreement, the Investor further represents that the Investor does not have any contract, undertaking, agreement or arrangement with any person to sell, transfer or grant participations to such person or to any third person, with respect to any of the Securities.[71]

   3.3. <u>Reliance Upon Investors' Representations</u>. The Investor understands that the Series A Stock is not, and any Common Stock acquired on conversion thereof at the time of issuance may not be, registered under the Securities Act on the grounds that the sale provided for in this Agreement and the issuance of securities hereunder is exempt from registration under the Securities Act pursuant to Section 4(2) thereof, and that the Company's reliance on such exemption is predicated on the Investor's representations set forth herein. The Investor realizes that the basis for the exemption may not be present if, notwithstanding such representations, the Investor has in mind merely acquiring shares of the Series A Stock for a fixed or determinable period in the future, or for a market rise, or for sale if the market does not rise, and the Investor does not have any such intention.[72]

   3.4. <u>Receipt of Information</u>. Without limiting the Company's representations and warranties set forth in Section 2 hereof, the Investor has received all the information the

---

[71] *A basic premise of most private placement exceptions used to enable a company to issue securities without conducting a registered public offering is that the shares are being purchased for investment purposes and not with a view to short-term resale.*
[72] *This confirms the investor's understanding that the company is relying on its representations to qualify the issuance of Series A stock under private placement exceptions.*
*430 –Growth Company Guide 4.0*

Investor considers necessary or appropriate for deciding whether to purchase the Series A Stock. The Investor has had an opportunity to ask questions and receive answers from the Company regarding the terms and conditions of the offering of the Series A Stock and the business, properties, prospects, and financial condition of the Company and to obtain additional information (to the extent the Company possessed such information or could acquire it without unreasonable effort or expense) necessary to verify the accuracy of any information furnished to the Investor or to which the Investor had access. [73]

   3.5.   <u>Investment Experience</u>.   The Investor is experienced in evaluating and investing in private placement transactions of securities of companies in a similar stage of development and acknowledges that the Investor is able to fend for itself, can bear the economic risk of the Investor's investment, and has such knowledge and experience in financial and business matters that the Investor is capable of evaluating the merits and risks of the investment in the Series A Stock.[74] Investor also represents the Investor has not been organized for the purpose of acquiring the Series A Stock.[75]

---

[73] *Another basic premise of a private sale is that the investor has been fully informed about the company in which it is investing or that it has had the opportunity to obtain descriptive information about the company. The later 'opportunity to obtain information' can be adequate when dealing with sophisticated, experienced investors such as an institutional venture capital fund.*

[74] *This representation documents the investor experience level used to justify reliance on the company's disclosure of information and access to information provided. The representations required of the company in section 2 of this agreement document the extensive amount of investigation the investor has undertaken. This investigation provides evidence of the investor's sophistication and experience in making venture capital investments.*

[75] *For securities law purposes, an investor who has been formed for the purpose of making a specific investment must be treated as if each of its investors is a direct investor in the company. This representation assures the company that it does not need to look*

3.6.　Accredited Investor.　The Investor is an "accredited investor"[76] within the meaning given to that term in Regulation D under the Securities Act.[77]

3.7.　Restricted Securities.[78]　The Investor understands that the Series A Stock (and any Common Stock issued on conversion thereof) may not be sold, transferred, or otherwise disposed of without registration under the Securities Act or an exemption therefrom, and that in the absence of an effective registration statement covering the Stock (or the Common Stock issued on conversion thereof) or an available exemption from registration under the Securities Act, the Series A Stock (and any Common Stock issued on conversion thereof) must be held indefinitely.　In particular, the Investor is aware that the Series A Stock (and any Common Stock issued on conversion thereof) may not be sold pursuant to Rule 144 promulgated under the Securities Act unless all of the applicable conditions of that Rule are met.　Among the conditions for use of Rule 144 may be the availability of current information to the public about the Company.　Such information is not now available and the Company has no

(..continued)
*through the investor organization to its individual investors when determining compliance with applicable securities laws.*
[76] *Accredited investors are a category of investors defined in Regulation D of the federal securities laws. They include individuals and institutions that meet certain minimum standards for assets or income and that were not formed for the purpose of making a single specific investment.*
[77] *The federal securities law Regulation D provides specific safe-harbor exemptions for selling securities without a public registration. It is easier to comply with these safe-harbors when dealing exclusively with accredited investors.*
[78] *This section describes the applicable securities law restrictions on the investors right to resell the Series A stock or the common stock issued upon conversion of the Series A stock. These restrictions are in addition to any contractual restrictions the investor may otherwise agree to.*
*432 –Growth Company Guide 4.0*

present plans to make such information available, except as contemplated by the Investor Rights Agreement in connection with a filing or public offering.

3.8. Legends.[79] To the extent applicable, each certificate or other document evidencing any of the Series A Stock or any Common Stock issued upon conversion thereof shall be endorsed with the legends substantially in the form set forth below:

(a) The following legend under the Securities Act:

"THE SHARES REPRESENTED HEREBY HAVE NOT BEEN REGISTERED UNDER THE SECURITIES ACT OF 1933, AS AMENDED, AND MAY NOT BE SOLD, TRANSFERRED, ASSIGNED, PLEDGED, OR HYPOTHECATED UNLESS AND UNTIL REGISTERED UNDER SUCH ACT, OR UNLESS THE COMPANY HAS RECEIVED AN OPINION OF COUNSEL OR OTHER EVIDENCE, REASONABLY SATISFACTORY TO THE COMPANY AND ITS COUNSEL, THAT SUCH REGISTRATION IS NOT REQUIRED."

(b) Any legend imposed or required by the Company's Bylaws or applicable state securities laws.[80]

3.9. Public Sale. The Investor agrees not to make, without the prior written consent of the Company, any public offering or sale of the Series A Stock, or any Common Stock issued upon the conversion thereof, although permitted to do so pursuant to Rule 144(k) promulgated under the Securities Act, until the earlier of (i) the date on which the Company effects its

---

[79] *The stock legend provides notice to potential purchasers of the limits of the holder's ability to transfer the stock.*
[80] *These legends might include rights related to electing board members. State securities laws require their own legends. They vary from state to state and depend on the exemption used to qualify the sale.*

initial registered public offering pursuant to the Securities Act or (ii) the date on which it becomes a registered company pursuant to Section 12(g) of the Securities Exchange Act of 1934, as amended, or (iii) five years after the Closing of the sale of the Series A Stock to the Investor by the Company.[81]

### 4. Conditions of Investor's Obligations at Closing.[82]

The obligations of the Investor under subsection 1.1(b) of this Agreement are subject to the fulfillment on or before the Closing of each of the following conditions, the waiver of which shall not be effective against the Investor unless Investor delivers a written consent to the Company with respect thereto:

4.1. <u>Representations and Warranties</u>. The representations and warranties of the Company contained in Section 2 shall be true at the Closing with the same effect as though such representations and warranties had been made on and as of the date of the Closing.[83]

4.2. <u>Performance</u>. The Company shall have performed and complied with all agreements, obligations, and conditions contained in this Agreement that are required to be performed or complied with by it on or before the Closing, including but not limited to the filing of the Restated Certificate with the Secretary of State of the State of Delaware.[84]

---

[81] *This provision restricts the investor's freedom to sell its shares. The investor is willing to agree to these restrictions because of the rights it has to require registration of its shares for sale in a public offering. These rights are contained in an investor rights agreement, which is referred to in section 4.9.*

[82] *This section details all of the things the company must do before the investor is required to purchase the first 1,000,000 shares of Series A stock.*

[83] *If the Stock Purchase Agreement is signed before the closing date, this representation requires the company to update the representations contained in section 2 on the closing date.*

[84] *If the company has breached this agreement or failed to file the 434 –Growth Company Guide 4.0*

4.3.    Compliance Certificate. The President of the Company shall deliver to the Investor at the Closing a certificate certifying that the conditions specified in Sections 4.1, 4.2, 4.4, 4.5, 4.6, 4.7, 4.9 and 4.10 have been fulfilled.[85]

4.4.    Qualifications. All authorizations, approvals, or permits, if any, of any governmental authority or regulatory body of the United States or of any state that are required in connection with the lawful issuance and sale of the Series A Stock pursuant to this Agreement shall be duly obtained and effective as of the Closing.[86]

4.5.    Proceedings and Documents. All corporate and other proceedings in connection with the transactions contemplated at the Closing and all documents incident thereto shall be reasonably satisfactory in form and substance to the Investor, which shall have received all such counterpart original and certified or other copies of such documents as it may reasonably request.[87]

4.6.    Voting for Directors. The Bylaws of the Company shall provide that (i) the authorized number of directors of the Company shall be five (5), two (2) of whom shall be elected by the holders of the Series A Stock, voting as a class, and (ii) the size of the Board of Directors of the Company shall not be increased beyond five (5) members without the prior approval of a majority of the holders of the Series A Stock, voting as a class.[88]

(..continued)
charter amendment that creates the Series A stock, the investor is excused from closing.
[85] This provision requires that the President of the company certify compliance with the closing conditions in writing at closing.
[86] In other words, the company is not lacking any required approval or authority to issue the Series A stock.
[87] Companies routinely share their corporate minute and stock books with the investor prior to closing so that investor's counsel can review the minutes of the company and its stock records.
[88] This is one way of assuring the investor that their representatives will be assured a seat on the board of directors. Agreements

4.7.   Board of Directors.  Effective as of the Closing, the directors of the Company shall be Dr. Alexander Priam, John P. Candaules, Lydia Gyges, Arthur Investor and Richard Investor.[89]  The Company shall reimburse the directors for their reasonable out-of-pocket expenses incurred by them in connection with their attendance at meetings of the Board of Directors.[90]

4.8.   Opinion of Company Counsel.  The Investor shall have received from Experienced & Effective LLP, special counsel for the Company, an opinion, dated the date of the Closing, in substantially the form attached hereto as Exhibit E.[91]

4.9.   Investor Rights Agreement.  The Company and the Investor shall have entered into the Investor Rights Agreement in the form attached hereto as Exhibit B.[92]

(..continued)

*among those shareholders who hold enough shares to elect directors are also effective to accomplish this objective. Sometimes the right to elect director representatives is assured by incorporating the right into the description of the Series A stock contained in the company's amended and restated articles of incorporation.*

[89] *This covenant assures the investor that the board will be configured immediately after the closing so that their two representatives, Arthur and Richard Investor are included on the board of directors.*

[90] *Investor representatives to the board will have their travel expenses reimbursed. No separate director's fee is required.*

[91] *This opinion requirement is relatively standard in venture financings. The opinion of the company's law firm typically addresses issues of company authority to enter into the agreements and issue the shares, the enforceability of agreements, and the capitalization of the company. A sample opinion is included with these documents. Investor counsel usually does not render opinions to the company.*

[92] *This agreement provides the investor with rights to register his shares for resale and, typically, contains agreements respecting the election of directors. Rights of first refusal and options to purchase*
*436 –Growth Company Guide 4.0*

4.10.  Co-Sale Agreements.  The Company and the Investor each shall have entered into a Co-Sale Agreement in the form attached hereto as Exhibit C.[93]

4.11.  Proprietary Information and Inventions Agreements.  Each employee and officer of the Company shall have executed a Proprietary Information and Inventions Agreement substantially in the form or forms that have been delivered to the Investor.[94]

4.12.  Material Adverse Change.  Since September 30, [Current Year], there has occurred no material adverse change in the business, condition (financial or otherwise), operations, performance, or properties of the Company.[95]

4.13.  Minimum Investment.  The Investor shall purchase an aggregate of at least 1,000,000 shares of Series A Stock at a price of $2.00 per share at the Closing.[96]

(..continued)

*management shares are also frequently included.*
[93] *The cosale agreement entitles the investor to include some of its shares with shares of a management shareholder when the management shareholder attempts to sell shares to a third party.*
[94] *This provides an essential and basic protection to the company for its trade secrets and inventions. Investors routinely use the event of financing to assure that all company employees are bound by written agreements that protect the confidentiality of company information and assure that any employee rights to inventions developed with company resources are transferred to the company.*
[95] *Nothing out of the ordinary and significantly adverse to the company has occurred since the date of the last financial statement included in the representations.*
[96] *In other words, the investor does not have to close unless all 1,000,000 shares contemplated by section 1.1 are sold. The company has a similar right not to close in section 5.3.*

**5.     Conditions of the Company's Obligations at Closing.**[97]

The obligations of the Company to the Investor under this Agreement are subject to the fulfillment on or before the Closing of each of the following conditions by the Investor:

5.1.    <u>Representations and Warranties</u>.    The representations and warranties of the Investor contained in Section 3 shall be true and correct on and as of the Closing with the same effect as though such representations and warranties had been made on and as of the date of the Closing.[98]

5.2.    <u>Qualifications</u>. All authorizations, approvals, or permits, if any, of any governmental authority or regulatory body of the United States or of any state that are required in connection with the lawful issuance and sale of the Series A Stock pursuant to this Agreement shall be duly obtained and effective as of the Closing.[99]

5.3.    <u>Minimum Investment</u>.    The Investor shall purchase an aggregate of at least 1,000,000 shares of Series A Stock at a price of $2.00 per share at the Closing and the Company shall have received the aggregate purchase price therefore.[100]

---

[97] *This section details all of the things the investor must do before the company is required to sell the stock.*

[98] *If the Stock Purchase Agreement is signed before the closing date, this representation requires the investor to update the representations contained in section 3 on the closing date.*

[99] *The investor does not lack any required approval or authority to purchase the Series A stock. For example, the sale does not require a federal or state securities agency approval.*

[100] *The company does not have to complete the transaction unless all 1,000,000 shares contemplated by section 1.1 are sold. The investor has a similar right not to close in section 4.13.*

## 6. Miscellaneous.[101]

6.1. <u>Entire Agreement</u>. This Agreement and the documents referred to herein constitute the entire agreement among the parties and no party shall be liable or bound to any other party in any manner by any warranties, representations, or covenants except as specifically set forth herein or therein.[102]

6.2. <u>Survival of Warranties</u>. The warranties, representations, and covenants of the Company and the Investor contained in or made pursuant to this Agreement shall survive the execution and delivery of this Agreement and the Closing.[103]

6.3. <u>Successors and Assigns</u>. Except as otherwise provided herein, the terms and conditions of this Agreement shall inure to the benefit of and be binding upon the respective successors and assigns of the parties (including permitted transferees of any shares of Series A Stock sold hereunder, including any nominee of the Investor as designated pursuant to the terms of Section 1.3 hereof, or any Common Stock issued upon conversion thereof).[104] Nothing in this Agreement,

---

[101] *The following provisions are frequently referred to as boilerplate. These are covenants that appear, in one form or another, in many contracts. Consequently, they are sometimes not reviewed as carefully as they should be during negotiations. Each provision deals with an issue that can be important to the interpretation of the contract or the rights of the parties.*

[102] *This says that side agreements or oral understandings that are not repeated in this agreement or any of the Ancillary Agreements are not intended to be effective or enforceable against the parties. In other words, if you have a secrecy agreement or other understanding between the parties to this agreement that you want to remain effective, you should specify here that the understanding survives or include the desired understanding in the terms of this agreement or one of the Ancillary Agreements.*

[103] *This holds the company and the investor to the accuracy of their representations after the transaction is closed.*

[104] *This permits a party to assign, or transfer, its rights under this agreement.*

express or implied, is intended to confer upon any party other than the parties hereto or their respective successors and assigns any rights, remedies, obligations, or liabilities under or by reason of this Agreement, except as expressly provided in this Agreement.

6.4. <u>Governing Law</u>. This Agreement shall be governed by and construed under the laws of the State of Delaware, without regard to conflict of law principles.[105]

6.5. <u>Counterparts</u>. This Agreement may be executed in two or more counterparts, each of which shall be deemed an original, but all of which together shall constitute one and the same instrument.[106]

6.6. <u>Titles and Subtitles</u>. The titles and subtitles used in this Agreement are used for convenience only and are not to be considered in construing or interpreting this Agreement.[107]

6.7. <u>Notices</u>. Unless otherwise provided, all notices and other communications required or permitted under this Agreement shall be in writing and shall be mailed by United States first-class mail, postage prepaid, sent by facsimile or delivered personally by hand or by a nationally recognized courier addressed to the party to be notified at the address or facsimile number indicated for such person below, or at such other address or facsimile number as such party may designate by ten (10) days' advance written notice to the other party hereto:

If to the Company:     Newco Incorporated
                       Atlanta, Georgia
                       Attn:   Dr. Priam

---

[105] *In case there is a dispute, the parties have specified Delaware law, the law of the state in which the company is incorporated, to be used to interpret the agreement.*

[106] *The parties do not all have to sign the same copy of the agreement for the agreement to be effective.*

[107] *If a section title conflicts with the agreements set forth in the text of the section, the meaning relayed in the text prevails.*

440 –*Growth Company Guide 4.0*

| with a copy to: | Effective LLP |
| | Atlanta, Georgia |

| If to the Investor: | Venture Fund LLC |
| | San Francisco, California |
| | Attn: Mr. Arthur Investor |

| with a copy to: | Investor Law Firm |
| | San Francisco, California |

All such notices and other written communications shall be effective on the date of mailing, confirmed facsimile transfer or delivery.

6.8. Finder's Fees.[108] Except for those fees and other consideration owed by the Company to TPG pursuant to that certain Consulting Agreement, dated May 30, 20XX, between the Company and TPG (a copy of which has been delivered to the Investor) (the "Consulting Agreement") or pursuant to any other agreement now existing or hereafter entered into between the Company and TPG which acts to amend, replace and/or rescind, in whole or in part, the Consulting Agreement (provided that such agreement does not increase the fees or other consideration originally existing under the Consulting Agreement), each party represents that it neither is nor will be obligated for any finder's fee or commission in connection with this transaction.[109] The Investor agrees to indemnify and to hold harmless the Company from any liability for any commission or compensation in the nature of a finder's fee (and the cost and expenses of defending against such liability or asserted liabili-

---

[108] *This section identifies all brokers fees and finders fees due as a consequence of the agreement and makes the company responsible for their payment.*

[109] *The investor or its counsel will review each of these agreements closely.*

ty) for which the Investor or any of its officers, partners, employees, or representatives is responsible. The Company agrees to indemnify and hold harmless the Investor from any liability for any commission or compensation in the nature of a finder's fee (and the costs and expenses of defending against such liability or asserted liability) for which the Company or any of its officers, employees, or representatives is responsible.[110]

6.9. Expenses. The Company shall pay all costs and expenses that it incurs with respect to the negotiation, execution, delivery, and performance of this Agreement. The Company shall, at the Closing, reimburse the reasonable fees of Investor Law Firm not to exceed $35,000.[111]

6.10. Attorneys' Fees. If any action at law or in equity is necessary to enforce or interpret the terms of this Agreement, the Investor Rights Agreement, the Co-Sale Rights Agreement, any Ancillary Agreement or the Restated Certificate, the prevailing party shall be entitled to reasonable attorneys' fees, costs, and disbursements in addition to any other relief to which such party may be entitled.[112]

6.11. Amendments and Waivers. Any term of this Agreement may be amended and the observance of any term of this Agreement may be waived (either generally or in a particular instance and either retroactively or prospectively), only with the written consent of the Company and the holders of more than 50% of the outstanding Series A Stock. Any

---

[110] *Each party will reimburse the other if the other is required to pay a finders fee based on an agreement the reimbursing party entered into.*

[111] *Investors typically require the companies they invest in to reimburse them for the fees they incur to lawyers for representing their interests in the transaction. A negotiated monetary limit on the company's obligation to reimburse is common.*

[112] *This attorneys' fee agreement makes it easier for the investor to sue the company by removing the expense of attorneys' fees if the investor prevails.*

*442 –Growth Company Guide 4.0*

amendment or waiver affected in accordance with this Section shall be binding upon each holder of any securities purchased under this Agreement at the time outstanding (including securities into which such securities have been converted), each future holder of all such securities, and the Company.[113]

6.12. <u>Severability</u>. If one or more provisions of this Agreement are held to be unenforceable under applicable law, such provision shall be excluded from this Agreement and the balance of the Agreement shall be interpreted as if such provision were so excluded and shall be enforceable in accordance with its terms.[114]

6.13. <u>Specific Performance</u>. [115] Each of the parties hereto acknowledges and agrees that the other party would be damaged irreparably in the event any of the provisions of this Agreement are not performed in accordance with their specific terms or otherwise are breached. Accordingly, each of the parties hereto agrees that the other party shall be entitled to enforce specifically this Agreement and the terms and provisions hereof in any action instituted in any court of the United States or any state thereof having jurisdiction over the

---

[113] *This is a common provision designed to make it easier to amend the agreement. Without such an agreement, amendment would require agreement of every investor who becomes a party to the agreement.*

[114] *A common provision to many types of agreements, this severability provision protects both parties from the risk that the entire contract could be voided if one provision is found unenforceable. Instead, this provision provides that the non-offending provisions will remain in effect.*

[115] *In the United States, a contract breach is usually remedied by a court with the awarding of a monetary judgment in an amount equal to the damage suffered by the non-breaching party. Specific performance, that requires a party to fulfill its agreements as stated in the agreement, is considered an extraordinary remedy and is only awarded when a party is irreparably damaged. This provision seeks to provide proof of this irreparable damage so that an aggrieved party can force the other party to perform.*

parties hereto and the matter, in addition to any other remedy to which they may be entitled, at law or in equity.

6.14. <u>Construction</u>. The parties hereto have participated jointly in the negotiation and drafting of this Agreement. In the event an ambiguity or question of intent or interpretation arises, this Agreement shall be construed as if drafted jointly by the parties hereto and no presumption or burden of proof shall arise favoring or disfavoring any party by virtue of the authorship of any of the provisions of this Agreement.

[signatures begin on following page]

IN WITNESS WHEREOF, the parties have executed this Agreement as of the date first above written.

**COMPANY:**

NEWCO INCORPORATED


By:

Dr. Alexander Priam, President


**INVESTOR:**

VENTURE FUND LLC

By:

Arthur Investor, Manager


**Exhibit A**
(Amended and Restated Articles of Incorporation)
**Exhibit B**
(Form of Investor Rights Agreement)
**Exhibit C**
(Form of Co-Sale Agreement)
**Exhibit D**
(Capitalization)

| Shareholder | Number of Shares of Common Stock |
|---|---|
| Dr. Alexander Priam | 3,000,000 |
| Venture Fund LLC | 1,000,000 |
| Total | 4,000,000 |

**Exhibit E**
(Legal Opinion of Company Counsel)
**Schedule of Exceptions**

# *About the Author*

Clinton Richardson is a partner with Womble Carlyle Sandridge & Rice PLLC, a commercial law firm with 500+ lawyers in offices throughout the Mid-Atlantic and Southeastern regions of the United States. For the last 30 years, Mr. Richardson has advised growing companies and their investors on issues impacting business growth.

In his practice, Mr. Richardson has helped companies raise and close venture capital financings, conduct private placements, establish licensing programs, acquire companies and products, structure joint ventures, develop business strategies, protect technology, structure borrowings, price stock offerings and go public. As counsel to private company investors and underwriters, he has structured venture capital funds and fund offering documents, closed investments in portfolio companies, and counseled on exit strategies, restructurings and conflicts issues.

Mr. Richardson is a co-founder of one of the oldest and largest trade association for venture capital and private equity investors in the Southeastern United States, the Atlanta Venture Forum, where he has served for more than a two decades as an officer and director. Mr. Richardson and his work have appeared in Venture, Inc, Entrepreneur and other business magazines.

A *phi beta kappa* and *summa cum laude* graduate of Economics from Albion College, Mr. Richardson obtained his law degree *with distinction* from Duke University School of Law, where he also served on the Editorial Board of the Duke Law Journal and the Moot Court Board. He has practiced law since 1975 in Atlanta, Georgia. He can be contacted at crichardson@wcsr.com.